MILEAH K. KROMER

Blue-State Republican

How Larry Hogan Won Where Republicans
Lose and Lessons for a Future GOP

TEMPLE UNIVERSITY PRESS
Philadelphia • *Rome* • *Tokyo*

TEMPLE UNIVERSITY PRESS
Philadelphia, Pennsylvania 19122
tupress.temple.edu

Library of Congress Cataloging-in-Publication Data

Names: Kromer, Mileah K., 1981– author.
Title: Blue-state Republican : how Larry Hogan won where Republicans lose
and lessons for a future GOP / Mileah K. Kromer.
Description: Philadelphia : Temple University Press, 2023. | Includes
bibliographical references and index. | Summary: "A political
scientist's perspective on the rise of Republican Larry Hogan as
governor of the heavily Democratic state of Maryland and what lessons
the Republican Party might learn from his success"—Provided by
publisher.
Identifiers: LCCN 2022012139 (print) | LCCN 2022012140 (ebook) | ISBN
9781439921883 (cloth) | ISBN 9781439921890 (paperback) | ISBN
9781439921906 (pdf)
Subjects: LCSH: Hogan, Larry J., 1956– | Republican Party (U.S. : 1854–)
—History—21st century. | Governors—Maryland—Biography. |
Maryland—Politics and government—1951– | United States—Politics and
government—21st century.
Classification: LCC F186.35.H64 K76 2023 (print) | LCC F186.35.H64
(ebook) | DDC 975.2/044092—dc23/eng/20220701
LC record available at https://lccn.loc.gov/2022012139
LC ebook record available at https://lccn.loc.gov/2022012140

Printed in the United States of America

9 8 7 6 5 4 3 2 1

To my late grandfather John E. Sobota.

Thank you for getting me interested in politics.

This one is for you, pap.

Contents

Preface

The Unofficial Start

Maryland's political season unofficially starts on a sweltering slab of asphalt along the edge of the Chesapeake Bay about three hours from anywhere. The J. Millard Tawes Crab and Clam Bake is an annual event in the fishing village of Crisfield that started as a fundraiser for local causes. Over the years, it improbably swelled into a sweaty confab of elected officials who wanted to prove their crab-picking bona fides and their fondness for the Eastern Shore. There was no doubt that Governor Larry Hogan would travel there in July 2018. The general election was four months away. It was an opportunity to flex his retail politics muscles and enjoy a moment where the focus was on affairs of the state rather than the foreboding presence of President Donald Trump.

The main intrigue of that July day was whether Hogan's Democratic opponent, former NAACP President Ben Jealous, would even show up.

Some politicians are tempted to bypass Tawes, deciding that a full day of driving and back-slapping in a remote town of 2,500 people isn't worth the time lost to tasks such as fundraising calls. But they do so at their own peril.

As I prepared to hit the road for Crisfield, I caught a new TV ad from the Republican Governors Association (RGA) titled "Big Spender." The ad asked Maryland voters, "How much would Ben Jealous cost you?" and answered, "Even he doesn't know." It was the same simple but effective economic message that Larry Hogan had won on four years earlier. Only this time, it was saturating the airwaves in July, and his Democratic opponent didn't have the means to counter it. Broke after winning the late June primary, Jealous couldn't afford a TV buy. Support from outside groups such as the Democratic Governors Association was nowhere to be found.

Four years earlier, it was Hogan who was being outspent three to one by the Democratic nominee, Anthony Brown, an eight-year lieutenant-governor. Yet Brown lost. I was a budding local pundit at the time, and I vividly remember sitting under hot lights inside the studio of the Baltimore Fox affiliate on election night, searching for the words to describe how Hogan had pulled it off. The explanation I settled on wasn't as good as the lines I had rehearsed during the drive to the station, practicing for a different outcome. Even though Hogan had made some clear gains during the campaign, Brown was supposed to cruise to victory. The Harvard-educated Iraq War vet was better known among voters and had led in the few public polls. After all, Maryland is one of the bluest states in the country. Democrats outnumbered Republicans by a margin of more than two to one and held every statewide elected position in 2014. President Barack Obama beat the Republican nominee, Mitt Romney, by twenty-six points in 2012. And Democratic Governor Martin O'Malley bested challenger and former Republican Governor Robert "Bob" Ehrlich by double-digits in the last statewide cycle in 2010. So while political insiders were certainly grumbling that the Brown campaign was a hot mess, few thought it messy enough to end in defeat at the hands of a little-known Republican.

That was November 4, 2014, and Lawrence Joseph "Larry" Hogan Jr., a developer who had never held elected office, won in arguably the biggest electoral upset in the country that year. *Politico* reported on the outcome with a "Hogan Shocks Brown" headline, and the *Washington Post* called it a "stunning upset." While Republicans cheered, Democratic leaders were dismissive. They called Hogan an "accidental governor" and banked on their supermajority in the state legislature to sideline the political novice until they restored order in 2018.

Fast-forward four years. Leaving my home in Baltimore City, where Democrats outnumber Republicans ten to one, I drove south to Annapolis, then across the Chesapeake Bay Bridge. One of Hogan's first moves was to lower tolls on roads and bridges across the state, so it was a little cheaper to cross now. Democrats decried this as shortsighted political showmanship. But the public didn't share their outrage. "Hogan for Governor" signs appeared as I crossed into Queen Anne's County on the Eastern Shore and did not relent as I drove past Easton over the Choptank River to Cambridge. More signs. And billboards, too. "The Eastern Shore Loves Hogan!" "Hogan Is the Champion of the Chesapeake!" "We Love Our Gov!"

My goodness, I thought. *How many staffers did this take?*

I made it to Salisbury, the largest city on the Eastern Shore and home of Perdue Farms, where I picked up Route 13 to head farther south. It was at about that point that it dawned on me I had yet to see a single sign for Jealous.

When I arrived in Crisfield, it took less than a minute to find a variety of political animals thriving in their natural habitat on a perfect low-eighties sunny summer day.

"Welcome Governor Larry Hogan!" screamed the huge sign on the front of the tent erected by one of Maryland's highest-paid lobbyists, Bruce Bereano—who almost single-handedly made Tawes a must-attend festival by chartering buses that would bring Democratic lawmakers from Baltimore to the Eastern Shore. Bereano was impossible to miss, with his peripatetic manner and well-worn "lobbyists have issues" T-shirt. His tent was the big top of Tawes and filled with elected officials, campaign professionals, wannabes, has-beens, and hangers-on. Reporters milled around outside, waiting to soak up the tea spilled after a few summer afternoon beers.[1]

Hogan soon arrived on the blacktop, surrounded by his entourage and Maryland State Police detail. His campaign volunteers assembled and cheered his arrival, creating an orchestrated photo op for television cameras. The governor made his way through the crowd, relishing the opportunity to shake hands and pose for selfies. Years removed from his long-shot nobody status, he still seemed delighted that random people wanted their picture taken with him. The diverse attendees were sweaty, some with hands and shirts spattered with Old Bay seasoning, and a little drunk. Hogan, a natural extrovert, was in his element.

Jealous did arrive after all to less fanfare but a warm reception from supporters uninterested in the Larry Hogan show. Taking the same route to Crisfield that I did (the only one available), he had just spent the past few hours looking at the same "Hogan for Governor" signs. He met with local Democratic clubs and volunteers but soon departed for a fundraising event. He had shown up and would benefit from the equal coverage the state media would give him when they ran their stories about the day, a solid return for an unremarkable campaign stop.[2]

Many people didn't seem to notice the Democratic nominee for governor amid the festivities. Others were likely happy to see him go—perhaps no one more than the state senator who represented Crisfield, Jim Mathias. Mathias was the last Democratic state senator on the Eastern Shore, where Republicans have a heavy advantage. He is a former mayor of the beachfront tourist town of Ocean City, and his visibility and energetic constituent service have kept his seat in Democratic control. The nomination of Jealous, a surrogate for the presidential candidate Bernie Sanders and a staunch progressive, was not making his competitive State Senate race any easier. The Hogan campaign and the RGA were already casting the race as a choice between a reckless ideologue and a steady pragmatist. Mathias knew which his constituents preferred and wanted to keep his distance. He would face a tough decision if Democratic leaders put the pressure on him to back Jealous. But the ask never came.

After almost two hours of socializing, Hogan escaped to a table deep inside the Bereano tent to eat crabs with his staff and key supporters. Politicians mingled. Staffers and aspiring political players jockeyed for face time with establishment powerhouses. Reporters wrapped up their takes. I made my way back through the crowd to grab a slice of Smith Island Cake—the official Maryland state dessert—from the Bereano tent for the drive home to Baltimore. As dominating a political presence as Trump had been since first descending that gilded escalator at Trump Tower, he was all but missing that day—just how Larry Hogan wanted it during his campaign and for the future of the Republican Party.

I decided to write this book in March 2018, as Democrats were jockeying to find the candidate who could take out the improbably popular Republican governor, as Trump was upending what we thought we knew about politics in the United States, and as many were postulating that the Trump effect would cost Hogan his reelection. Measuring attitudes toward and related commentary on the governor had become a big part of my professional life. As the director of the Goucher College Poll, which during Hogan's first term in office moved from fledgling institute to staple in the state's political coverage, I was asked by nearly every Maryland reporter to explain the mechanics of Hogan's political success. My primary goal in writing *Blue-State Republican* was to provide a definitive answer to that question; secondarily, given the governor's growing profile within national Republican Party politics, it was to consider whether any of it matters outside of Maryland.

I've been fortunate enough to have access to the state's key political leaders. Their insights, along with public and internal polling, campaign finance data, electoral returns, focus group reports, and the views of several leading conservative political commentators, help me tell the story of how Hogan won where Republicans lose and consider whether the "Hogan coalition" offers any lessons for a future GOP.

At the end of our interview for this book, the governor and I turned to his future ambitions. I noted that, considering his frequent appearances on national cable news, his recent autobiography, and the rumors of a presidential run, it certainly looked like he would take a shot at the White House. Not willing to give me a more definitive answer than he'd given to any prominent national journalist, but delighted by the prospect, he deflected, "It would at least help you sell some books."[3] I guess we'll see.

Acknowledgments

This book would not have been possible without the editing suggestions of David and Karen Nitkin. In killing all my darlings, they turned word salad into prose, and I'm forever in their debt. The small but mighty members of the State House press corps in Maryland are among the best in the business. Their essential work of reporting our state's politics is the backbone of this book. I owe a special thank you to Bryan Sears, a reporter for the *Daily Record*. Bryan was the first journalist who covered the results of my fledging polling operation and provided me with hours of free lessons on Maryland politics. Every lawmaker, political insider, and journalist who spoke with me, on and off the record, played a vital role in this book. Thank you for sharing your diverse insights and perspectives with me.

I'm grateful to Doug Mayer, who lived up to his reputation and never stopped spinning but also was generous with his time and paved the way for me to access key players in the Hogan world: Russ Schriefer, Ashley O'Connor, and Jim Barnett, as well as Lieutenant-Governor Boyd Rutherford and Governor Larry Hogan.

My friend Sophia Silbergeld helped me better understand the realities of Maryland's political landscape from an insider's perspective and was kind enough to make introductions when I needed them.

Catalina Byrd and Nyasha Grayman-Simpson were two friends always up for a phone call and willing to provide feedback. I'm thankful to have them in my life.

Geoffrey Kabaservice of the Niskanen Center lent me his expertise and access to Washington insiders. Their frank assessments of the current state of the Republican Party helped me better understand what its future might be.

Thank you to Goucher College—specifically, former Provost Scott Sibley—for granting me a sabbatical to do this work and Aaron Javsicas of Temple University Press for taking a chance on a new author.

Blue-State Republican

Introduction

Building a Durable Republican Majority

It was almost 10 P.M. on Tuesday, November 6, 2018, and Larry Hogan was restless. The Associated Press had declared him a victor nearly an hour earlier, making him the first Republican governor in Maryland to win reelection in more than half a century. Hogan was eager to ascend the stage at the Westin hotel in Annapolis and bask in the cheers of supporters, rejoicing that he transcended the divisiveness and unpopularity of his party's leader, President Donald Trump.

But he couldn't just yet.

Voters were still waiting in line in Prince George's County, the majority-Black, heavily Democratic jurisdiction outside Washington, DC, long after the polls were supposed to close.[1] Local officials had miscalculated the ballots needed to meet the demand driven by anti-Trump sentiment. Couriers rushed through rain and traffic to deliver more, but crowds were growing, and Hogan's opponent, former NAACP President Ben Jealous, was urging voters to stay. Declaring victory before the lines cleared would produce horrible optics. Hogan and his team didn't make mistakes like that.

Soon enough, the last voters were entering their precincts and the State Board of Elections was updating results. The governor turned to his advisers and announced, "It's time to go."[2]

His team readied the stage, and Hogan walked out around 10:30 P.M. to deliver his victory speech. Flanked by his wife, his running mate, and members of both families, the sixty-two-year-old governor beamed before the crowd: "Tonight, in a deep-blue state in this blue year, with a Blue Wave, it turns out I can surf!"[3]

That night, the families onstage at the Westin represented a far more diverse portrait than is typically found at Republican victory parties. The governor's wife, Yumi, an immigrant, and her daughters are Korean American; Lieutenant-Governor Boyd Rutherford, his wife, Monica, and their daughters are Black. Together, the families reflected the coalition that Hogan built and maintained in one of the most diverse states in the country.

Dressed in a dark suit and a purple tie, Hogan was jubilant but more physically weathered than when he took the same stage four years earlier. The aftermath of cancer treatments left him heavier and with a buzz cut where a full head of silver hair had been. He thanked Marylanders for putting aside partisan politics and voting for civility, bipartisanship, and commonsense leadership. He lauded the independents and "hundreds of thousands of Democrats" who crossed over and delivered him a second term.

Blue-State Republican is the story of how Larry Hogan, a lifelong member of a Republican Party now more defined by Donald Trump than Ronald Reagan, made it to that stage while many other Republicans across the country, and down-ballot in Maryland, were making concession calls. The GOP lost control of the U.S. House of Representatives, six state legislative chambers, more than three hundred State House and Senate seats, and seven governorships in that cycle. In Maryland, Republicans lost winnable races for county executive and fell well short of their goal to break the veto-proof Democratic majority in the Maryland State Senate. Other Republican candidates running for statewide office in Maryland lost their bids to unseat a U.S. senator, an attorney-general, and a state comptroller by an average of thirty-six points.

Hogan's rejection of culture wars and Trump-style populism and rhetoric that has consumed much of the Republican Party enabled him to win the votes of Democrats and make significant inroads with key elements of their electoral coalition: college-educated voters, suburbanites, women, and racial minorities—notably, Black voters. And his fiscally conservative values, mixed with a carefully messaged, pragmatic approach to governance, helped maintain the support of his base while appealing to the center-right voters who continue to make up a majority of the country.[4] The result was a double-digit victory built by voters who abhorred Trump and the GOP, as well as those who were full-on Trumpian in a Democratic wave year.

Hogan's victory has since catapulted him onto the national stage, but the journey to a second term didn't get much attention or close examination outside of Maryland. He was a well-funded, popular incumbent in a state that most voters thought was heading in the right direction. He led in every preelection poll, despite a hostile national climate for Republican candidates. The widespread perception that Hogan was always going to win belied what it took to get there.

Maryland: Where Republicans Lose

The significance of Hogan's 2018 reelection victory and his first win in 2014 become more apparent in the context of Maryland's political history and demographics.

Simply put, Democratic dominance defines Maryland's politics.[5] In a state with twice as many registered Democrats as Republicans, Hogan had to earn at least a quarter of the Democratic vote to win, even if his opponent did not receive any Republican votes. It also meant that while an enthusiastic GOP base could not deliver Hogan the election, a low turnout among those voters could lose one. The state's two population centers—the Baltimore metropolitan area and the Washington, DC, suburbs of Montgomery and Prince George's counties—are overwhelmingly Democratic.

History is also on the Democrats' side. Since 1960 the state has chosen only three Republicans for president: Richard Nixon in 1972 (with former Maryland Governor Spiro Agnew as vice president), Ronald Reagan in 1984, and George H. W. Bush in 1988. In presidential elections since 2008, the Old Line State has gone for the Democratic presidential candidate by an average of twenty-eight points.

Maryland has sent just two Republicans to the U.S. Senate in the past fifty years: James Glenn Beall, who served from 1971 to 1977, and Charles "Mac" Mathias, who served from 1969 to 1987. Republicans consistently filled three and sometimes four of the state's eight seats in the House of Representatives from 1963 to 2012. Democratic gerrymandering after the 2010 Census left Maryland with a single Republican-held congressional district.

Republican governors haven't fared any better. Agnew served from 1967 to 1969 before resigning to become vice president. It would be thirty-four years before another Republican, Robert L. Ehrlich Jr., occupied the second floor of the State House. Only two Republicans in the history of the state—Theodore R. McKeldin, who served from 1951 to 1959, and Hogan himself—have ever served a second term.

Democrats have held veto-proof majorities in both legislative chambers of the Maryland General Assembly since 1922. The presiding officers of these chambers during Hogan's rise and through his reelection bid, House of Delegates Speaker Michael E. Busch and Senate President Thomas V. Mike Miller Jr., were veterans adept at controlling the state's policy agenda.

The Maryland Republican Party has never matched Democrats in organization, leadership, or fundraising. The deficiencies in the Maryland GOP are so pronounced that they have sometimes left the party without high-quality staff to run operations or candidates to challenge Democrats in high-profile races. In other words, it's always an uphill climb for Republicans in Maryland, and Hogan could never rely on his state party to support his general election candidacy in any meaningful way. He had to build an organization outside of the party structure to achieve success.

Of course, Hogan was not the only Republican governor to win in a blue state in the 2018 cycle. Phil Scott of Vermont and Charlie Baker of Massachusetts won their reelection bids by large margins and earned similarly high job approval ratings in office. But Hogan has demonstrated more than the ability to win Democratic voters and like-minded independents. What sets his victory apart from his blue-state Republican contemporaries, and therefore makes Hogan a uniquely compelling study, is how he triumphed given Maryland's racial diversity.

According to the 2020 U.S. Census, 48.7 percent of Maryland's population identifies as white alone, and 29.5 percent of the population is Black alone. Almost 7 percent of Marylanders are Asian, and other races, including Marylanders who identify with multiple racial backgrounds, make up the remaining 14.5 percent. The state's Hispanic population of any race is 11.8 percent. That makes Maryland the fourth most racially diverse state in the country, measured by the Diversity Index developed by the U.S. Census. Vermont is ranked forty-eighth, and Massachusetts is twenty-fifth.[6]

Given the history of near-unified support of Democratic candidates among Black voters and Democratic advantages among other racial minorities, Hogan faced not only an unfavorable political environment but also a demographic disadvantage.[7] *Blue-State Republican* focuses primarily on how Hogan earned support from Black voters, who are a significant voting bloc in the state and produce the most robust support for the Democratic Party among any demographic group.[8]

Maryland's population creates additional challenges for Republicans outside of just the dynamics of party and race. There is a "diploma divide" in the electoral behavior of American voters, particularly among white voters.[9] Polling by Gallup shows a significant and growing Democratic advantage in party and voter preferences among college-educated white voters since 2014.[10] Exit polling from 2016, 2018, and 2020 shows a similar trend. Maryland is among the most college-educated states in the country, with 40.2 percent of residents twenty-five and older holding a four-year college degree.

The state's proximity to Washington, DC, also presents a uniquely nationalized state political environment. According to the Maryland Department of Labor, Licensing, and Regulation, the state ranks first for federal jobs per capita, at 240 jobs per 10,000 residents.[11] Residents who live near the District are inundated with DC-centered news even when tuned in to local outlets. In other words, decisions in Washington have an immediate economic impact on many residents—and therefore on the state's electoral politics.

All told, Maryland presents some of the toughest political terrain in the country for Republicans. Understanding how Hogan won is not only useful for understanding Maryland's politics; it can also provide insights into how Republicans can win in a diversifying America.

The Republican Autopsy and the Hogan Coalition

In fact, broadening the electoral map and moving the GOP toward a new center-right coalition that could gain the support of a majority of voters was once an explicit goal of the Republican Party. In the Growth and Opportunity Project, a soul-searching postmortem ordered by Republican National Committee Chair Reince Priebus in the aftermath of Mitt Romney's loss to Barack Obama in 2012, GOP analysts advocated moving away from "ideological reinforcement to like-minded people" and toward appealing to "more people, including those who share some but not all of our conservative principles." To realize that goal, the "autopsy report," as it was dubbed, recommended that the party modernize its campaigns and invest in outreach to Black, female, Asian, and Pacific Islander voters, as well as to gay Americans, and urged immigration reform to win over Hispanics and Latinos.[12]

A necessary first step was to suppress the power of Tea Party and fringe right-wing candidates, who many party leaders believed were the source of their most immediate electoral woes and presented a long-term problem. Establishment Republicans and affiliated advocacy groups, such as the U.S. Chamber of Commerce, actively vetted and supported more business-friendly and traditional Republicans during the 2014 primary cycle.[13]

Establishment favorites went on to run the board in U.S. Senate Republican primaries, though some victories were by a narrow margin, and won most contested House primary races.[14] The GOP dominated the 2014 general election cycle, taking control of the U.S. Senate and expanding its majority in the House of Representatives by fourteen seats. Republicans also added governors in the Democratic strongholds of Massachusetts and Illinois, in addition to Hogan's win in Maryland. Tim Miller, a former Republican strategist who helped write the autopsy report and served as the communications director for Jeb Bush's 2016 presidential campaign, describes this cycle as a "momentary glimmer of hope" that the GOP could move in the direction proposed in the autopsy report.[15]

Even Barack Obama recognized that "Republicans had a good night" after the 2014 midterms.[16] But the veteran GOP pollster Whit Ayres wasn't all that sanguine. The wins, he contended, were a "repudiation of the Democratic message and not an endorsement of a Republican alternative."[17] Still, Ayres and others believed that the Republican Party was poised to recapture the voter enthusiasm of the Reagan and George W. Bush years by building a policy platform grounded in conservative principles but appealing to a broad swath of the electorate.

Ayres's book *2016 and Beyond* (2015), widely read in Republican circles, showed that majorities of Americans agreed with the general concepts of limited but present government, fairness of opportunity, lower deficits, and reducing tax burdens while preserving popular programs such as Social Security and Medicare. In an interview about the 2016 presidential cycle, Ayres—who soon after signed on to Florida Senator Marco Rubio's presidential campaign—told the *Washington Post*'s Jonathan Capehart that the party was one transformational candidate away from resurrection.[18]

Then, almost exactly one year later, *Politico* ran a story with the headline, "Trump Kills GOP Autopsy."[19]

Donald Trump, the New York developer turned reality television star turned Republican presidential candidate, was certainly transformational. But he had no interest in creating a broad and durable coalition like the one imagined in the autopsy report. Establishment Republicans were horrified—or at least feigned horror—in the months that followed Trump's entrance into GOP politics. But one by one, their preferred candidates faltered while Trump gained momentum, reenergizing the party's Tea Party wing under his populist rallying cry: Make America Great Again.

Trump handily won the Republican primary and, surprising political analysts and insiders of all stripes, edged out the Democratic nominee, Hillary Clinton, in key battleground states to win the presidency. He dismantled the so-called blue wall of Wisconsin, Michigan, and Pennsylvania by appealing to primarily white voters. Analysis by political scientists and others concluded that Trump owed his win to some combination of white identity politics, authoritarian attitudes, racial animosity, sentiment about immigration, economic anxiety, and negative partisanship (Abramowitz and McCoy 2019; Green and McElwee 2019; Knuckey and Hassan 2020; Reny et al. 2019; Tolbert et al. 2018). They also credited Trump's personal celebrity and media savvy, as well as Democratic strategic mistakes and the personal unpopularity of Hillary Clinton (Bordo 2018; Happer et al. 2019).

Still, Clinton earned 2.87 million more votes than Trump, making him the third straight Republican nominee to lose the popular vote. A shift of fewer than eighty thousand votes in Michigan, Pennsylvania, and Wisconsin would have made her president. And that is exactly what happened in the next presidential cycle, when the Democratic nominee, Joe Biden, beat Trump by carrying the same trio of blue-wall states Clinton had lost while adding narrow victories in racially and ethnically diverse, but reliably Republican, Georgia and Arizona. Biden also improved on Clinton's total vote share. The former vice president earned about 81 million total votes, the most in American electoral history, eclipsing Trump's votes by more than 7 million.

Trump became the tenth elected president to run a second time and lose. And Democratic wins in the pair of Georgia's U.S. Senate runoff races made him the first elected president since the Great Depression to lose control over the House, Senate, and presidency in a single term.

The electoral results of the 2018 and 2020 cycles and evidence from public polling and the 2020 U.S. Census brought to life some of the warnings of the GOP autopsy report. The number of white voters is shrinking. A failure to broaden the Republican Party's base to include more racially diverse voters and close the gender gap will be a liability if the GOP continues its current course.

Exit polling conducted for CNN by Edison Research suggests that many demographic groups voted similarly in 2016 and 2020. While Trump's marginal gains among Black and, particularly, Hispanic voters (mostly among men) in key states drove headlines, the big picture is that he and most Republicans lost heavily among voters of color. For example, 90 percent of Black voters, 65 percent of Latinos, 61 percent of Asians, and 55 percent of other racial groups backed Biden.[20]

Moreover, America's youngest and most racially diverse generations of voters—millennials who are now reaching their forties and Gen Zers who have just reached voting age—both lean heavily Democratic and will eventually become the majority of the electorate. Most troubling for Republicans, voting patterns of the eldest millennials do not indicate they are growing more politically conservative with age.[21]

The most immediate cause for concern for Republicans comes from the populous suburbs of major metropolitan areas, including key Rust Belt and Sun Belt states. An analysis by the Brookings Institution demographer William H. Frey showed a Democratic advantage in these areas for the first time since Obama's 2008 victory. Moreover, a Pew Research Center analysis found that Trump only narrowly won white suburban voters in 2020, whereas in 2016 he won this group by sixteen points. College-educated voters, women, and the growing racial diversity of the suburbs all contributed to this result.

Still, disproportionate rates of turnout and ballot access for some minority voters, as well as the structural advantages built into the Electoral College and some of the heavily gerrymandered House of Representatives and state legislative districts that favor Republicans, will protect the GOP, at least for a time, from the immediate effects of demographic change.[22]

It's still likely that Trump-style populism, culture wars, and conservative identity politics that appeal predominantly to white voters can win the Electoral College and majorities in the U.S. Congress over the next few cycles, particularly if Republican-led efforts to restrict ballot access are successful. At the same time, the 2020 election demonstrated that Democratic turnout operations that focus on dense and diverse metro areas such as Atlanta, Philadelphia, Milwaukee, Detroit, and Phoenix can offset GOP gains among predominantly white voters in must-win Electoral College states.

The dynamics of the coalition Hogan built in Maryland, by contrast, offer the GOP the prospects of a durable majority where demographics are still destiny but not demise. Moreover, the ability for Republicans to compete for votes from a broader swath of American voters decreases the incentive to try to hang on to power through nonmajoritarian means—such as voter-suppression tactics bolstered by false claims about the integrity of American elections—which threaten liberal democracy.

Indeed, the autopsy report called for "Republicans on the federal level to learn from successful Republicans on the state level."[23] Hogan is undoubtedly one of the GOP's success stories from this era. He has stood as one of the most outspoken and visible among a handful of elected Republicans who have remained steadfast in their opposition to Trump and Trumpism. At the same time, unlike party defectors who believe that Trump and his seemingly unshakable support among many GOP voters have rendered the party beyond redemption, Hogan is committed to building a future for the Republican Party.

Speaking at the Ronald Reagan Presidential Foundation and Institute shortly after the 2020 election, Hogan reaffirmed his belief that "the party of Lincoln and Reagan is the last best hope for our nation" and asked, "Are we going to be a party that can't win national elections, or are we willing to do the hard work of building a durable coalition that can shape our nation's destiny?"[24] Hogan's ability to build a national Republican following around these notions, as well as whether his appeal to Democrats and independent voters can reach outside of Maryland is, as of this writing, untested.

1

They Even Taxed the Rain

Maryland sits almost entirely in the watershed of Chesapeake Bay, the largest estuary in the United States and third biggest in the world. For decades, suburban sprawl and agriculture have choked this national treasure and the fishing and tourism industries that depend on it. Rain that falls onto roads, driveways, turf fields, and other impervious surfaces flows into streams, rivers, and, eventually, the bay, carrying pollutants harmful to wildlife and water quality.

Environmentalists had demanded action on stormwater runoff for years. They finally scored a victory in 2012, when lawmakers approved a plan requiring Baltimore City and Maryland's nine largest counties to launch projects to prevent runoff while creating incentives to reduce or replace impervious surfaces. Supporters, including Governor Martin O'Malley, said the fairest way to pay for the cleanup was through a levy on homes and businesses with paved surfaces: a stormwater utility charge.

Republicans saw it differently. Democrats were so out of touch with average Marylanders, they contended, they felt empowered to even tax the rain. A week after the legislative session ended, that view was articulated in an op-ed in the *Baltimore Sun*. "Why do Annapolis leaders do these things?" it asked. "Because they can."[1] The piece argued, "Governance in Maryland reflects the arrogance, unaccountability and reform aversion you would expect in a one-party monopoly regime."

Its author was a politically connected developer named Larry Hogan.

Changing Maryland, Not Tea Partying

Hogan had spent the previous year needling O'Malley and other Democrats through Change Maryland, a nonpartisan, anti-tax advocacy organization he cofounded with Steve Crim in 2011.

Run by a small, volunteer team working from Hogan's home and office, Change Maryland was initially limited in its influence to acerbic Facebook comments about the fiscal policies of O'Malley and the Democratic-led state legislature, shared with its few thousand followers.[2]

Hogan was a social media novice, admitting that in the beginning he didn't know much about Facebook other than "Obama used it" and "it seemed like you could reach a lot of people for free." But like any burgeoning influencer, he remembers feeling excited with each new "like" and comment when "people I don't even know like what I said!"[3]

But Change Maryland soon expanded beyond Facebook posts. It became a public platform. As the owner of Hogan Companies, Hogan was just a businessman complaining about taxes and the business climate. As the leader of an advocacy group, he could speak for Marylanders and business owners "fed up" with the "failed leadership in Annapolis," a refrain the governor still uses today. He began to appear regularly on local talk radio and in local newspaper stories and eventually managed some hits on national outlets such as Fox Business.[4] The exposure continued with speaking appearances at local Republican clubs and to business advocacy organizations. It all helped build name recognition and the beginnings of a political base for his rumored run for governor. Hogan and Change Maryland also helped fill the void left in the wake of former Governor Robert Ehrlich's double-digit loss to O'Malley in 2010. The Maryland GOP was left broke and rudderless, causing some party leaders to openly speculate that they might not see "another Republican governor of Maryland for the next 40 years."[5]

The rise of Change Maryland and Hogan's political ambitions also came at a crucial moment for the Republican Party nationally. The Tea Party, a powerful mobilizing force during the first half of President Barack Obama's first term, had reached its apex of power during the 2010 midterm elections, only to precipitously decline after the 2012 presidential election cycle and the backlash to its role in the 2013 government shutdown.[6]

The decentralized mix of local groups helped organize and motivate mostly white voters around issues including taxes and deficits; grievances toward "government handouts" to "undeserving" groups such as immigrants, low-income earners, and young people; distrust of government; a conservative interpretation of the U.S. Constitution; and outrage over the Affordable Care Act (Williamson et al. 2011). Polling showed that those who identified as Tea Partiers were overwhelmingly Republicans, and the Republicans who viewed the Tea Party favorably were more likely to identify as conservative than moderate.[7] Kevin Arceneaux and Stephen P. Nicholson (2012), Christopher S. Parker and Matt A. Barretto (2014), and Daniel Tope, Justin T. Pickett, and Ted Chiricos (2015), among others, suggest that the core of the Tea Party movement was white racial resentment rather than fiscal responsibility. This notion is further supported by Theda Skocpol and Vanessa Williamson in *The Tea Party and the Remaking of Republican Conservatism* (2020), which notes that, despite claiming to be against "big government," many Tea Party activists supported Social Security, Medicare, and benefits for military veterans. Rachel Blum, in *How the Tea Party Captured the GOP* (2020), describes the movement as an insurgent faction of the Republican Party primarily motivated by the perception that the country was changing in ways that threatened the status of white Christians.

Hogan and Change Maryland focused on tax relief and built a grassroots following online. And that's where similarities to the Tea Party effectively end.

Hogan is clear on this point: Change Maryland had nothing to do with the Tea Party or the style of populism it advanced. He didn't want to be an insurgent faction within the Republican Party; nor did he want to engage in politics or rhetoric that would exclude voters, including Democrats and members of their racially diverse coalition, from hearing his message. Hogan believes that traditional Republican free-market, pro-growth economic policies are not only better than liberal alternatives but are popular with most Americans.

A driving force of Hogan's worldview, even during the infancy of Change Maryland, was that Republicans already have the right ideas. They just need to do a better job talking about them to moderate Democrats, independents, and racial minorities—and spend less time focusing on divisive social issues that turn people off. The Tea Party and, later, Trumpism looked to win by inciting the worst—often racist and nativist—instincts of the GOP base, whereas Hogan wanted to win by expanding the base.

By the end of 2012, Change Maryland had amassed twenty-five thousand followers.[8] In early January 2014, when it began carrying the authority line, the legal designation that it was raising and spending campaign funds, of the Hogan for Governor campaign, it was closer to seventy-five thousand and growing.

In his formal campaign announcement on January 20, 2014, Hogan touted his status as a "political outsider" and "small-business man," oft-repeated claims that are debatably true but certainly tenuous. The "small business" Hogan owns is Hogan Companies, a land and real estate development firm that, according to its website, "has completed $2 billion in real estate transactions" and sold "40,000 residential lots to home builders and developers."[9] And his status as a "political outsider" wasn't for lack of trying. Hogan ran in 1981 and 1992 to represent Maryland's 5th district in the U.S. House of Representatives and was a rumored candidate for governor in the 2010 cycle. He also served as appointments secretary under Governor Ehrlich and grew up on his father's successful campaigns for Congress and Prince George's County executive.

The elder Larry Hogan stands as the central figure in the younger's political development. Lawrence Joseph Hogan Sr. served in Congress from 1969 to 1975, and shades of what would become Change Maryland's core messaging are easily found in Hogan Sr.'s campaign rhetoric. He often spoke of the "forgotten man," a voter he described as "the hardworking, taxpaying, law-abiding citizen who goes on year after year financially supporting his government and is generally ignored."[10] Representative Hogan is best remembered as the first Republican on the House Judiciary Committee to support the impeachment of President Richard Nixon, an ideologically similar ally he supported during Nixon's presidential campaigns. Hogan ultimately became the only Republican member of Congress to vote for all three articles of impeachment brought against Nixon.

The moment when Representative Hogan announced his support for impeachment, saying, "No man, not even the President of the United States, is above the law," earned renewed attention on cable television during the first impeachment proceedings against President Trump in 2019. Liberal commentators such as MSNBC's Lawrence O'Donnell held Representative Hogan and his statement up as the bar the current crop of congressional Republicans failed to meet.[11] Hogan's position on impeachment is now generally lauded as an example of putting country over party. However, it made him a pariah among Republicans in Congress and in his home state in the immediate aftermath. Republicans, some of whom were longtime friends and allies, and Democrats alike accused him of playing politics and using the impeachment to boost his political profile. At the time, Hogan was running and favored to win the Republican nomination in Maryland's 1974 gubernatorial contest. His support among Republicans plummeted after the impeachment vote, and he eventually lost the primary contest to Louise Gore, a state senator from Montgomery County. Gore lost handily to the incumbent Democratic Governor Marvin Mandel in the general election.

Hogan told the *Washington Post* in a 1987 interview, "I assumed that in coming out for impeachment I would lose the nomination, which I did. It had absolutely nothing to do with politics. I still resent people saying that now."[12] The willingness to buck party lines and take an independent stance proved to be an essential lesson for his son, particularly after the election of Donald Trump. Hogan often notes that he "probably learned more about integrity in one day when my dad read that vote than most people learn in a lifetime."[13]

But there were more, albeit far less well known, lessons from his father. In 1978, after the wounds from Watergate and his failed gubernatorial run had healed, Hogan Sr. once again entered the political arena as a candidate for Prince George's County executive. From that race, a twenty-two-year-old Larry Hogan—who volunteered on the campaign—saw firsthand the unifying power of pocketbook issues and the merits of adopting policy ideas from across the partisan aisle. Hogan Sr. embraced the Tax Reform Initiative by Marylanders (TRIM), a ballot referendum that would freeze the property tax the county could collect at the $143.9 million it raised in 1979.[14] Two Democratic lawmakers originally championed TRIM and modeled it after California's Proposition 13.

Fueled by anti–property-tax public sentiment of the era and a smart campaign, Hogan and the TRIM referendum won in the heavily Democratic and increasingly racially diverse Prince George's County. He would be the last Republican to hold that office, and TRIM remains the central part of his legacy as county executive. Economists and public policy wonks argue that budgetary shortfalls resulting from TRIM have hurt public schools and the ability of the county to compete with Montgomery County, its more affluent neighbor. Others credit the low property tax rate for the population and economic growth, noting that Prince George's County is one of the most affluent Black-majority counties in the country. Lawmakers have modified TRIM over the years, but efforts to repeal it have failed.

In a *Washington Post* profile during the race for Prince George's County executive, Eugene Meyer described candidate Hogan as a "Republican propelled to Congress three times in a county that is overwhelmingly Democratic, he is a driving, magnetic and often combative politician, outgoing and gregarious. His present wife once described him as a 'short dumpy guy,' yet he nonetheless evokes the word 'charisma.'" Meyer went on to write that the "public Larry Hogan projects a dynamic image. He comes across as a man who is knowledgeable about a variety of subjects and is seldom at a loss for words. He is a good media candidate who enjoys the limelight."[15]

Reporters have since used similar descriptions to describe the younger Hogan. Though Yumi Hogan, who is reserved and has a reputation among Hogan staffers for being exceedingly kind, would never describe her husband as "dumpy" to the press, even in jest. Hogan Sr.'s political career was ended in 1982 when he lost a bid for U.S. Senate against the incumbent Democrat Paul S. Sarbanes.

There are shades of gray and forgotten nuance to iconic moments in American political history and the legacies of politicians. Elected leaders are rarely as virtuous or self-serving as their respective cheerleaders and detractors remember them. Hogan Sr. is no different.

Still, any complexities in his political motivations or overall evaluations of his time in elected office don't diminish the influence of his legacy on the son. Hogan holds his dad up as a hero, and his father's influence undoubtedly shapes his politics and public persona.

The Primary Message: Electability

Hogan's entry rounded out a field of four men seeking the Republican nomination. Some felt the candidate to beat was David Craig, the county executive of Harford County, northeast of Baltimore City. The other candidates were Ron George, a state delegate from Anne Arundel County, and Charles Lollar, a Black businessman and former Marine. Hogan wasn't interested in highlighting his negligible policy differences with the rest of the field. He wanted to talk about electability. He flatly told the *Baltimore Sun* reporter Tim Wheeler that his opponents "haven't generated much enthusiasm or excitement or raised any money. That's one of the reasons why people were trying to encourage me to get into the race. Because they feel like this is an opportunity to have a competitive race in November, and they felt that I was the only one that could give that."[16]

Hogan announced Boyd Rutherford as his running mate at his first campaign rally on January 29, 2014. Rutherford had served with Hogan in the Ehrlich administration as secretary of the Department of General Services and later was assistant secretary in the U.S. Department of Agriculture under President George W. Bush. A reserved technocrat who is Black, Rutherford offered a personal contrast to the gregarious Hogan but shared his fiscally conservative politics.

On the Democratic side, millions of dollars were pouring into the contest between Lieutenant-Governor Anthony Brown, Attorney-General Doug Gansler, and State Delegate Heather Mizeur. Brown announced first, in early May 2013, but Gansler, twice elected to statewide office, held a fundraising advantage when he officially entered the race a few months later.[17] Brown closed the money gap when he selected as a running mate Ken Ulman, the popular Howard County executive contemplating his own run for governor, and the two combined their campaign accounts. The ticket also quickly picked up endorsements, including O'Malley and Barbara A. Mikulski, the longest-serving female senator and dean of the Maryland congressional delegation.[18] Brown, the son of Jamaican and Swiss immigrants, had had deep experience in state government and, if successful, would be the first Black governor of Maryland.

The race between Gansler and Brown was hotly contested and, at times, even personal. Gansler's campaign emphasized that Brown represented a continuation of the status quo and highlighted Brown's role as manager of the botched rollout of the Affordable Care Act health-care exchange in Maryland. Gansler's campaign also voiced some of the arguments Change Maryland had been making during the previous two years concerning the "entrenched political establishment" and said that the "hard-working people feel nickel-and-dimed, and the entrepreneurs we need are not building here in Maryland."[19]

Brown highlighted Gansler's missteps—notably, allegations that he misused the state police officer and vehicle assigned to him and a viral photograph of Gansler at a high school graduation beach party attended by his son and other friends who were drinking.[20] Mizeur, the most progressive candidate, mostly stayed above the fray, building a cadre of followers but without the resources to pose a serious challenge.

Hogan ran his primary race as if Brown were already his opponent. He hammered the "O'Malley-Brown administration" and reframed the previous eight years of Democratic policy victories as mismanagement of the budget at the expense of Maryland taxpayers. His attacks centered on the list of tax and fee increases that Change Maryland had been chronicling and a Gallup poll that found nearly half of Maryland residents wanted to move to a different state.[21] He also honed his messaging pièce de résistance: turning the stormwater remediation fee into a malevolent and politically powerful "rain tax."

He was the only GOP candidate with enough money to run television ads and raised enough through small donations to qualify for the state's public campaign funding.[22] If victorious in the primary, he would be guaranteed about $2.6 million in public financing for the general election. That qualifying for public money was the goal for the Hogan campaign further illustrates the general state of Republicans in Maryland.

Polling in February by the *Baltimore Sun* and *Washington Post* had Hogan up in the primary field by six and nine points, respectively. By early June, those same polls had him up by double digits. He ultimately won by fourteen points, earning 43 percent (92,376 votes) in the primary, where only Republicans were allowed to vote. Brown collected 51 percent (249,398 votes) in the Democratic primary, besting Gansler by double digits. In comparison, Hogan earned 12,345 fewer votes in his primary victory than Mizeur won in her third-place finish in the Democratic primary.

Many thought Hogan's victory was all but meaningless. The *Baltimore Sun* noted that the entire Republican field had spent less than $2.3 million and that Hogan still had little statewide name recognition. The article's last line belonged to a Republican voter who described her party's odds against the Democrats as a "snowball's chance in hell."[23]

The O'Malley Challenge

Brown spent mightily—arguably foolishly—to achieve what amounted to a landslide primary win, and he entered the general election contest underfunded. His herculean fundraising team raised more than $11 million leading up to the June primary. The decisions of his strategists left the campaign with about a half-million dollars in campaign funds.

Hogan, meanwhile, approached the summer with his public financing cash, and he would use it to build name recognition and drive home the point that electing Brown would effectively mean a third term of O'Malley. This presented a unique challenge to the Brown campaign.

O'Malley, who became the mayor of Baltimore City at thirty-six and went on to serve two terms as governor, had been the dominant political force in the state for more than a decade. As the 2014 cycle ramped up, he was preparing for an impending presidential run and racking up as many progressive victories as possible during his last two years in office.

He signed legislation that banned the death penalty, legalized same-sex marriage, enacted arguably the most sweeping gun control measures in the country, prohibited discrimination based on gender identity, and expanded reproductive health access for low-income women.

Those policy victories had the unintended consequence of clearing the field of the most pressing social issues, allowing Hogan to focus his gubernatorial campaign exclusively on economic issues where Republicans had crossover appeal with some Democrats.

During the Great Recession, O'Malley had chosen the path of investment over austerity and raised revenue in various ways. The Hogan campaign had added up every increase. By their count, O'Malley and Democrats increased or created forty different taxes and fees, including the rain tax.

As with many two-term governors, there was undoubtedly some O'Malley fatigue at the end of his term. According to polling conducted by the *Washington Post*, O'Malley's approval ratings peaked at 55 percent a month before he won reelection in 2010, then hovered around the 50 percent mark until falling to an eight-year low of 41 percent in October 2014, just as voters were making up their minds on a successor. Among Democrats, who are the majority of the state's voters, O'Malley's approval rating was 56 percent. The Brown campaign wanted to keep O'Malley at arm's length, but the Hogan campaign would not let that happen. The effort paid off: 63 percent of Maryland voters viewed Brown's agenda as "very" or "somewhat" like O'Malley's.

O'Malley and his supporters later faulted the Brown campaign for not embracing the two-term governor's record of progressive victories. And O'Malley later told Robert McCartney of the *Washington Post* that the Brown campaign "made a tactical decision not to defend the record or talk about it, and we saw the results that we saw."[24]

A Defining Summer

The day after Hogan's primary victory, his team dropped a web-only ad highlighting Brown's connection with O'Malley, the rain tax, and the failures of what should have been Brown's signature accomplishment: managing Maryland's health-care exchange under the Affordable Care Act.

The ad labeled Brown the "most incompetent man in Maryland," reminding voters that Brown "was put in charge of the health care rollout—and promptly wasted $125 million, on a website." It was a fair point: the Maryland Health Connection enrollment website crashed on its first day, October 1, 2013, and was slow to improve. It got so bad that the inspector general for the U.S. Department of Health and Human Services launched an investigation.

The same ad used an image of Brown and his running mate, Ulman, flexing their biceps. Hogan's team didn't realize that the pose was an homage to an eighteen-year-old University of Maryland student, Zachary Lederer, who had flexed while in a hospital bed to show friends his strength following brain cancer surgery. Lederer died in March 2014, and the pose became known as "Zaching." A web-only ad wouldn't have received much traction on its own. But the Brown campaign publicly criticized Hogan for being insensitive. The criticism, in turn, drove attention to it. "The lieutenant governor didn't dispute any facts in the ad, that he raised taxes forty times, wasted more than $125 million on the single biggest job entrusted to him, nearly doubled unemployment and has demonstrated no managerial competence," Hogan told reporters. "He only took issue with a picture in it, so we changed it for him."[25]

Giving underdog Hogan the opportunity to earn free media was a mistake that Brown repeated throughout the course of the campaign. Hogan capitalized on these opportunities while working to introduce and define himself to voters over the summer. Anyone speaking for the campaign stuck to messages on jobs, fiscal responsibility, and economic growth. There was no room for mistakes or missed opportunities. While Brown tended to limit his media availability, reporters could walk right up to Hogan and ask him questions. He was a fixture at public events, where he repeated his attack line to anyone who would listen: "They even taxed the rain." And as summer wore on, Hogan's internal polling showed him gaining name recognition and steadily narrowing the gap with Brown.

The Momentum Shift

The drumbeat of the rain tax, the forty tax hikes, and the botched health-care rollout was driving the campaign narrative, and Brown's people desperately wanted to change the conversation. They believed they could stop Hogan's momentum by painting him as a right-wing extremist who would restrict reproductive rights and roll back gun control measures. Democrats across the country had used similar tactics against ideologues and Tea Party extremists with some success. But it backfired against Hogan.

Brown's first television ad, launched in September, claimed Hogan opposed a woman's right to access an abortion even in cases of rape and incest. It cited Hogan's support of an order issued by his father, then the Prince George's County executive, to ban abortion in county hospitals except to save the life of the mother. It also described Hogan's prior support for a "human life" amendment giving civil rights to unborn infants.[26] The positions were more than thirty years old.

Hogan cut a response ad within a few hours. It was a simple, single-camera shot of his adult daughter, Jaymi Sterling, telling voters that "anti-woman" attacks against Hogan were misplaced. The ad informed voters of Hogan's positions on reproductive issues, which included requiring insurers cover over-the-counter birth control and a commitment not to change Maryland law regarding abortion access, and showcased his diverse family.[27]

Hogan's wife, the former Yumi Kim, grew up on a chicken farm in South Korea and immigrated to the United States at eighteen with her then husband. The marriage didn't work out, and Yumi and her three daughters—Kim, Jaymi, and Julie—eventually settled in Howard County because of the good public schools. Hogan first met Yumi at an art show, where she was showcasing her work, in 2001.[28] Yumi is a devout Presbyterian who worked as a cashier and was singularly focused on raising her girls. She initially brushed off Hogan's interest in her, taking his business card but never calling. The following year, Hogan returned to the same art show and tried his luck again, with far greater success. They soon began dating and married in 2004. After their marriage, Hogan supported his wife's dream of attending art school, which elated her daughters, with whom he shares a close relationship and considers his own.

Brown's ad opened the door for Jaymi to tell the Hogan family story, which could appeal to groups the GOP often has trouble reaching, such as immigrants, people of color, and single mothers.

A second Brown ad attempted to paint Hogan as an extremist on guns. The thirty-second spot, which ran in Baltimore and DC markets, showed images of assault rifles juxtaposed against children playing, set to ominous music and a human heartbeat. Hogan was on record as saying he opposed the gun control legislation signed by

O'Malley in 2013 but would not try to repeal it. The ad allowed him to remind voters—specifically, reachable Democratic voters—that he had no intention of changing current gun laws.

Brown's focus on social issues gave Hogan a broader opening to argue that the lieutenant-governor didn't want to address the O'Malley-Brown administration's tax increases or Brown's own economic plans. Three debates provided more of the same. Brown tried to force Hogan to talk about social issues. Hogan responded by accusing Brown of not wanting to talk about his record on taxes and the health insurance exchange. Brown argued that Hogan was a right-winger, but Hogan charted a moderate course by reiterating he did not intend to change current laws.

And although Hogan had spent a good part of the previous three years criticizing Democratic leaders in Maryland, he used the debates to stress his willingness to work across party lines while pointing out that Brown (or O'Malley) never did the same.

A Picture Perfect Finish

In the last week of October 2014, viewers in the Baltimore media market started seeing an ad called "Picture Perfect." The thirty-second spot featured a fast-talking narrator listing all the tax and fee increases during the two-term O'Malley-Brown administration presented in a series of snapshots of the items and called Brown "the second string for O'Malley's third high-tax term."

The authority line: the Republican Governors Association (RGA).

Getting the RGA to pay attention to Maryland was a coup. The state had not been on its target list for 2014. That would change, thanks to Hogan's campaign adviser Russ Schriefer.

Schriefer had worked for Ehrlich, producing ads for congressional victories and three runs for governor. He knew Hogan from his time in the Ehrlich administration and believed that the Republican had a chance. Schriefer is a powerful and connected political operative who worked on behalf of several high-profile Republican senatorial and gubernatorial campaigns and the presidential campaigns of George H. W. Bush, George W. Bush, and Mitt Romney.

The RGA could give Hogan the boost he needed. New Jersey Governor Chris Christie, the RGA's chair, was a political celebrity and a powerhouse fundraiser, drawing media attention wherever he went.[29] For months, Hogan's staff begged Schriefer to make the case to the RGA to invest resources in Maryland. It was a persistent chorus of "You gotta talk to Christie! Can you call him? What are you going to do about getting the RGA involved?"[30]

Schriefer's response was always, "That's not the way they operate."

The RGA's priorities are simple: first, protect incumbents; then identify places where investment has a realistic shot of paying off. The RGA had researched each state by early 2014. According to Executive Director Phil Cox, Illinois, Massachusetts, and Connecticut were chosen as the blue states that could go red. Maryland didn't make the cut.[31] Most polling from just before the June primary had Hogan down by almost twenty points in the general election, though an early July poll from the conservative-leaning *Rasmussen Reports* had Hogan down by thirteen.

The pitch from Schriefer finally came in late July, on a plane to a campaign event for Oklahoma Governor Mary Fallin, another Schriefer client. After listening to Cox give an overview on governors' races across the county, Schriefer interjected, "I want to talk you to about Maryland." Nobody was particularly open to this conversation. Christie couldn't even remember who the GOP's nominee was. Undeterred, Schriefer laid out the Hogan campaign's progress since winning the primary: *Anthony Brown is not very popular. There's a real desire for change. Hogan's message on taxes and economic development is resonating. He is a good candidate. Our polling shows that the race is winnable. It reminds me of your [Christie's] 2009 race against Jon Corzine.*

Schriefer had clout. And Christie was intrigued.

The New Jersey governor made his first trip to Maryland on September 17, headlining an event that raised more than $400,000 for Hogan. "In the beginning it didn't look like a race that was going to be tight, but it is tight now," said Christie. "That's why I'm here, and that's why the RGA is going to be here to help him."[32]

Christie would make four visits to Maryland in 2014, forging strong ties with Hogan.

The "Picture Perfect" ad encapsulated the points Hogan had been making for a year and the message that Change Maryland had delivered since its inception in 2011. The final push was enough to get a surging candidate over the finish line.

The Hogan campaign released top-line numbers from its internal polling on October 29. The data showed that the campaign had moved from a twelve-point deficit in July to a five-point advantage the week before the election. Forty-four percent of voters planned to vote for Hogan; 39 percent, for Brown; and 14 percent were still undecided.[33] And on October 31, the *Cook Political Report* moved Maryland's gubernatorial race from "leaning Democrat" to "toss-up."[34]

When the votes were counted on Tuesday, November 4, 2014, Hogan had bested Brown by a four-point margin, 51 to 47 percent. Turnout was a dismal 47.2 percent.

An Accidental Governor

The finger-pointing among Democrats started before the shock wore off.

Most outside—and some inside—the Brown campaign disparaged the strategic decisions of campaign manager Justin Schall and other high-level advisers. Many others placed the blame squarely on Brown, noting that he was rigid, inaccessible to the press, bad on TV, unwilling to defend O'Malley's accomplishments, and uninspiring to voters. Just 46.8 percent of Democrats had cast a ballot that cycle compared with 58.7 percent of Republicans.

The consensus among the political class in Maryland wasn't that Hogan won. It was that Brown lost and Hogan was an accidental governor.

Schriefer scoffs at this notion, arguing that "no Republican wins statewide by accident in Maryland."[35] In his view, Hogan's victory was more about a disciplined candidate tapping into the economic concerns held by most Marylanders that capitalized on Brown's shortcomings. The refusal to recognize Hogan as a formidable politician would hinder Democrats' efforts to sideline him over the next four years.

To that point, Hogan campaigned and made inroads with voters in the urban and suburban areas that had handed O'Malley his two victories against Ehrlich while still paying attention to the state's less populated areas. Brown won in the three populous Democratic strongholds—Montgomery County, Prince George's County, and Baltimore City—and smaller, racially diverse Charles County. But Brown's vote share, particularly in Montgomery and, to a lesser extent, Baltimore City, was smaller than expected, as was overall turnout in his home county of Prince George's. Unfortunately, no exit polling was conducted in Maryland in 2014 to provide a close look at the results by demographics.

Hogan earned 36.7 percent of the votes in Montgomery County, 14.9 percent in Prince George's County, and 21.9 percent in Baltimore City, a majority-Black jurisdiction where Democrats outnumber Republicans ten to one. He won in suburban Howard, Baltimore, and Anne Arundel counties, which cast nearly a third of the total votes in Maryland. The rural parts of the state broke hard for Hogan.

Learning from Ehrlich's Mistakes

Hogan was sworn in as Maryland's 62nd governor on January 21, 2015. He took his oath on a Bible used by Theodore R. McKeldin, the only Republican in Maryland history to serve two terms as governor. Christie delivered introductory remarks at the outdoor ceremony. "They said it was going to be a cold day in hell before we elected a Republican governor," Hogan quipped under heavy snowfall.[36]

His speech highlighted the economic themes of his campaign and contained fiscally conservative messaging but also emphasized bipartisan cooperation. "Too often, we see wedge politics and petty rhetoric used to belittle our adversaries and inflame partisan divisions. But I believe that Maryland is better than this," he said. "It is only when the partisan shouting stops that we can hear each other's voices and concerns."[37]

After a day of pomp came the realities of governing a state that had just elected a Democratic state comptroller and attorney-general—and, once again, a veto-proof majority in the General Assembly. Winning wasn't easy. Governing would be harder.

As governor, Hogan could shape some state policy by executive order, and the budget authority he had was considered among the broadest in the nation, according to a widely used measure of gubernatorial powers developed by the political scientist Thad Beyle (2004).[38]

But Democratic legislative leaders, holding a veto-proof majority, have greater say on public policy in Maryland.

Mike Miller entered his twenty-eighth year as Senate president when Hogan was inaugurated. He was a commanding presence—broad-shouldered, his once fiery red hair white with age. His tenure as a presiding officer had already overlapped with four other Maryland governors. Executives came and went. Miller endured.[39] Pragmatic and transactional, Miller was a master at controlling his chamber. An old Annapolis adage says, "Mike Miller has the votes to do anything he wants, including burning down the State House."

On the other side of the State House, the House of Delegates was led by another long-serving and powerful lawmaker: Speaker Michael Busch. Busch was more progressive than Miller, and, as a former running back at Temple University and local recreation department official, was affectionately called "coach" by members of his chamber.[40] Busch was Miller's equal in command of his respective chamber and ability to advance a Democratic agenda. For example, Busch repeatedly blocked legalized gambling during the administration of the previous Republican governor, Ehrlich, only to allow its passage under O'Malley's first term.[41] The maneuver served a dual political purpose: denying the Republican governor a significant policy victory and driving the narrative that Ehrlich was unable to work with the Democratic legislature.

Many Democrats told themselves that Hogan was little more than a shorter and less charismatic version of Ehrlich and that "Mike and Mike," as the presiding officers were often called, would render Hogan ineffective and subsequently deny him a second term—just as they did to Ehrlich.

There were similarities between the two Republican governors. Both ran on themes of change and fiscal responsibility. Both tapped Black men—Michael Steele for Ehrlich and Rutherford for Hogan—as lieutenant-governor. Both won their first gubernatorial contests by besting a sitting lieutenant-governor. Both have similar outgoing personalities. These surface similarities mask the consequential differences between them.

Journalists and political insiders generally agree on the three biggest mistakes by Ehrlich as governor: he made some poor staffing decisions; he couldn't communicate effectively to the public through the statewide media; and he fought unnecessary battles with the legislature that he couldn't win. Hogan learned from these mistakes and did not repeat them.

One of the most controversial episodes of Ehrlich's tenure was the hiring of an eccentric campaign operative, Joe Steffen, into an administration job to root out Democrats in state agencies and replace them with Republican loyalists.[42] Steffen favored black trench coats and unlit offices, calling himself the "Prince of Darkness." He started making the rounds of agencies and reviewing their rosters. The firings began. Democrats, including Busch, were outraged and formed a committee to examine whether Ehrlich's firing practices violated state employment laws. But before the committee could meet, Steffen himself was fired: he had been outed as a participant on a conservative message board, FreeRepublic.com, that was spreading rumors about O'Malley's personal life.[43]

No longer a state employee, Steffen acknowledged in testimony that the terminations had been "informed by party affiliation" and that he met regularly with top state officials to receive lists of at-will employees to review. Those officials, Steffen claimed, were Ehrlich's Chief of Staff Steven L. Kreseski and Appointments Secretary Larry Hogan.

Hogan denied any involvement with Steffen during sworn testimony, and the committee never implicated Hogan in any wrongdoing, though some Democrats still believe he was directly involved. Hogan maintained that he simply did his job as appointments secretary, which included replacing the appointees of former Democratic Governor Parris Glendening. The controversy generated by Steffen consumed Annapolis for months during an election year. C. Fraser Smith, a longtime journalist and opinion writer, referred to Steffen as "the Ehrlich administration's Katrina," arguing that the news surrounding Steffen had helped to tarnish Ehrlich's "well-liked, a nice guy" image.

Ehrlich would go on to lose his reelection bid to Martin O'Malley.

Being close to a political storm that could have ended his future political ambitions was enough. There would be no room for staff that detracted from Hogan's public image or those who made publicly embarrassing mistakes in his executive branch.

"It's a massive undertaking to get elected, and then ninety days later, you submit a budget, a legislative package, and you have to hire staff. I identified people who were loyal, capable, and talented. And I didn't care whether they were Republicans or Democrats," Hogan recalls. He goes on to note, "I also rounded up people from the private sector, those who never worked in state government and could run things like a business. And we did national searches on some positions."[44]

Rutherford, who helped advise Hogan on staffing decisions, adds, "We were looking for competence and people who weren't overtly political but were politically savvy. We wanted people who were respected across the partisan aisle and did not want partisan bomb throwers."[45] Rutherford also points to managerial differences between the two Republican governors: "Hogan is much more hands-on, while Ehrlich relied a lot more on his chief of staff and his deputy chiefs of staff to engage with the executive departments."

Hogan and Rutherford also agreed that they wouldn't comment on every piece of legislation or matter. They were not going to testify in front of legislative committees. "If the legislation gains enough traction to get to us," Rutherford says, "we'll go through our legislative shop to work on it, but we're not going to be rolling out all the cabinet secretaries to testify on every bill." This tack was different from how Ehrlich chose to engage. The former governor would battle with the Democrats both in the press and by personally testifying to legislative committees even on issues he was almost certain to lose. The Hogan administration does most of its public communication on legislative matters through press statements. This practice has resulted in criticism that the governor is disengaged from the policy-making process and uninterested in building relationships with lawmakers.[46]

Ehrlich also had trouble communicating through the State House press. Some reporters described his communications team as not particularly good at their jobs. The same could not be said for the team Hogan assembled. His first communications director, Matthew Clark, set a standard for fierce loyalty, disciplined messaging, and professionalism. Clark stayed in his role for eighteen months before returning to the private sector. He rejoined Hogan a year later as chief of staff.

David Nitkin, the State House bureau chief at the *Baltimore Sun* during the Ehrlich years, notes that when Ehrlich was running for governor, he was accessible to the press that followed him on the campaign trail. That changed, especially for print media, soon after he was sworn into office. In Nitkin's view, Ehrlich did not take well to criticism. Responding to what he considered unfair coverage over a deal to sell off state-owned land to a politically connected developer, Ehrlich took the unprecedented step of banning Nitkin and the *Baltimore Sun* columnist Michael Olesker from speaking with state executive branch employees. The *Baltimore Sun* sued the Ehrlich administration for an infringement of the reporter's First Amendment rights. Courts later ruled in favor of Ehrlich, but the ordeal drew increased public scrutiny to his administration and further highlighted the differences between Ehrlich and the Democratic leadership on environmental and land-use issues. The ban lifted, Nitkin notes, "when O'Malley became governor."[47]

Hogan is still guarded, sometimes prickly, and often terse with the media. While he holds frequent, structured press conferences and gives media opportunities to ask him questions directly during informal gaggles at his public events, he regularly refuses to grant one-on-one interviews with certain reporters or entire outlets. Herein lies a difference with Ehrlich: Hogan will privately refuse to engage but would never publicly ban a reporter or outlet.

At the same time, Hogan is a frequent guest on outlets and with interviewers he likes, such as Clarence "C4" Mitchell IV, a former state senator and host on WBAL AM radio who is a cousin of the top Hogan adviser Keiffer Mitchell. But his communications team, even though adversarial and aggressively on-message, recognizes that the media plays an important role and makes sure their boss is fully prepared for interviews and press conferences. Even Hogan's harshest critics admit that he assembled a top-notch communications team from the infancy of his administration. He has also proved difficult to push off-message, even by seasoned State House reporters, and rarely makes verbal gaffes or slip-ups.

Josh Kurtz, a reporter who covered the first Ehrlich campaign and now the founding editor at *Maryland Matters*, an independent news website that focuses exclusively on state politics, notes that "Hogan is not Mr. Open to the press, quite the contrary." He adds, "In all my time covering politics on Capitol Hill, I've never experienced the type of defensive or attack posture that I saw out of Hogan's press shop." Kurtz also says that Hogan dealt with a completely different, arguably more advantageous, media environment: "The economy of the news business in the state has changed a lot since Ehrlich was governor. Even major outlets have fewer resources and reporters covering the state politics."[48] Moreover, Kurtz contends, the rise of social media, which Hogan's communications team is adept at using, meant that he didn't have to rely solely on the press to get his message out.

A First Look at Governing

One of Hogan's first acts as governor was to add "We're Open for Business" to Maryland's highway welcome signs. The longtime *Baltimore Sun* columnist Dan Rodricks wasn't impressed. "The greeting is supposed to make it clear that Maryland will . . . what?" he wrote. "Give free pedicures to any executive who locates a business here? Further reduce industrial regulation? Hand out massive tax breaks? Is that what we're all about?"[49]

The first real view of Hogan's priorities came days after his swearing-in, when he released his first budget proposal. As expected, he cut into spending—but not as deeply as some Democrats had feared—to produce a balanced budget, as required by law. Among other things, he called for cuts to Medicaid and a freeze on salary increases for state employees.

Hogan's primary goals were to make room for a series of targeted tax cuts and to address the state's structural deficit by making payments into an underfunded pension system. Republicans were thrilled. Democrats were determined to claw back as much funding for their priorities as possible. The state legislature cannot add to or move money around within the governor's proposed operating budget in Maryland. However, lawmakers can make cuts and ask the governor to give them a supplemental bill that adds money back to legislative priorities. Democratic leadership offered a budget counterproposal that increased pay for state employees and added education funding while eliminating Hogan's proposed tax cuts.

Hogan responded with a supplemental budget that ignored the top priorities of General Assembly leaders. Busch, the House speaker, at one point refused to let his chamber even consider the supplemental budget, creating immediate tension.

As the session came down to the last days, Hogan told reporters, "We made a proposal to them we think is fair, that accomplishes many of the things they're trying to get done and is a little more fiscally responsible."[50]

But things did not end smoothly. In the final budget agreement, Hogan returned about half of the money that lawmakers had tried to steer toward schools, but refused to release $68 million more that lawmakers had cut—an affront to Democratic leaders.

In response, Democrats hastily passed a bill that in future years would require the governor to give more money to school districts where the cost of education is higher. Hogan decided not to veto it. Unlike Ehrlich, he didn't dig his heels in on losing battles. Allowing bills that he opposed to go into law without his signature, instead of fighting with the legislature and taking a public loss when his veto was overridden, became a common practice.

In the weeks that followed, Democratic leaders and teachers' unions hammered the governor for "short-changing Maryland," a twist on his Change Maryland brand, and accused him of declaring war on Maryland's children. The rift between Hogan and public education advocates would never heal.

But it was unclear whether the conflict was resonating with voters.

Polls from Goucher College and the *Washington Post* during the first few weeks of Hogan's tenure in office showed that he was still largely unknown, with 40 percent approving of his job performance, 17 percent disapproving, and 43 percent saying they didn't know. But Marylanders were significantly more positive on the state's direction since he took office. Majorities said they didn't want cuts to education and schools but supported other cost-saving measures, such as reducing payments the state makes to doctors who participate in Medicaid, forcing state agencies to cut 2 percent from their budgets, and freezing salaries for state employees.[51] Residents also supported some of Hogan's proposed tax cuts.

Even though many of his proposals were killed, tabled, or watered down, Hogan ended the session with a positive spin. "We didn't get everything we wanted, they're not going to get everything they wanted, but overall it was a strong session," he said. "I think it's good for the taxpayers of Maryland."[52]

Perhaps most significant, he fulfilled his promise on stormwater, at least to some extent. Earlier in the legislative session, Democrats had killed Hogan's version of the rain tax repeal. However, they eventually got behind a bill sponsored by Miller that made the program voluntary and gave more flexibility to each jurisdiction but required that local governments report on how they were funding the mandated bay cleanup.

"It doesn't matter to me who gets the credit, or whose name is on the bill," Hogan told reporters when asked about Miller's bill. "Everybody knows I'm the leading driver behind this entire movement. We called it the 'rain tax.' I got 100,000 people involved in the effort. I was elected mainly on this issue. The senate president agrees with us. The bills essentially do the same thing."[53]

The bill eventually passed through both legislative chambers, and Hogan signed it into law on May 12, 2015. In an accompanying statement, he said that "charging Marylanders for the rain that falls on the roof of their homes made the rain tax the most universally detested tax throughout the state and I am pleased to finally declare an end to it."[54]

2

The Uprising and the Honeymoon

On April 12, 2015, a day before the adjournment of Hogan's first legislative session as governor, Freddie Gray was arrested in Baltimore City for possession of a switchblade. He died a week later from the injuries he sustained at the hands of the police. Like Eric Garner, Michael Brown, and Sandra Bland before, and Philando Castile and George Floyd after, Gray instantly became a national symbol of systemic racial injustices plaguing policing in America. The events that followed Gray's death, about eight months after protests and violence over police brutality in Ferguson, Missouri, were the first real test of the fledgling governor's leadership.

Public demonstrations over Gray's mistreatment and eventual death began on August 18. The first instances of unrest occurred on Saturday, April 25, when a peaceful march that brought nearly 1,200 people to City Hall earlier that day ended with a tense standoff between a smaller group of protesters and police outside of Camden Yards, the home of the Baltimore Orioles. Police cruiser windows were smashed and downtown businesses were vandalized.[1] The incident drew massive national attention, partly because fans attending the baseball game were briefly locked inside the stadium as announcers warned of an "ongoing public safety issue."[2] In a press conference that evening, Baltimore Mayor Stephanie Rawlings-Blake spoke to the balance between order and respecting free speech, telling reporters,

> We've had these kinds of conversations before, and I made it very clear that I work with the police and instructed them to do everything that they could to make sure that the protesters were able to exercise their right to free speech. It's a very delicate balancing act. Because while we try to make sure that they were protected from the cars and the other things that were going on, we also gave those who wished to destroy space to do that as well. And we worked very hard to keep that balance and to put ourselves in the best position to de-escalate, and that's what you saw this evening.[3]

The context of her comments was quickly lost, leaving only "we also gave those who wished to destroy space to do that" to dominate local and national media coverage while drawing harsh criticism from conservative commentators.[4]

The governor put his entire executive team, including Major-General Linda Singh of the Maryland National Guard and Colonel Bill Pallozzi of the Maryland State Police, on alert after the incident at Camden Yards. Gray's funeral was held two days later, at New Shiloh Baptist Church in West Baltimore. Along with Gray's grieving family, the service was attended by Baltimore's political and civil rights leaders, members of the Obama administration, and thousands of Baltimoreans.

There remain differing perspectives on what ultimately pushed a city on edge and plagued by systemic racism to the arson and violence that followed. Some point to rumors of a planned "purge," a period of lawlessness modeled after the movie series by the same name, set to start at Mondawmin Mall and continue downtown to the Inner Harbor on the day of Gray's funeral.[5] The threat caused downtown businesses such as T. Rowe Price and historic Lexington Market to close for the day. Public transportation was halted, and police were sent to Mondawmin Mall, adjacent to a transportation hub where students would normally catch their buses to head home.

When school let out, young Baltimoreans, already anxious, were met by police in riot gear. With no way to leave and tensions rising, some threw bricks and bottles at officers. Most were just scared school-age children trying to find a way home caught in a situation created by adults. Meg Gibson, a teacher at Belmont Elementary School, witnessed the scene from a stoplight in front of Frederick Douglass High School and directly across from Mondawmin Mall at 3 P.M. "There were police helicopters flying overhead. The riot police were already at the bus stop on the other side of the mall, turning buses that transport the students away, not allowing students to board," she posted on Facebook. "Those kids were set up, they were treated like criminals before the first brick was thrown."[6] Other teachers and parents recounted similar experiences to reporters, though some community members and business owners interviewed that day were more angry than sympathetic.

The afternoon confrontation between students and police and the continued civil unrest in different parts of the city marked the start of the worst violence the city had experienced since 1968, when riots broke out nationwide following the assassination of Dr. Martin Luther King Jr.[7] In the hours that followed, there was looting, property destruction, and confrontations between protesters and police.[8] A CVS pharmacy and a community center were set on fire. This was the image most outside Baltimore would see on cable television news over the next few days. By morning, police had made 235 arrests (201 adults and 34 minors), and twenty police officers had been injured.[9]

Keiffer Mitchell, a senior adviser to Hogan, was sent to Baltimore to establish a direct line of communication with Mayor Rawlings-Blake on the day of Gray's funeral. Mitchell had known the mayor since middle school and was a former Democratic member of the Baltimore City Council. Mitchell met up with Rawlings-Blake at City Hall, where the mayor and her senior staff were fielding a barrage of phone calls and attending meetings, including one with a group of Baltimore City students. Rawlings-Blake briefly stepped out to speak with the governor during the meeting with the students.

Soon after, the mayor and core staffers departed City Hall for the Emergency Operations Center on Calvert Street, where Mitchell was supposed to meet them.[10] But first Rawlings-Blake stopped at police headquarters for a meeting with Police Commissioner Anthony Batts and her law department regarding the state of emergency and to iron out details of the citywide curfew. This put the mayor and Mitchell at different locations for about ninety minutes, resulting in reports that Rawlings-Blake was "out of touch" with the governor. Staff to Rawlings-Blake push back on this notion, arguing that Mitchell knew where they were and could have reached them by cell phone. Mitchell contends that no one answered his calls.

Hogan had already put the National Guard on standby and canceled leave for all state troopers following the events outside of Camden Yards. He had two versions of an executive order ready to sign to deploy the National Guard to Baltimore City: one said that the mayor requested the help, and the other did not. Hogan wanted to release the former. Mitchell, at one point, advised Hogan that he might have to make the call without the mayor. But Rawlings-Blake connected with Hogan soon after at 6:30 P.M. and asked him to declare a state of emergency and send in the National Guard. Hogan did so immediately.

The mayor and the governor spoke to the press separately that evening, then appeared together around midnight. There was obvious friction. During Hogan's earlier press conference declaring the state of emergency, he noted that he was "trying to get in touch with the mayor for quite some time" before adding, "she *finally* made that call, and we immediately took action." Rawlings-Blake, reportedly frustrated by the inexperienced governor, was angry that he insinuated she was out of contact when she was working out details of a state of emergency.

Hogan held a morning press conference the next day and vowed to restore order. "We're not going to have another repeat of what happened last night," he said. "It's not going to happen tonight." And it didn't. While there were scattered instances of property damage and confrontations between protesters and police in the days that followed, most damage and unrest was limited to that single day. The national media that had descended on the city gave the governor largely positive coverage for his leadership and decision to send in the National Guard.

Hogan moved state government operations to his offices in Baltimore City, where they remained for ten days until the state of emergency was lifted on May 6. During that time, he visited injured police officers in the hospital, was a visible presence in the city, and met with community leaders and residents. He also chose his words carefully, a disciplined style that became a hallmark of his public communications. He told David Collins, a reporter for WBAL-TV, "My heart goes out to the family and everyone involved in the entire incident, and like everyone else, we are hoping to get to the bottom of it and find out the facts."[11] On May 3, Baltimore City State's Attorney Marilyn Mosby brought charges against all six officers involved in Gray's arrest, a rapid development that came before a police investigation was complete, but was lauded by some Baltimore City residents. Hogan responded: "With respect to the indictment, we believe in the criminal justice system. The process is going to play itself out. I don't have much role in that process, but we're focused on keeping the city safe. We understand that emotions are still high, that there's a lot of frustration out there. I've been incredibly impressed with the people of Baltimore. They care about their community, they're concerned about their neighbors. I want to continue to ask for calm and peace."[12]

The deployment of the National Guard helped prevent prolonged violence and certainly brought a sense of order for many city residents and business owners. Others resented a military presence in their city. But the deployment was only one part of the larger response. Black community and church leaders stepped up and calmed their streets; Democratic elected officials helped organize clean-ups and reached out to their constituents; and, perhaps most importantly, everyday citizens, who wanted justice for Gray, also demanded that the violence stop. Reverend Alvin Hathaway, the head pastor at Union Baptist Church, credits Colonel Melvin Russell, chief of the Baltimore City Police Community Collaboration Division, for playing a key role in bringing together a coalition, including the faith community and gang leaders, to help stop the violence. Hathaway also lauds the leadership of Singh, the National Guard chief. He notes that the National Guard created a sense of order but was restrained in its interactions with the community.[13]

The contrast between Hogan's response to Baltimore's unrest in 2015 and President Donald Trump's comments and leadership five years later, during the protests in 2020 over the murder of George Floyd, is stark. During an appearance on CNN's *State of the Union* on May 30, 2020, Hogan told Jake Tapper, "I think one of the most important things that a leader can do right now, and I went through this in 2015 during the riots in Baltimore, one of my primary focuses was to try to lower the temperature." Referencing Trump's tweets, including one that said, "When the looting starts, the shooting starts," Hogan added, "It's sort of continuing to escalate the rhetoric. I think it's just the opposite of the message that should have been coming out of the White House."[14]

Hogan was less judicious in the retelling of the events in Baltimore in his 2020 memoir *Still Standing.* He described Rawlings-Blake as "paralyzed with fear and indecision, . . . [and] making some very poor decisions: ordering the police to stand down and missing in action when her city was desperate and needed her most" and Freddie Gray as a "street-level drug dealer with a long criminal rap sheet, well known to these Baltimore City police." Regarding the outcome of the trials against the police officers, he wrote, "Mosby, the 'no justice, no peace' prosecutor, was 0 for 6."[15]

As expected, there remain mixed reactions to and accounts of Hogan's leadership during the Baltimore Uprising, as these events came to be called. As part of lawsuit against Baltimore City brought by small-business owners affected by the 2015 unrest, Baltimore City leadership, including Rawlings-Blake and her staff, as well as Batts, offered a critical view of Hogan and the state's actions in depositions concerning the content of their communications and actions during the afternoon and into the early evening of April 27, 2016.[16] Others maintain that the governor acted decisively and effectively navigated a precarious situation that could have escalated as in Ferguson.

A Golf Ball–Size Lump

A month later, Hogan, along with his wife, Yumi, and a delegation of Maryland business executives and higher-education leaders, kicked off a twelve-day economic development and trade mission to Asia. The trip included meetings with South Korean President Park Geun-hye, Chinese Vice Premier Liu Yandong, and Japanese Prime Minister Shinzo Abe during stops in Seoul, Beijing, and Tokyo. Hogan hoped to attract foreign investment to Maryland, including a pitch for Korea Air to add service to Baltimore-Washington International Thurgood Marshall Airport.

But the most talked-about moment of the trip came from Hogan's ride on a magnetic levitation (maglev) train at the Yamanashi Maglev

Test Track near Mount Fuji. Hogan had campaigned on a transportation platform focused on roads and highways, but he was enamored with the possibility of traveling from Baltimore to Washington in less than fifteen minutes. He later signed a memorandum of cooperation with Abe to explore a partnership with the Japanese government to bring maglev high-speed rail to the state.

Hogan was mentally energized by the trip, but physically he was unwell. On the day before the delegation's return to Maryland, the governor found a golf ball–size lump in his neck while shaving. The pain and sickness he felt the entire trip wasn't extended jet lag or the pains of late middle age. Doctors confirmed the worst when he returned home: he had an abdomen full of tumors that were now pushing against his spine.

On June 22, surrounded by his family and members of his cabinet, Hogan told a room full of reporters and shocked staffers he had "very advanced and very aggressive" non-Hodgkin's lymphoma. He said he planned to remain in office with the help of Lieutenant-Governor Boyd Rutherford while he underwent chemotherapy treatment. Ovetta Wiggins and Jenna Johnson of the *Washington Post* described the emotional scene:

> He gripped the lectern and spoke openly, saying that he had noticed a lump in his neck while shaving, and that it turned out to be one of more than 30 tumors. He struggled while listing the medical terms: "An aggressive B-cell, non-Hodgkin's lymphoma, to be specific." To his left, his wife, Yumi Hogan, clenched her hands into fists.[17]

The governor faced his mortality with a dose of political spin, telling the room:

> The best news is that my odds of getting through this and beating this are much, much better than the odds I had of beating Anthony Brown to become the 62nd governor of Maryland. The odds are better than finally doing away with the rain tax mandate. The odds are better than delivering tax relief for the families of Maryland. Better than the odds of passing a budget that doesn't include tax hikes and reins in state spending. Better

than the odds of negotiating enhanced PMT [Phosphorus Management Tool] regulations with both the agricultural community and the environmental community to help save our bay. Better than the odds of reducing tolls for the first time in 50 years. And definitely better than actually having the *Baltimore Sun* name me as Marylander of the Year.[18]

The governor's chemotherapy regimen began almost immediately after the press conference. He received treatments throughout the summer and into the fall. It was unquestionably physically and mentally brutal, but he endured it while working from his hospital room, very publicly, with humility and humor.

The day after Hogan announced his diagnosis, presidential candidate Donald Trump headlined the Maryland Republican Party's annual Red, White, and Blue Dinner. Hogan didn't attend the event for obvious reasons. Trump had entered the race a few weeks earlier. At the event, Trump said, "I've met your governor, I respect your governor, and he is going to beat this. Give him my regards."[19] These were the first and last public comments Trump would make explicitly about Hogan until the two men clashed over the response to the COVID-19 pandemic in 2020. Trump was also wrong about meeting Hogan. The two men didn't meet in person until the annual Governors' Dinner at the White House in 2017.

Hogan would have liked to be anywhere but somewhere sick with cancer. But missing the photo op with Trump, thus depriving opponents of a visual weapon, would ultimately benefit his reelection campaign. Democrats later had to settle for a picture of Hogan with Secretary of Education Betsy DeVos for attack ads. But like most elected Republicans at the time, Hogan didn't personally give Trump or his candidacy much serious thought. Even Doug Mayer, who was serving as Hogan's deputy director of communications at the time and is paid to worry about that kind of thing, did not see Trump as a problem for Hogan. "At that point in time, the crisis was the cancer and not the Trump candidacy," he recalls.[20]

For the Republicans running for president, however, Trump was nothing but major problems from the moment he got into the race. His racist and off-color comments drove the discussion on every major cable TV show that gave him, a candidate who was then averaging less than 5 percent in national GOP primary polls, a disproportionate amount of crucial early attention.[21]

Still, most seasoned Republican observers believed attention would soon turn away from the Trump circus and to any one of the Republican stars who were either already in the primary race or said to be thinking about it.

The Red Line: Boon for Baltimore, or Boondoggle?

On June 25, 2015, three days after he went public with his cancer diagnosis, Hogan officially pulled the plug on the Red Line, a long-planned east-west light-rail line in Baltimore City. And this wasn't just any project. Former Governor Martin O'Malley and other Democrats had worked to secure $900 million in federal funds for the transit line, and the Maryland Transit Administration had invested more than a dozen years and $288 million in planning, design, engineering, and land acquisition. Proponents of the project, including Baltimore business leaders and transportation and community activists, argued that the rail project would secure a strong future for the city by bolstering jobs and economic development.

Rawlings-Blake, who had already clashed with Hogan over the unrest in Baltimore City, released a statement saying, "Although the governor has promised to support economic growth in Baltimore, he canceled a project that would have expanded economic development, created thousands of jobs, increased access to thousands more, and offered residents better health care, child care, and educational opportunities." Democratic elected officials in the region were furious.[22]

Hogan dismissed the project as a "wasteful boondoggle" that was fatally flawed in design and was "not the best way to bring jobs and opportunity to the city."[23] His biggest gripe with the project was the billion-dollar price tag for a portion that required a downtown tunnel. Pete Rahn, Hogan's secretary of transportation, who came from New Mexico, shared the governor's preference for investment in roads and highways. Rahn believed that the Red Line's $2.9 billion cost estimate "wasn't realistic" and that the costs associated with tunneling would have "ballooned by an additional $1 billion."[24] Ron Cassie, a journalist with *Baltimore Magazine* who extensively covered the Red Line and city transportation issues, noted, "Hogan is great with language, calling it a 'boondoogle,' but the Hogan administration has not produced a report or study about cost overruns, ridership, economic impact, or racial equity to this day."[25] After the decision, Hogan dismissed requests to discuss the project further and eventually reallocated funds that would have paid for the Red Line to various highway improvement projects in other parts of the state.

At the same time, and although he campaigned against it, Hogan approved a public transportation project in Montgomery and Prince George's counties known as the Purple Line, earning praise from Democrats and other local business leaders. Speaking to Robert McCartney of the *Washington Post*, Montgomery County Executive Ike Leggett, a Democrat, noted that the governor's decision-making process "had no hint of politics or partisanship whatsoever" and added, "You have to give him very much credit that he was willing, open and ready to listen."[26]

Hogan would later allocate $135 million to Baltimore City for a revamped bus system called BaltimoreLink, a move that Don Fry, the president and chief executive of the Greater Baltimore Committee, a pro-business group, called "not an adequate substitute for a multibillion-dollar project that would have provided thousands of jobs and connected significantly disadvantaged parts of the city."[27] Sheryll Cashin, a law professor at Georgetown University, wrote in a 2020 article for *Politico*, "[For] Black Baltimoreans and allies watching, the pattern of investing public funds in white areas and disinvesting from Black neighborhoods could not have been more obvious."[28] Democratic State Delegate Robbyn Lewis, who at the time of the cancellation was an environmental activist and head of the political action committee Red Line Now, maintained that "the impact of [Hogan's] decision will color social, economic and environmental outcomes in this city for a generation."

Cassie also notes that "there is a political class that benefits from constantly throwing Baltimore City under the bus, arguing that the money spent in Baltimore is a waste whether it's on transit or education. Larry Hogan has often used language that implies that Baltimore City isn't part of the state."[29] The cancellation of the Red Line, as well as some of Hogan's later rhetoric on schools, crime, and various problems facing Baltimore City, is central to the belief held by some city residents, Democratic lawmakers, and progressives that Hogan is uninterested in bettering, and even adversarial to, the city.

But lawmakers and residents from other parts of the state were, not surprisingly, far less concerned. Instead of building the Red Line, Hogan allocated $160 million to widen Route 404, a gateway to beaches in Maryland and Delaware, in rural Caroline and Talbot counties. Another $90 million went to realign U.S. 219 between Interstate 68 and the Pennsylvania line in Garrett County, the westernmost jurisdiction in the state. And $100 million went to a new interchange at Routes 295 and 175 near Fort Meade and reconfigured the Severn River bridge on U.S. 50 near Annapolis in Anne Arundel County. The Democratic stronghold of Prince George's County received $135 million to rebuild a Capital Beltway interchange leading to the Greenbelt Metro station.

A few months after the cancellation of the Red Line, a coalition of civil rights groups that included the National Association for the Advancement of Colored People (NAACP) and the American Civil Liberties Union (ACLU) filed a federal complaint against the Hogan administration with the U.S. Department of Transportation. "The cancellation of the Red Line, rather than being a cost-saving measure, was simply a naked transfer of resources from the project corridor's primarily African American population to other rural and suburban parts of the state," it said.[30] On behalf of Hogan, Mayer fired back. "Ultimately, this so-called complaint has absolutely zero credibility or legal standing, and is essentially nothing more than a press release," he said. "The Red Line didn't move forward because it was poorly designed and simply unaffordable, with at least a billion-dollar tunnel running through the heart of the city." Trump's Department of Transportation closed the complaint in mid-2017 "without finding."[31]

Hogan's 2014 victory exposed weaknesses and divisions festering within the Maryland Democratic Party, reflecting ideological struggles between moderates and progressives now prominent at the national level. But the most significant divisions are grounded in the changing regional power dynamics of the state. Nearly a million people called Baltimore City home in the 1950s, but the population has since steadily declined. By the time Hogan took office, only about

620,000 residents called the city home, approximately 10 percent of all eligible statewide voters by 2018. That population loss, coupled with growth in the suburbs around Washington, DC, has severely diminished the political power of the state's largest city.

A poll conducted in February 2018 by Goucher College found that only a quarter of Maryland residents viewed Baltimore City as the economic engine of the state, a frequent assertion made by state leaders across the political spectrum.[32] The Maryland region or county-level jurisdiction that can claim status as the state's economic engine depends on the measure. The populous counties in the Washington, DC, metro area—Montgomery and Prince George's—generate more state revenue from income and sales taxes. Still, Baltimore City is home to a vibrant port and internationally known health-care companies. The Baltimore metro area, which includes Baltimore City and the surrounding counties, accounts for about half of all state gross domestic product (GDP); Montgomery and Prince George's counties account for slightly more than a third.[33] In 2021, Montgomery County was home to the headquarters of three *Fortune* 500 companies, as was Baltimore City and surrounding Baltimore County.[34]

Hogan has navigated these dynamics to his advantage throughout his time in office. For example, a poll conducted a few months before the Red Line cancellation found that 82 percent of Maryland residents had heard "a little" or "nothing at all" about "the proposed Red Line public transportation project in Baltimore."[35] Throughout Hogan's first term, Marylanders were consistently divided over whether the state should invest more money in "roads and highways" or "public transportation," suggesting that how residents viewed the governor's transportation priorities very much depended on where they lived and how they commuted. A poll by Goucher College conducted three months after he canceled the Red Line found that 50 percent of Marylanders approved of the job Hogan was doing on transportation and 29 percent disapproved.

Developing and Controlling the Message: Polls and Media

Hogan's careful attention to public sentiment and media relations helps him maintain popularity even when bucking ideas supported by huge swaths of Democratic voters and their elected representatives. His team frequently conducts internal polling, and the information he gathers has helped him determine which initiatives to highlight. Polling has helped him understand when to go to battle with Democrats, when to compromise, and when to take the loss. His critics disparage this as "governing by the polls." Hogan views it as governing. And a focus on promoting popular policy issues has contributed to his political success. For a Republican governor of a blue state, public support and executive powers are the only real check on a Democratic legislature with a veto-proof majority.

But what sets Hogan apart is how effectively he's incorporated public opinion into his media strategy. Earning and keeping the support of Democratic voters is much harder for a Republican elected official than a Democrat, so Hogan needed to continually remind them—and, to a lesser extent, independents—why they took a chance on him in the first place. Every communications team wants to frame the discussions to advance its agenda. Hogan's team took it a step further during his first months in office and throughout his first term. They didn't just control the narrative; they also controlled the clock.

An early and illustrative example is an announcement that tolls would be reduced at Maryland's bridges and tunnels. In January 2015, Hogan, as governor-elect, told reporters that he planned to "try to reduce tolls" sometime after the first legislative session, which ended the following April. Little was publicly said after that, until Bryan Sears, a reporter for the *Daily Record*, got a tip in early May that the Maryland Transportation Authority would take up the proposed reductions of tolls at a meeting hastily scheduled for a few days later.

Sears approached the governor's staff at a public event in Baltimore and told them he had enough information to write the story. The press staff said they wouldn't comment. "But later," Sears said, "when the governor was getting lunch at Faidley's in Lexington Market, he came over, leaned across the table, and asked me, 'Why are you trying to ruin my press conference?'"[36] The *Daily Record* ran the story, which included a detail that the transportation authority would meet in a building near the Chesapeake Bay Bridge, miles away from its typical meeting spot in Baltimore. Backups at the bridge toll plaza were notorious and infuriating, but no one would say why that meeting location was chosen.

The transportation authority met at 8 A.M. and quickly voted to decrease tolls. Hogan's communications team was setting up just across the street in front of the Bay Bridge toll plaza. Less than a half-hour after the vote, Transportation Secretary Pete Rahn walked out of the building and over to the toll booth, where the governor was ready to announce the cuts to the public. With a busy Bay Bridge tolling plaza as the backdrop, Hogan gave brief remarks and then, using a big bright-red marker, crossed out the old fees on the toll sign and wrote in the new, lower number as the television cameras rolled.

Democratic leaders knew Hogan was planning to make cuts but were caught off guard by the compressed time frame and lack of courtesy consultation before the public announcement. By the time Democrats put together a response, television reporters were putting the finishing touches on their packages for the evening news. The toll reductions received positive statewide media coverage, but the TV coverage was especially favorable. For example, a story on NBC4, the station with the highest viewership in the Washington, DC, metro area, did not include a single oppositional viewpoint. The reporter introduced the segment by saying, "This is pretty incredible. In fact, Maryland Governor Larry Hogan said this is the first decrease in tolls in the state in almost fifty years."[37] The coverage must have been infuriating for Democratic leaders. Making matters worse, as they fumed, Hogan staffers were putting up posters announcing the reductions at the various toll plazas across the state.

The toll reduction rollout became a familiar operating procedure for Hogan's communications team. They would run the same playbook later that summer when the governor announced the closure of a Baltimore jail without informing or including a single Baltimore City elected official. The decision garnered support from the ACLU and the Justice Policy Institute, which are often allied with Democratic leaders.[38] A year later, Hogan mandated that schools could not open before Labor Day, a position long advocated by the state's beach-based tourism industry. He touted "real, commonsense, bipartisan solutions" supported by an "overwhelming majority of Marylanders," and polls by Goucher College and the *Washington Post* backed him up.[39] Democrats were furious but had to let the issue go until after the election. Not only were they on the wrong side of public opinion, but some lawmakers had supported the idea when it was initially proposed and studied under Democratic Governor Martin O'Malley.

There's a repeated mechanism that Hogan used early on and frequently thereafter to control the message and co-opt Democrats. For announcements such as the toll reduction and school start date, the Governor's Office sends out a vague media advisory, often with little more than a time and location. Reporters call for more information but are almost always rebuffed by the tight-lipped team. Even without specific details, someone will be assigned the story. Short-staffed television news outlets might send just a cameraman and no reporter to ask questions. The event is timed to make it difficult for reporters to get an opposition voice on camera before the package is due at about 2 P.M. Democrats, for all their dominance in Maryland's legislative arena, have relatively few lawmakers available to speak to an issue at a moment's notice. Moreover, television stations often operate with a skeleton crew at night, so there's no guarantee another voice would be added, even if one were found. Newspaper deadlines and interviews by phone allow more time to get a dissenting opinion. But print publications are woefully understaffed, so it doesn't always happen. The decline of local media across the country has undoubtedly made it easier for governors and other elected officials to escape some scrutiny. And many in Maryland have complained that Hogan has benefited from an uneven media playing field that advantages the governor. In many respects, they're right. But it's the same incumbency advantage that all governors, regardless of party, can enjoy if they have a competent communications staff.

A Cancer Bump

Speculation over how the heavily Democratic electorate viewed Hogan was intense among Maryland politicos by the end of the summer. The first independent measure of Hogan's approval rating after the unrest in Baltimore City; his cancer diagnosis; and decisions regarding transportation policy, tolls, and education funding was released by the Goucher College Poll in early October 2015.[40] And the snapshot in time was nothing short of remarkable. Hogan was more popular among Marylanders than President Barack Obama, who was now well into his second term.

TABLE 2.1. HOGAN JOB APPROVAL RATING, CHANGE FROM FEBRUARY TO SEPTEMBER 2015			
	Approve	Disapprove	Don't Know
Maryland adults			
February 2015	39%	17%	43%
September 2015	58%	18%	25%
Change	+19	+1	−19
Republicans			
February 2015	72%	2%	26%
September 2015	78%	11%	12%
Change	+6	+9	−14
Democrats			
February 2015	27%	21%	51%
September 2015	48%	23%	29%
Change	+21	+3	−23
Independents			
February 2015	32%	11%	55%
September 2015	57%	11%	32%
Change	+25	+1	−23

Source: Goucher College Poll, Maryland adults
February 15–19, 2015 (n = 619, +/−3.9%)
September 26–30, 2015 (n = 636, +/−3.9%)

Fifty-eight percent of Maryland residents approved of how Hogan was handling his job as governor, and 18 percent disapproved. By comparison, 53 percent approved and 38 percent disapproved of the job Obama was doing as president. That represented a nineteen-point jump in approval for Hogan since February, primarily driven by an increase in name recognition and approval among Democrats and independents. It is worth noting here that the Maryland State Board of Elections used "unaffiliated" as the official designation for voters who are registered to vote but do not identify with a political party. Political reporting and polling in the state often use the term "independent" to describe these unaffiliated voters, as I do in this book. Table 2.1 above includes the results from the February and September Goucher College polls by party identification.

The *Washington Post* released its poll of Marylanders a few weeks later, in October, and found a similar result: 61 percent approved, and 22 percent disapproved. The *Post*'s top-line results also provided important historical data. Hogan was more popular than two-term Democratic Governor Martin O'Malley and about as popular as Republican Governor Robert Ehrlich were at the same point in their first terms. But reports of his high job approval rating were immediately met with speculation of a "cancer bump" that extended the traditional honeymoon period with the public.

There's no denying his battle with cancer positively influenced how the public saw Hogan. How could it not? Every year, more than 1.5 million new cases of cancer are diagnosed in the United States. The disease has touched nearly everyone in some way. And Hogan endured his treatments in a way that appealed to the average Marylander: he was sick, exhausted, and going to work. He shared the bald, blotchy, and swollen version of himself instead of retreating behind press releases or spokespeople, and the public loved him for it. The *Washington Post* poll found that half of Maryland residents (56 percent) had heard "a lot" or "some" about his diagnosis, and among those residents his approval rating hit 70 percent.[41]

While most Democrats are hesitant to say it publicly, many buy this "cancer bump" theory—they attribute Hogan's popularity and even reelection to the fact that he had cancer. They contend that it solidified a "nice guy" public image at odds with his harsh, conservative policies. But it's an oversimplification, or flatly incorrect, to view his cancer diagnosis as the driving force behind his popularity throughout his first term and beyond. The laudable public handling of the disease boosted his initial baseline approval, but Hogan's other actions contributed to and, eventually, sustained it. The same *Washington Post* poll measured his approval rating among those who indicated they'd heard only "a little" about the cancer at 58 percent. Hogan also earned a net-positive approval rating on five specific issue areas, including his handling of education. Most Marylanders approved of his handling of transportation issues and how he worked with Democrats in the legislature. Almost half approved of the job he was doing on taxes. Most important, given the focus on Hogan's messaging, 59 percent of residents approved of his handling of the economy.

On November 16, 2015, about a month after his last round of chemotherapy and after eighteen weeks of treatment, Hogan announced he was in remission. His approval ratings continued to climb and averaged in the mid-sixties to low seventies for the remainder of this first term. In other words, the "cancer bump" was a temporary boost that helped define Hogan but not a stand-alone reason for his consistently high and seemingly unshakable job approval ratings.

3

The Nontransferable Endorsement

New Jersey Governor Chris Christie formally entered the race for president on June 30, 2015. At a campaign stop in New Hampshire a few days later, a voter asked him about the neon-green bracelet he was wearing on his wrist. Christie explained that it was to show his support for his friend Larry Hogan, who was battling cancer. "I'm hoping that I'm going to be able to cut this thing off once the doctors give Larry the good news that he's in remission," Christie said.[1] The connection that Christie and Hogan had forged the previous year, after the New Jersey governor helped the long shot Hogan, had grown into a genuine friendship.

Hogan officially endorsed Christie less than a month later at the Double T Diner in Annapolis, soon after finishing five straight days of chemotherapy. Chase Cook of the *Capital Gazette* noted that the roles of the two men were now reversed: Christie endorsed Hogan when he was the underdog candidate, and now Hogan was doing the same for Christie. Hogan, dressed in a light-gray suit and blue tie, had not yet begun to lose his hair or show the outward physical signs of his cancer treatments, but he was feeling them. "I happen to believe that he's exactly the leader that we need," Hogan said of Christie. "I think that he should be the next president. And I think he will be the next president. I would not be governor of Maryland if it were not for this guy right here."[2]

As the primary campaigns entered the fall of 2015, Donald Trump's incendiary comments and refusal to apologize for them continued to be the driving narrative. It got so bad that even Republicans not running for president began to feel pressure to respond to Trump's racism, sexism, and personal insults. Hogan largely avoided dealing with Trump due to his early endorsement of Christie and his ongoing cancer treatments.

A Missed Call

Things took a sharp turn for Hogan and the rest of the Republican Party at the beginning of 2016. Christie ended his presidential run a little more than a month into the new year, after receiving just 7 percent of the New Hampshire primary vote.

Under normal circumstances, Christie's exit wouldn't have mattered for Hogan. Not picking the winner from a crowded primary field isn't exactly a significant event. But Christie didn't just drop out. On February 26, 2016, he became the first of Trump's former competitors to endorse the candidacy of the New York developer and reality show star. Throughout most of his career, the New Jersey governor would embrace his made-for-YouTube moments to bolster his image as a politician who didn't shy away from "telling it like it is." He had berated a critic on the Seaside Heights boardwalk ("You're a real big shot shooting your mouth off!"), scolded a reporter during a press conference ("You know, Tom, you must be the thinnest-skinned guy in America. . . . You should really see me when I'm pissed"), and yelled at a public-school teacher ("I am tired of you people. What do you want?").

These moments did more political good than harm and raised his national profile. People viewed his brashness as authenticity. And the historically bad public approval ratings of his second term overshadow the fact that Christie was a twice-elected blue-state Republican governor who enjoyed strong public approval ratings through most of his time in office before the Bridgegate scandal.[3] That's perhaps why the visual of Christie endorsing and then standing behind Trump as the candidate answered questions about tax returns and an endorsement from the former Grand Wizard of the Ku Klux Klan David Duke was a stunning moment. The expression on his face would almost immediately be likened to someone in a hostage video and became instant Twitter fodder when set to the song "The Sound of Silence." Hello darkness, indeed.

Christie called Hogan twice to say he planned to endorse Trump, but Hogan missed the calls. "I knew he wasn't going to be happy about it," Christie recalls.[4] An understatement, to be sure. Christie's endorsement, along with Trump's status as the front-runner, moved Trump out of the "not a problem" column for Hogan and into the "potentially huge problem" category. His political rivals had been waiting for an opportunity to knock the governor and his now-mid-sixties approval rating down a few notches. With Hogan's cancer in remission and Christie out of the way, they finally had an opportunity. And this wasn't some disagreement over policy. This was salient, sensational, and divisive. Trump was the lead story on every major news network, and he was well on his way to being the Republican nominee.

U.S. Representative John Delaney, a Democrat representing Maryland's 6th congressional district, was the first elected official to draw the comparison between Hogan and Trump in earnest. For two weeks in mid-March, Delaney funded a billboard to be driven around downtown Annapolis, including in front of the governor's mansion. It featured a large picture of Trump with the words "Silence Is an Endorsement." One side posed the question: "Will you support Trump as the Republican nominee?" The other side was a statement: "Because everyone in Maryland will lose if Trump wins."[5]

Delaney, a political moderate with enough money to fund roving billboards and a statewide gubernatorial campaign, was discussed as a potential challenger to Hogan in 2018. He would later forgo State House hopes for White House dreams.

When Ovetta Wiggins of the *Washington Post* asked Hogan about the billboard, the governor said he "thought it was cute" and added, "I don't think every day about what Donald Trump is doing or what John Delaney has to say. I don't really care. I only endorsed one guy and he's out of the race."[6] Hogan expanded on his position a few weeks later. "I'm not a Trump fan," he told the Associated Press in an interview carried in the *New York Times*. "I don't think he should be the nominee. At this point in time, I have no idea who the candidates are going to be or who I'm going to vote for." He described the entire 2016 primary election season as a "mess" and said, "I hate the whole thing. I don't think we have the best candidates in either party that are being put up. I don't like the dialogue. I don't like the things that are going on, and I'm sick of talking about it, because it's not anything I have anything to do with."[7]

Business as Usual

Hogan would catch one last respite before Trump officially became a constant, irritating presence in his life. Senator Barbara A. Mikulski, the longest-serving woman in the U.S. Congress, announced her retirement from the Senate in early March 2015, giving Democratic hopefuls ample time to mull over and launch campaigns for her replacement. Chris Van Hollen, a congressman with deep campaign coffers and strong support from the Maryland and national Democratic establishment, was always considered the favorite, despite polling that showed a close contest. The campaign dominated the media coverage in the state and earned national attention due to its historic nature: the other candidate on the Democratic side, Maryland Congresswoman Donna Edwards—had she been successful—would have been only the second Black woman in history to serve in the U.S. Senate.

At this point, Democrats knew Trump could be used to needle Hogan, but they, and the statewide media, were focused on the legislative session and the race between Edwards and Van Hollen. There was little bandwidth to spare for tying Hogan to a candidate who many still believed would fail to secure the Republican nomination. Thus, roving billboards aside, it was business as usual for the last part of the ninety-day legislative session in Annapolis in 2016. Democratic lawmakers and Hogan sparred over a deal to give Marylanders an income tax break. Hogan would eventually lose this fight but found common ground with Democrats on other issues.

He signed into law the Maryland Justice Reinvestment Act of 2016, which, among other things, shortened maximum sentences for numerous nonviolent offenses and steered users of illegal drugs to treatment instead of prison. The framework for the bill was established by the Justice Reinvestment Coordinating Council, a bipartisan mix of lawmakers and members of the judicial and executive branches, working under the auspices of the Governor's Office of Crime Control and Prevention.[8] Progressive lawmakers and the American Civil Liberties Union, while noting that flaws remained in the legislation, were nonetheless happy to advance criminal justice reform. In an official statement, Hogan touted it as "a balance between our most important duty of protecting public safety and the cost savings that result from a more efficient criminal justice system."[9]

Democrats and Hogan also worked together to address the opioid epidemic, an issue that was an early part of the governor's agenda. He signed into law the Opioid-Associated Disease Prevention and Outreach Act, a bill that authorized local health departments and community-based organizations to establish sterile syringe exchange programs. The state had experienced a 70 percent increase, the largest on record, in opioid-related deaths between 2015 and 2016, after five years of modest increase. The proliferation of nonpharmaceutical fentanyl and heroin was the primary driver of the overall rise in opioid-related deaths, and the problem crossed racial, regional, and generational lines. The next year, Hogan used his executive powers to declare a state of emergency and committed $50 million more over five years to improve treatment services, enforcement, and prevention.

Hogan was not able, however, to make progress on one of his signature issues: legislative redistricting. Despite the work of the Maryland Redistricting Reform Commission, which he had established by an executive order earlier that August, Democratic leaders dismissed the proposal to create a nonpartisan, independent commission to draw Maryland's state legislative and congressional districts. The redistricting that occurred after the 2010 U.S. Census made Maryland's congressional and legislative districts among the most gerrymandered in the country. The state legislative map is a misshapen hodgepodge of multi- and single-member districts drawn so that many legislative elections are effectively decided in the primary rather than the general election. At the congressional level, where Maryland's congressional delegation was once evenly split, there is now a single Republican member of Congress.

Privately, and to some extent publicly, Democratic lawmakers admitted that the redistricting process needed reform and that Maryland's district lines give them an unfair advantage. Democrats just had no intention to unilaterally disarm while Republican-led legislatures in other states were busy drawing districts for their own electoral advantages. About three-quarters of Marylanders supported the adoption of an independent commission, according to a Goucher College poll.[10] But Hogan was never able to convert this public support into real political pressure on legislators during any of the four legislative sessions in his first term.

The last day of the legislative session was April 11, 2016. Maryland's primary would be held two weeks and a day later, on April 26. In the Senate race, Van Hollen bested Edwards by double digits to win the Democratic nomination, and Kathy Szeliga, a state delegate who represents the conservative suburbs northeast of Baltimore and parts of Harford County, won on the Republican side. Hillary Clinton beat Bernie Sanders by nearly thirty points. Trump went five for five on all the Republican primary contests held that day and won a majority of the Republican votes in Maryland.

Faced with the electoral math and fundraising realities, the last two hopes of the Republicans seeking to stop Trump—Texas Senator Ted Cruz and Ohio Governor John Kasich—threw in their respective towels on May 3 and 4. Trump was now the presumptive Republican nominee for president of the United States. Members of the Republican establishment, even those vocally opposed to his candidacy, began to coalesce behind him. Elections are binary choices, and the voters had spoken.

There were still holdouts, of course, particularly among Republican governors. To capitalize on their lack of definitive stances, the Democratic Governors Association started a public pressure campaign called "The Silent 9" to inform voters which GOP governors had not said whether they would support Trump for president.[11] Hogan was on the list, but not for long. Unmoved by pressure to get behind his party's nominee and annoyed by the entire process, he told the *Washington Post* on May 5, "I said I was not going to get involved, and I would not endorse any candidate and that I was going to stay focused on Maryland. And I'm not going to take any more stupid questions about Donald Trump."[12]

A few weeks later, he clarified his stance when asked by reporters whether he'd vote for Trump or the presumptive Democratic nominee, Hillary Clinton. "No, I don't plan to [vote for Trump or Clinton],"

Hogan said on June 17. "I guess when I get behind the curtain, I'll have to figure it out, maybe write someone in. I'm not sure. It's a tough choice. I don't like either one of them." In mid-July, Hogan announced he was skipping the Republican National Convention (RNC), held that year at the Quicken Loans Arena in Cleveland, and would instead attend the annual J. Millard Tawes Crab and Clam Bake, scheduled for the same time. This move was called "the most Maryland way possible" to skip the convention and made *Rolling Stone*'s list of "27 Best Republican Excuses for Skipping Trump's RNC."[13]

Hogan wasn't the only Maryland Republican forgoing the convention for Tawes. Howard County Executive Allan Kittleman, who had attended the RNC four years prior, opted for an afternoon at Sommers Cove instead. Reporting from the event, the veteran *Baltimore Sun* State House reporter Michael Dresser observed that Hogan "shook hands, posed for pictures, greeted old friends, drank beer and generally seemed to be having a superb time."[14] Dresser noted that the Somerset County Republican Party was distributing Trump signs at its tent and that someone asked Hogan directly why he was declining to support Trump. Hogan's response was a terse "I don't like him."

The First Look at the Trouble with Trump

Kathy Szeliga, the minority whip in the Maryland House of Delegates, had the right stuff to win the Republican nomination for U.S. Senate. She got her start in politics as a staffer for U.S. Representative Andy Harris of Maryland (now one of Trump's biggest supporters in Congress) and represents one of the most conservative state legislative districts. Szeliga, as minority whip in the House of Delegates, was the highest ranking elected female Republican in the state.

Hogan endorsed Szeliga's candidacy on July 19, 2016, outside of a restaurant in Annapolis. This was his first statewide endorsement and a test of his coattails. The timing of the endorsement, the same time the RNC was happening in Cleveland, was also a smart political move. It allowed Szeliga to symbolically distance herself from Trump without criticizing him and gave Hogan another opportunity to remind Marylanders that he had shunned the convention. When asked by a reporter what he thought of the primetime speeches at the RNC—specifically, that of Milwaukee County Sheriff David Clarke, who directly criticized Baltimore City State's Attorney Marilyn Mosby for bringing charges against the six officers involved of the death of Freddie Gray—Hogan responded, "I didn't watch any of the convention at all."[15]

Later that September, Hogan endorsed Amie Hoeber, a former Army deputy undersecretary during the Reagan administration, challenging Democratic incumbent Representative John Delaney in the 6th congressional district. This race was the only potential, even if still very unlikely, pickup for the GOP. Hogan also endorsed Mark Plaster, a physician running against the incumbent Democratic Representative John Sarbanes. Plaster didn't have a realistic shot, as the heavily gerrymandered 3rd congressional district was emblematic of Hogan's calls for redistricting reform.

Any chance that Szeliga or Hoeber had at an upset victory was shattered by Trump's nomination. Unlike Hogan, neither candidate rejected Trump outright; they maintained their intention to "vote for their party's nominee." Questions about Trump overshadowed their campaigns. The candidates were pressed to comment on controversies such as Trump's racist comments about a federal judge with a Latino surname; suggestions that the election would be rigged; and, of course, the infamous *Access Hollywood* tape. It left little opportunity for the candidates to make their case to voters. "Hogan endorsed" might have shown up on all of Szeliga's and Hoeber's yard signs and was a favorite talking point of their campaigns, but the governor didn't spend a significant amount of time on the campaign trail with either.

Szeliga tried to follow Hogan's 2014 campaign themes by focusing on fiscal responsibility, reducing business regulation, economic policy, and other issues popular across party lines. But she also didn't shy away from expressing her opposition to gun control (Szeliga was endorsed by the National Rifle Association) and other socially conservative positions. By contrast, Hogan had kept his campaign promise from 2014 and stayed away from social policy issues. In fact, during Hogan's first legislative session, he allowed a bill that made it easier for transgender people to change the gender marker on their birth certificates to become law without his signature.[16]

An exchange among Szeliga, Van Hollen, and the radio host Kojo Nnamdi during the October 7, 2016, Senate debate offered a glimpse of the problems Trump could cause for a Republican candidate in a blue state:

> Van Hollen: Delegate Szeliga has invoked Governor Hogan a couple times. And he does have high numbers. He made the decision not to support Donald Trump because he decided, in this case, to put country over party and not elect someone who is erratic and could be dangerous for the country. And there are a whole range of other issues, from a woman's right to choose to commonsense gun safety to marriage equality, where Delegate Szeliga is on the other side of those issues. That is very out of touch with a great majority of the Maryland public.
>
> Nnamdi: The Donald Trump issue: Delegate Szeliga, you have indicated that you will be supporting your party's nominee. The party's nominee is Donald Trump. Some people don't make a distinction between supporting the party [nominee] and endorsing him. The bottom line is he is the party's nominee and therefore you are supporting him. Care to defend that?
>
> Szeliga: So, just like Congressman Van Hollen is supporting his nominee, I am supporting my nominee.
>
> Nnamdi: I haven't heard you say his name [Trump] yet.[17]

Given the state's political demographics, Szeliga already needed the absolute best of political circumstances to beat Van Hollen. In reference to the fact that she was running for the seat previously held by Barbara Mikulski, the longest-serving female senator, Szeliga while on the campaign trail would ask, "Why not send a taller Baltimore Polish woman to Washington?" It was a great one-liner. But her commitment to voting for Trump in November ensured that most voters outside of the Republican base wouldn't be a bit interested in what she had to say.

To be sure, Democratic leaders and lawmakers were not impressed by Hogan's stance on Trump. But Hogan's public approval ratings indicated that Democratic voters in Maryland were happy with Hogan's positioning. According to a Goucher College poll, half of the Democratic voters approved of the job he was doing in February 2016, and nearly 70 percent did by the following September. The governor came out of the Trump campaign not only unscathed but politically stronger. And, like most of America, he was preparing for a Clinton presidency.

A New Political Order

Hogan cast his ballot for president during Maryland's early voting. Late on Election Day, Mayer told reporters that Hogan had written in the name of his father, Larry Hogan Sr. "The governor is extremely disappointed in the candidates from both major parties and decided to write in the name of the person who taught him what it meant to hold public office with integrity," he said. Hogan didn't attend any parties the night of the election. He watched the electoral returns—and the dynamics of American politics, his Republican Party, and his reelection chances dramatically shifting—from home.

Most Democratic elected officials and insiders started election night in 2016 at various victory parties, only to leave in stunned disbelief. Sophia Silbergeld, a political operative who spent the better part of her career strong-arming powerful Democratic politicians to make fundraising phone calls, was at a party for Catherine Pugh, the Democratic candidate for mayor of Baltimore, as returns began to come in. She remembers people at the event were brimming with excitement to see Clinton become the first female president—until Florida was called. That's when the ballroom at the Radisson Hotel downtown emptied in a sad, hurried fashion. Silbergeld had cohosted a similarly deflated election night party for the O'Malley and Brown staffers two years earlier.

Like their counterparts across the country, Democrats in Maryland were anguished in the days that followed the election. But the hardened political professionals among them had found hope in the general despair. Maryland decisively reaffirmed its standing as a state that quashed statewide Republican ambitions. Clinton won Maryland by twenty-six points. More important, she won Anne Arundel and Baltimore counties, the two swing counties where Hogan had earned 66 percent and 59 percent of the vote in 2014, respectively.

Sure, Hogan boasted a 70 percent approval rating in October. But he had no discernible coattails in November. The three candidates he endorsed—Szeliga, Hoeber, and Plaster—lost by sizable margins. The speculation that he had somehow "purpled" the state or that there was a real change in voter preferences was largely silenced, and talk of reelection vulnerability was quickly emerging in its place.

State House reporters immediately started writing about whether the Trump victory would hurt Hogan's reelection effort. It was a safe assumption: the party that holds the presidency tends to lose ground during the midterms, and those losses can sometimes extend beyond Congress to the states. Hogan didn't support or vote for candidate Trump, and that earned him admiration among Democrats and other left-leaning voters. But the dynamics had shifted. Trump was no longer a temporary annoyance that Hogan could ignore as a fringe element. He was the president-elect. Most Republicans, including those in Maryland, had voted for and were now willing to embrace their new president.

Silbergeld notes that there was a real sense among Democratic insiders that 2018 had shifted in their favor: "Before that election night, it was said tongue-in-cheek among Maryland Democratic operatives—because no one believed Trump would win and no one wanted him as president—that the best thing that could happen for Maryland Democrats electorally in 2018 was a Trump victory. People were certain that when Trump won, Hogan would lose because of the backlash."[18]

Hogan recalls receiving an onslaught of texts from his inner circle and replying, "Life as we know it is about to change. Trump is all we're going to hear about."[19] The day after the presidential election, the *Washington Post* ran the headline "Not Much in the Way of Coattails: All Three of Hogan's Candidates Lose."

4

Moderating the Trump Effect

When the Maryland Economic Development Association met on January 12, 2017, at the Governor Calvert House in Annapolis, Hogan was ready to answer questions about commerce-related laws slated for the upcoming legislative session.

He got questions about Donald Trump instead. That morning, news had broken that the City of Baltimore and the Justice Department had reached an agreement on a court-enforceable consent decree to institute reforms in Baltimore's police department, stemming from the death of Freddie Gray.

There was real fear that the incoming president and his soon-to-be attorney-general, Alabama Senator Jeff Sessions, would undermine, if not entirely disregard, the long-sought agreement. Reporters wanted to know whether Hogan would encourage the Trump administration to support the consent decree. The governor responded that he had recently met the Baltimore City mayor and had discussed several topics, including the decree, but had not yet fully reviewed the document. Pamela Wood, a State House reporter with the *Baltimore Sun*, pressed Hogan. His response was as curt as it was familiar: "I'm just really tired of being asked to answer stupid questions about the Trump administration."[1]

Managing Trump

A *Politico* headline early in Trump's tenure perfectly captured the political reality from inauguration to the midterms: "Trump Makes Blue-State Republicans Squirm."[2]

Hogan attended Trump's inauguration on January 20, 2017. Through his spokeswoman Amelia Chassé, he said he was "committed to working with the incoming Trump administration just as he has successfully worked with the Obama administration to promote what is in Maryland's best interest" and that he "look[ed] forward to having an open dialogue with the president-elect and his team."[3] He offered similar remarks in the immediate aftermath of Trump's victory but little else in the way of public statements. Even if tempered and indirect, any show of support to the new president could hurt his reelection efforts less than two years away.

The governor held on to hope that Trump would leave the bombastic campaign persona behind and rise to (or at least be constrained by) the traditional expectations of the office. That didn't last.

A week after his inauguration, the new president issued an executive order banning foreign nationals from seven predominantly Muslim countries from visiting the United States. Among the first detained: a five-year-old Maryland resident at Dulles International Airport.[4] The "Muslim ban" met immediate backlash and court challenges, including a multistate lawsuit that included Maryland Attorney-General Brian Frosh.[5]

Protests were organized by activist groups at Baltimore-Washington International Thurgood Marshall Airport.[6] Prominent Maryland Democrats attended, including Representatives Elijah Cummings, C. A. "Dutch" Ruppersberger, and John Sarbanes, as well as former Governor Martin O'Malley. Smaller protests took place elsewhere, including in front of the governor's mansion. Hogan's social media accounts were flooded with messages insisting he denounce Trump. Democratic leaders demanded to know where he stood.

The governor's response was tepid. "Implementation and enforcement of immigration law and policies is the sole purview of the federal government," he said, adding that his administration "continues to support strengthened and more clarified vetting processes for those entering the country. Improving our national security can and should be done in a defined and concise manner that upholds our American values."[7]

This position was in line with that of leading Republicans in Congress, who also affirmed their commitment to better vetting but rejected the ban as overly broad and a threat to religious freedom. It was not a clear rebuke like those offered by Republican governors Charlie Baker in Massachusetts and Phil Scott in Vermont.[8] In a *Baltimore Sun* op-ed, Delegate Eric Luedtke, a Montgomery County Democrat and a sharp critic of Hogan, called the statement "mealy-mouthed" and "transparently an attempt to avoid taking a position."[9] The Maryland Democratic Party asked, "How can Maryland families count on the Governor to stand up for them when he's too afraid to stand up to Donald Trump?"[10]

Hogan was frustrated by the political landscape distorted by Trump. "I'm not a defender of the administration, but we're certainly going to work as best we can to make sure that Maryland (has) got a good relationship with our federal officers," he said on February 14, 2017, at a forum hosted by the Greater Salisbury Committee, a business and civic organization. "And that includes the president and administration and the cabinet secretaries."[11]

A week later, during an appearance on Baltimore-based WBAL radio, he said it wasn't his "role" to criticize Trump and noted that Maryland's elected representatives in Washington are "supposed to deal with those problems."[12] Democrats responded with a web ad highlighting comments Hogan made during the Obama administration about "fighting back" against the federal government. The ad gained some media mentions but failed to rack up a significant number of views.

But Democrats were sure that they had finally landed a punch on the governor.

A mid-March poll from the *Washington Post* found that nearly two-thirds of Maryland residents opposed the Muslim ban; a third supported it. Moreover, three-quarters of those who opposed the ban thought it was "absolutely necessary that Governor Hogan speak out in opposition." Taken together, that meant that about half of Maryland residents both opposed the ban and wanted Hogan to rebuke Trump over it. That same poll put Hogan's job approval rating in the mid-sixties, a small but negligible drop from the fall.

Democrats would have more opportunities to tie Hogan and Trump together; the president proved impossible to ignore.

As the party's de facto leader, Trump was remaking the GOP in his image, disempowering traditional forces. Most Republican leaders, even those who vehemently opposed the Trump candidacy, boarded the Trump train after he was elected. Any remaining lines between Trumpism and the Republican Party blurred, particularly in the eyes of Democrats.

Coverage of the daily drama of his unconventional presidency dominated cable TV. One tweet from @realDonaldTrump drove the news cycle, and never in a way that was helpful to Hogan—at least at first.

The Muslim ban was soon followed by the firing of James Comey, director of the Federal Bureau of Investigation (FBI); investigations into Russian interference in the election; indictments of Trump campaign associates on charges of conspiracy and money laundering; the removal of the United States from the Paris climate agreement; and comments blaming "both sides" for the overtly racist rally in Charlottesville, Virginia.

Some early Trump administration actions hit close to home for Marylanders: a proposal to withhold pay raises for federal government employees (Maryland is home to one of the highest percentages of federal employees in the country) and deep budgetary cuts to the Environmental Protection Agency's Chesapeake Bay Program. Even much-hyped federal tax cuts Trump signed into law in December 2017 came with a cost to middle-class Maryland families because the cuts eliminated the deductibility of state and local income and property taxes.[13]

Trump didn't get any semblance of the honeymoon typically enjoyed by incoming presidents, nationally or in Maryland. His approval rating never rose above the mid-twenties to low-thirties among all Maryland voters, and it languished in the single digits among Democrats. Polling also showed that, as Democrats hoped, Trump had the potential to bring Hogan down.

In an early poll on Hogan's reelection prospects, conducted by Goucher College in late February 2017, 55 percent of voters said that their views toward Trump would have "some" or "a lot" of influence on how they would vote in 2018—and a majority of those voters indicated they were leaning toward or said they would definitely vote for Hogan's still very hypothetical Democratic challenger.[14]

Another poll by Goucher College, conducted just two months before the gubernatorial primaries on June 26, 2018, had Hogan in the lead against potential challengers but losing among those who thought the governor had kept "too little" distance from the president and voters who said that Trump would have at least some influence on how they cast their vote in November.

Democrats gleefully recalled that former Governor Robert Ehrlich was personally popular when an unfavorable national political climate and a sinking Republican president contributed to his loss to O'Malley in 2006. Only a third of Maryland's likely voters approved of the job George W. Bush was doing as president in weeks leading up to that election, while 55 percent still held a favorable view of Ehrlich and just as many thought the state was heading in the right direction.[15] Hogan's eventual Democratic opponent, Ben Jealous, later echoed this sentiment, telling a reporter for the *American Prospect*, "There's literally nothing happening in the Hogan campaign that wasn't happening in the [Robert] Ehrlich campaign, and Ehrlich was a one-term bird, and Hogan will be a one-termer, too."[16]

Unlike Ehrlich, who had friendly ties to the Bush administration, Hogan eventually demonstrated that he could distance himself from an unpopular president who shared his party affiliation. His responses to Trump never rose to the harsh lambasting by Democrats. But he did push back, and in a measured way that offered a stark contrast to the president in terms of personal style.

At the same time, the governor frequently criticized Democrats for "playing politics" in trying to tie him to the president and often blamed "both sides" for Washington's dysfunction. One early example was over Trump's attempts to repeal the Affordable Care Act, a longtime goal of Republican members of Congress. At a press event held on March 20 in Annapolis, Representative Sarbanes, joined by Democratic Representatives Steny Hoyer, Elijah Cummings, and Jamie Raskin, asked the governor "to stand up as many governors have done . . . to say that the repeal of the Affordable Care Act makes no sense for America and it certainly makes no sense for Maryland." Hogan, who had earlier signed on to a bipartisan letter of governors opposing the so-called skinny repeal of Obamacare, responded by calling the rally "grandstanding" and the reason "why Congress has an approval rating in the single digits."[17]

Later that summer, after another effort to repeal the Affordable Care Act failed, Hogan again joined a bipartisan group of governors requesting that Congress "immediately reject" efforts to repeal the Affordable Care Act and focus instead on stabilizing insurance markets. Democrats chided the governor for waiting "until the 11th hour to take a firm stance."[18]

Hogan also broke with Trump over the decision to abandon the Paris climate agreement. "This is not an action the governor would have taken," the official statement said, describing Hogan as a "strong advocate for protecting Maryland's environment, including cleaner air and water," and a supporter of efforts to fight climate change. Democrats blasted Hogan for not initially joining an alliance of state and city leaders who pledged to uphold the goals of the Paris climate accord, but he would later sign on to it.[19]

The Resistance Session

Trump was sworn into office—and unleashed his disruption—just days into the third state legislative session of Hogan's term. This lawmaking period is the most crucial of the four-year cycle in Maryland: new legislators have settled in, and big ideas and spending plans can gain traction without fear of immediate election-year backlash.

But Democrats had a heightened sense of urgency, given Trump's standing and Hogan's persistent popularity, and were ready to corner the governor whenever they saw an opportunity.

Hogan, a capable but not gifted orator who comes across more "Larry" than "Lawrence" even in formal settings, delivered his third State of the State address on February 1, 2017. Noticeably missing from the speech was any mention of the new president. Hogan highlighted accomplishments from previous legislative sessions and asked lawmakers to work with him to address a growing opioid problem, pollution in the Chesapeake Bay, an aging transportation infrastructure, and the need for redistricting reform. Mixed in were familiar messaging on economic growth and development, another push for targeted tax breaks, and a boast about the "record funding for education" enacted during his time in office.

This claim about education funding drove public school advocates and Democratic lawmakers crazy. While technically correct—each of Hogan's budgets allocated more toward public education than any of his predecessors'—it wasn't simply a function of his priorities.[20] Education spending in Maryland is mandated under formulas defined in the Bridge to Excellence in Public Schools Act of 2002, which ties state funding for public education to enrollment and inflation. Every governor who held office since the 2003 fiscal year could make the same claim as Hogan. Moreover, Hogan is a proponent of school choice and the expansion of charter schools. He advocated for several bills aimed at private school funding and charter school expansion during his first term. These efforts were mostly rebuked by Democratic lawmakers.

The day after Hogan delivered his State of the State, despite an attempt to pick off votes from Democratic senators in swing districts, the Democratic majority in the General Assembly overrode his veto of the Clean Energy Jobs bill from the previous session, raising the requirement for renewable-energy sources in Maryland's electricity supply from 20 percent by the year 2022 to 25 percent by the year 2020.[21] Hogan called this a "sunshine and wind tax."

Then Democrats got to the work of resistance.

Under Maryland law, the attorney-general needed permission from the governor to sue the federal government. Democrats wanted to remove the possibility that their Republican governor could be a roadblock, so the presiding officers fast-tracked through their respective chambers the Maryland Defense Act, which would give the attorney-general power to take legal action against the federal government without permission from the governor.[22]

The resolution came after Attorney-General Brian Frosh, the state's chief lawyer, requested permission to take legal action against Trump's Muslim ban and was met with silence from Hogan. Senate President Mike Miller maintained it was "aimed at Capitol Hill" and had "absolutely nothing" to do with Hogan.[23] Republican lawmakers, none of whom supported the resolution, complained that it was an attempt to tie Hogan to Trump.[24] Democrats also introduced a bill that would set aside money in the state budget to support Frosh's efforts. Hogan voiced opposition, at one point calling it "rank partisanship," but allowed the bill to become law without his signature.

There was a political upside for the governor: when Frosh, a slim and mild-mannered man with a Ned Flanders–style mustache, used the power of his office against the Trump administration, Hogan could stay above the fray. Frosh would later lead an effort to sue Trump over violations of the Emoluments Clause, the inclusion of a citizenship question on the 2020 U.S. Census, and changes to federal tax law.

Democrats also moved to protect the state against any impact the Trump administration would have on the Affordable Care Act and access to reproductive health. A bill that triggered state funds to reimburse Planned Parenthood clinics if Congress cut its federal funding sailed through the General Assembly and landed on the governor's desk. Hogan allowed it to become law without his signature. The legislation received national media attention and made Maryland the first state to take such action.[25]

Democrats also advanced a measure, the Maryland Health Insurance Coverage Protection Act, to monitor any federal changes to the Affordable Care Act, Medicaid, the Maryland Children's Health Program, and Medicare, and recommend state and local response. They also issued a joint resolution expressing "sharp disagreement" with attempts to repeal Obamacare and "urging the Governor of Maryland to join in urging the U.S. Congress to promptly protect specified provisions of the federal Affordable Care Act."[26]

Hogan, again, allowed these measures to pass without his signature.

A tactic Hogan often used to bolster bipartisan and moderate credentials was to support—or, in the view of Democratic leaders, co-opt—popular parts of the Democratic agenda. He learned this lesson from his friend Governor Chris Christie, who contends, "When you're the governor, you're held responsible for when things go wrong. But every victory, regardless of who first championed it, is your victory."[27]

A common refrain from the governor was that he didn't care what side of the aisle a good idea came from. He told reporters he was "taking things [Democrats] say they support and saying, 'This is how we can make it better.'"[28] Democrats complained to reporters that the governor wasn't leading but, rather, putting his name on the public policies they had long worked to advance.

He put the tactic to use during the 2017 assembly session, positioning himself as a supporter of paid sick leave and a ban on hydraulic fracturing, known as fracking, after Democrats had laid the groundwork for those initiatives.

After years of trying, paid sick leave legislation—championed by Baltimore Delegate Luke Clippinger and backed by unions—finally had the momentum to make it to Hogan's desk. He had tried to get ahead of it by imploring lawmakers earlier in December to compromise and accept his version, which would apply to businesses with fifty or more employees, instead of fifteen. The two versions enjoyed similar levels of public support, suggesting that the average voter didn't see much difference between them.

Democratic lawmakers and progressive groups viewed the governor's bill as a watered-down policy that would leave hundreds of thousands of Maryland workers without the benefit. They passed their version. Hogan, who positioned his proposal as a business-friendly compromise, eventually vetoed it. In response, Democrats overrode his veto during the first week of the 2018 legislative session. Never one to allow a loss to occupy more than a single news cycle, his spokeswoman Amelia Chassé told reporters after the override that "now that the political posturing is over, it's time for the legislature to get down to the business of fixing the serious flaws in the bill." The governor urged legislators to fast-track a Small Business Relief Tax Credit to "ensure employers aren't forced to close their doors and lay off their employees."[29]

Hogan found a clear win on the fracking ban, simultaneously outflanking Democrats and strengthening his environmental credentials. A three-year moratorium on hydraulic fracturing—the practice of injecting water, chemicals, and sand at high pressure to release natural gas from below the earth's surface—was set to expire in October 2017. Hogan, who had supported fracking during his 2014 campaign, allowed the moratorium bill to go into law without his signature two years earlier; now there was a push to ban the practice permanently.

The bill sailed through the House of Delegates with a vote of 97 to 40—a veto-proof majority that included eight Republicans—but stalled in the Senate. Miller and Senator Joan Carter Conway, who chaired the Education, Health, and Environmental Affairs Committee, told Senator Robert A. "Bobby" Zirkin, the sponsor of the Senate version of the bill, that he needed twenty-nine votes (a veto-proof majority) to get the bill on the Senate floor. Zirkin had secured twenty-four Senate co-sponsors, but the rest were, as he put it, "roadblocked."

On March 17, Zirkin received a call from the Governor's Office inviting him to attend a press conference. Less than an hour later, the senator was standing next to Hogan as the governor announced support for the fracking ban. Hogan called it "an important initiative to safeguard our environment" and told hastily assembled reporters he did not believe that the environmental risks of fracking outweighed any potential benefits. No other Democrats knew the announcement was coming.

Hogan's embrace of the fracking ban didn't come easily. Zirkin had lobbied the governor over the previous year through Chris Shank, Hogan's chief legislative officer, presenting a full range of environmental and public health research. He appealed to Hogan directly at a Baltimore Ravens tailgate party, telling the governor, after a friendly conversation about approval ratings and a few shots of Fireball Cinnamon Whiskey, "You want to know what's popular, Governor? Banning fracking."[30]

Polling from the *Washington Post* in September 2016 found that 60 percent of Marylanders opposed fracking, including majorities of independents (66 percent) and Democrats (69 percent). Two-thirds of state residents thought that the drilling practice posed significant risk to the environment. Maryland Republicans, by contrast, supported fracking by a margin of 49 percent support to 36 percent opposition.

The five votes Zirkin needed were now unblocked, and the bill passed. A few weeks later, Hogan signed the fracking ban, making Maryland the first state with natural gas reserves to ban the practice via the legislative process.[31] Zirkin, in his words, "caught hell" from his caucus for handing the governor a bipartisan win but maintains that without Hogan the bill would have died that legislative session.

As the lawmaking session drew to a close, Hogan secured victories on a handful of his priorities: tax breaks for manufacturing firms that bring jobs to areas with high unemployment and tax breaks for some retirees and law enforcement. Democrats agreed to delay the implementation of transportation legislation that would require the

Governor's Office to publicly score and rank transportation projects. Hogan dubbed this legislation the "roadkill bill," but that moniker, like the "sunshine and wind tax," never captured the messaging magic he found with the "rain tax."

Deeper Breaks

With lawmakers done for the year, Hogan could turn more attention to his coming reelection. And as he did, there were more opportunities to break with the president.

Hogan's first substantive rebuke of Trump came in the aftermath of the Unite the Right rally on August 12, 2017, in Charlottesville, Virginia, one of the defining moments of the Trump presidency. Protesters gathered to oppose the removal of the statue of General Robert E. Lee from Charlottesville's former Lee Park and unify the white nationalist movement. The protest turned violent when white nationalists clashed with counterprotesters. A white supremacist rammed his car into a crowd, killing thirty-two-year-old Heather Heyer and injuring nineteen others.

Hogan's response was markedly different from the heavily criticized statement offered by Trump. Instead of seeing "very fine people on both sides," the governor said that "hate and bigotry only lead to violence and death, and there is no place for it in our society." He added that Trump had made a "terrible mistake" in his response.

Within days, Hogan supported the removal from the State House grounds a statue of Supreme Court Chief Justice Roger Taney, writer of the 1857 *Dred Scott* decision that upheld slavery and denied citizenship to Black Americans. A vote in favor of removal was quickly taken by the State House Trust, a four-member board that includes the governor, the two presiding officers of the General Assembly, and the chair of the Maryland Historical Trust. The statue was quietly removed overnight two days later, less than a week after the events at Charlottesville.

Hogan's Facebook page was flooded the next day with angry comments calling him a "RINO" (Republican in name only), accusing him of "siding with liberals," and worse. Hogan ignored them, and polling conducted after the removal showed no difference in his levels of support among Republicans.

Hogan's support for removing the Taney statue represented a shift. In 2015, he had called efforts to remove Confederate statues "political correctness run amok." But in the aftermath of Charlottesville, he told reporters, "The time has come to make clear the difference between properly acknowledging our past and glorifying the darkest chapters in our history."[32]

He also considered the issue from a practical perspective. "If we didn't do it [remove the statue], we were going to have people tearing it down," he says. The quick removal also prevented possible protests in support of keeping the statue. The governor clarifies that he does not support the carte blanche removal of other historical monuments but does support the rights of states or localities to undertake a process to reach their own decisions.[33]

As months went on, Hogan's rhetoric in response to Trump grew more pointed, and he began to draw sharper contrasts. This was comparatively more than most other Republicans, except for other blue-state governors and a handful of others, were willing to do.

When reports came out that the federal government was separating immigrant children from their families, Hogan, along with other mostly Democratic governors, recalled National Guard troops at the U.S.-Mexico border. (The move was largely symbolic: Maryland's unit consisted of just a handful of crew members and a helicopter.)

When the president proposed canceling pay raises for federal employees, Hogan called the move "simply wrong" and urged "Congress to take bipartisan action to protect these hardworking employees and keep the promises made to them."[34]

When Trump called Haiti and African countries "shithole countries," Hogan called the comments "beyond unacceptable, beneath the office, and unrepresentative of the American people."[35]

When Trump sided with President Vladimir Putin over his own intelligence agencies regarding Russian interference in the 2016 election, Hogan tweeted, "I remember when President Ronald Reagan called the Soviet Union the evil empire. . . . President Trump failed to stand up for our country yesterday."[36]

When Trump endorsed Roy Moore for the Alabama Senate seat vacated by Attorney-General Jeff Sessions, despite credible allegations that Moore had pursued relationships and sexual encounters with teenagers when he was in his thirties, Hogan said the Republican candidate was "unfit for office and should step aside. Americans are better than this."[37]

When Trump's U.S. Supreme Court nominee faced allegations of sexual assault against Christine Blasey Ford while they were both in high school, drawing stark condemnation from Democrats, Hogan, along with four other GOP governors, called on the U.S. Senate to delay a confirmation vote until an independent investigation was conducted.

Hogan didn't comment on Trump's tweets, the early-morning musings and personal attacks that seemed to replace a White House communications strategy, other than to say, "I wish he would stop tweeting."[38]

At some point, and even the Hogan camp can't pinpoint precisely when, the nature of the Trump effect in Maryland came into focus.

Democratic pressure on Hogan and Democrats' comparisons of him to Trump didn't make the governor guilty by shared party affiliation. Instead, it made Hogan look reasonable, moderate, and steady-handed by contrast. Polls suggested voters were broadly satisfied with how Hogan handled the president. But Democratic elected officials, candidates, and operatives continued to ignore the warning signs that asking voters to compare Hogan to Trump was backfiring. They kept hoping for a messaging misstep on Trump that never came.

Managing Trump was only part of the reelection puzzle. To win, Hogan also needed to convince voters that he was a "different kind of Republican," a rare moderate among GOP elected officials, through governance. And he'd use the last legislative session of his first term to strengthen his image as a pragmatist looking for common ground with Democrats on policies supported by most Marylanders.

Last Chance to Moderate

The virtues of bipartisanship and moderation were major themes of Hogan's fourth State of the State address, delivered in January 2018. He decried the ills of "wedge politics and petty rhetoric" and drew contrasts between the productive governance in Annapolis and the dysfunction of Washington.

In that spirit, Hogan and Democratic leaders put together a competitive—but ultimately unsuccessful—bid to bring Amazon's new headquarters to the state. They also hashed out a deal to stabilize the Obamacare marketplace in the face of surging premiums; approved targeted tax cuts to offset the impact of the new federal tax law; and worked out a compromise, along with lawmakers from DC and Virginia, to give the DC Metro a permanent funding increase.[39]

Hogan signed bills to overhaul sexual harassment policies in the State House, allow prior sexual predatory behavior to be used in criminal prosecutions of alleged sex offenders, ban retail pet stores from selling puppies and kittens, and establish a targeted free community college program. He also secured modest victories on taxes and economic development, expanding his tax breaks for correctional officers and retired military veterans and increasing the number of counties eligible for the manufacturing tax credit.

But the session wasn't all puppies, funding, and tax breaks.

Democrats, tired of the "bipartisan bromance" between Hogan and Democratic State Comptroller Peter Franchot that had developed since Trump's election, flexed their significant legislative muscle.[40] They mandated more money for school construction while simultaneously stripping the state's Board of Public Works of its power to oversee how that money was spent. The board comprises three members—the governor, state comptroller, and state treasurer (who is appointed by the legislature)—and reviews, approves, and oversees state expenditures.

State Treasurer Nancy Kopp noted that the board had become "political theater" in recent years, with Hogan and Franchot using its meetings as opportunities to criticize the state legislature. Hogan vetoed the school construction bill and complained that it was "a personal vendetta against my colleague, the Comptroller."[41] The veto was quickly overridden.

Democrats and Hogan also went another round on education spending, the most persistent source of tension between them. Democrats were set to create a "lockbox" for casino revenues and use the money to increase education funding beyond levels required by legal formulas. Without discussing it with Democratic leaders, Hogan publicly announced a similar proposal. Both plans ensured that casino revenues would supplement—instead of supplant—money already budgeted for schools, fixing earlier legislation. But the Democratic version looked to codify the "lockbox" in the state constitution, while

Hogan argued that passing a law to create the lockbox was more expedient than a ballot referendum.

The Democratic proposal won out, even earning support from Republican lawmakers. Hogan signed the bill. Later that summer, he released a web ad asking voters to support "his important ballot initiative," dubbing it the "Hogan lockbox."

Hogan's most defining moments of moderation came, improbably, on social issues.

At 7:57 A.M. on March 20, 2018, at Great Mills High School in suburban St. Mary's County, Austin Rollins approached his sixteen-year-old classmate Jaelynn Willey and murdered her with his father's Glock 9 mm pistol. The bullet also struck another student before Rollins, after being confronted by a school resource officer, turned the gun on himself. The incident came on the heels of the mass shooting at Marjory Stoneman Douglas High School in Parkland, Florida, and less than six months after a mass shooter on the Las Vegas Strip left sixty people dead and wounded hundreds more.

During his 2014 campaign, Hogan had earned an "A-" grade and an endorsement from the National Rifle Association (NRA) for opposing a ban on the sale of assault-type weapons, a limit on magazines, and a fingerprints and license requirement to buy a handgun, among other measures.

In response to a renewed national push for gun reforms, Democratic lawmakers introduced legislation to ban the sale and possession of bump stocks, the accessory used by the Las Vegas shooter to make semiautomatic rifles fire faster, and to allow judges to temporarily order gun owners to surrender firearms if they are deemed dangerous to themselves or others. Hogan called them "commonsense bipartisan measures" and signed them into law, despite protests from gun rights activists and many in his party.

A few months later, he told students from Great Mills High School that he would not accept any support or money from the NRA. That fall the NRA downgraded its rating of Hogan to a "C" and declined to endorse him. The move earned national media attention.[42]

Hogan's most socially progressive stance as governor was perhaps his support of a bill to ban "conversion therapy," the practice of trying to change an individual's sexual orientation or gender identity through psychological or faith-based interventions. The already profoundly personal debate on the issue took a dramatic turn when Delegate Megan Simonaire, a first-term Republican delegate from Anne Arundel County, testified in favor of the ban. Simonaire recounted the "significant pain, self-loathing and deep depression" she experienced when her parents recommended a conversion therapy provider after she came out to them as bisexual.[43] Less than a week earlier, her father, Republican Senator Bryan Simonaire, had argued passionately to keep conversion therapy legal.

At the signing ceremony, Hogan handed one of the ceremonial pens to Delegate Simonaire. Spokeswoman Amelia Chassé later told reporters, "The governor was pleased to sign this bill, and believes it's the right thing to do."[44] Hogan's position on conversion therapy put him at odds not only with Republican lawmakers in Maryland but also with the 2016 Republican Party platform, which included language that supported "the right of parents to determine the proper medical treatment and therapy for their minor children."[45] This was widely viewed as a tacit endorsement of conversion therapy, particularly given Vice President Mike Pence's long-standing opposition to LGBTQ+ rights.[46]

Assessing the Power of (Perceived) Moderation

As they looked toward the election, it was abundantly clear to political insiders that perceptions of Hogan's ideology—whether voters viewed him as conservative or a moderate—mattered. And it appeared that the positions and public messaging during his first term, particularly in the last two legislative sessions and in response to Trump, had solidified Hogan's moderate credentials to Maryland voters.

Table 4.1 includes three polls conducted by Goucher College in 2018 that asked whether voters viewed Hogan as a conservative, moderate, or progressive. In all three, a plurality of Democrats and majorities of independent (unaffiliated) voters and Republicans viewed him as a moderate.

The degree to which perceptions of the governor's ideology influenced his approval ratings and the likelihood of reelection differed across party identification. Republicans who viewed Hogan as a moderate expressed similar levels of approval for the job he was doing and

TABLE 4.1. PERCEPTIONS OF HOGAN'S IDEOLOGY BY PARTY AFFILIATION											
	February 2018				April 2018				September 2018			
	D	I	R	All	D	I	R	All	D	I	R	All
Conservative	30%	20%	36%	30%	30%	25%	25%	27%	27%	25%	29%	27%
Moderate	47%	59%	50%	50%	51%	55%	57%	54%	46%	57%	56%	50%
Progressive	7%	5%	4%	6%	8%	6%	10%	8%	12%	5%	7%	9%
$n =$	384	101	162	658	269	99	134	522	387	105	181	696

Source: Goucher College Poll, Maryland voters
February 12–17, 2018 ($n = 658$, +/–3.8)
April 14–19, 2018 ($n = 522$, +/–4.2%)
September 11–16, 2018 ($n = 696$, +/–3.7)
Note: Table does not display "don't know" or "refused" responses or from individuals who are registered with a third or other party. D = Democrat; I = Independent; R = Republican.

support for his reelection as Republicans who viewed the governor as a conservative. In other words, Republican voters weren't turned off by political moderation, suggesting that, at least in some circumstances, GOP candidates can still tack toward the middle without losing their base.

But the most significant finding was how dramatically the perception of moderation changed attitudes toward Hogan and support for his reelection among Democrats and independent voters. In each of the three polls, Democrats and independents who viewed Hogan as a moderate, compared with those who viewed him as a conservative, were significantly more likely to approve of the job he was doing and support his reelection. For example, in the poll conducted in mid-September 2018, there was more than a thirty-point difference in support for Hogan's reelection among both Democrats and independents between those who thought the governor was a conservative compared with those who viewed him as a moderate.

Table 4.2 includes Hogan's approval rating and support for his reelection by perceptions of his ideology across party affiliation. The small number of respondents who considered Hogan a progressive are not included.

Overall, the results indicate that moderation was central to Hogan's political strength among the Democratic and independent voters he needed to secure a second term. Hogan's team knew it, and so did his Democratic opponents.

TABLE 4.2. HOGAN APPROVAL AND SUPPORT FOR REELECTION BY PERCEPTIONS OF IDEOLOGY ACROSS PARTY AFFILIATION

	February 2018 Perception of Hogan's Ideology				April 2018 Perception of Hogan's Ideology				September 2018 Perception of Hogan's Ideology			
	C	M	Diff.	Total	C	M	Diff.	Total	C	M	Diff.	Total
Approve of the job Hogan is doing												
Democrat	39%	76%	+37	56%	40%	81%	+40	65%	31%	72%	+41	56%
Independent	30%	78%	+48	60%	28%	89%	+61	64%	64%	92%	+28	73%
Republican	95%	89%	−6	87%	91%	91	0	81%	94%	89%	−5	89%
Will vote for/lean toward voting for Hogan in the upcoming election												
Democrat	20%	42%	+22	29%	17%	29%	+12	25%	10%	47%	+37	38%
Independent	25%	61%	+36	50%	26%	50%	+24	42%	38%	72%	+34	61%
Republican	95%	94%	−1	88%	84%	89%	+5	86%	89%	92%	+3	88%

Source: Goucher College Poll, Maryland voters
February 12–17, 2018 (*n* = 658, +/−3.8)
April 14–19, 2018 (*n* = 522, +/−4.2%)
September 11–16, 2018 (*n* = 696, +/−3.7)
Note: C = conservative; M = moderate

A Real Moderate, or a Conservative Who Strategically Moderates?

Eric Cortellessa, a digital editor for the *Washington Monthly*, succinctly summarized the case against Hogan's moderation that Democrats were making in an October 31 op-ed for the *Washington Post*. He argued that the governor has "vetoed bills to restore voting rights to returning citizens; prohibit state colleges and universities from asking about applicants' arrest or conviction records; remove criminal penalties for possession of marijuana paraphernalia; mandate a larger portion of electricity sold in Maryland to come from renewable sources; and require companies to offer paid sick leave."[47] While this argument made by Cortellessa and Hogan's rivals has merit, the governor also supported liberal policy positions such as a ban on fracking, modest gun control measures, and a ban on conversion therapy.

The conflicts over state funding provide an additional layer to the debate over the governor's ideological leanings. His unwillingness to allocate extra state money toward Democratic budgetary priorities, such as public education and transit, is more evidence of a conservative streak, but frequent public communications touting "record government spending" stand counter to those of most conservative leaders. The necessity of working with Democrats, given their immense power over the state's politics and the constraints of the Maryland electorate, further blurs the picture of the policies Hogan might pursue under different political circumstances. Still, holding a mix of liberal and conservative policy positions is also consistent with how moderation is characterized—arguably mischaracterized—among the voters in the mass electorate. Douglas Ahler and David Broockman (2018), for example, find that those who identify as moderates are just as likely as liberals or conservatives to hold extreme political views, and their mix of positions simply average out when placed on the traditional ideological scale.

Moreover, ideology is no longer simply the expression of a set of coherent issue positions defined by Philip Converse (1964) as a "system of beliefs" or Lloyd Free and Hadley Cantril (1967) as "operational ideology." The ideological labels of "liberal" and "conservative," much like party identification, are now a social identity (Devine 2015; Malka and Lelkes 2010; Mason 2018) or a "symbolic" construct (Ellis and Stimson 2012). And much like the well-established "loathing" of Democrats and Republicans toward members of the opposing political party, the consequence of identity-based ideology contributes to heightened levels of affective polarization against outgroup ideologues (Mason 2018).

The clear signals from political elites on which ideology best aligns with the party—Democrats are liberals and Republicans are conservatives—have led to increased rates of voters identifying with the ideology most consistent with their partisanship (Halliez and Thornton 2021). Based on this research, it's likely that public perceptions of Hogan's moderation are grounded not fully in a robust consideration of his policy positions, but in his willingness to challenge the orthodoxy of his partisan and ideological social group, the Republican Party, or its leader, Donald Trump. Hogan's personal popularity, evidenced by consistently strong favorability ratings, might also play a role. The plurality of Maryland voters view themselves as moderates, and research by Karyn Amira (2018) finds that voters tend to "project" liked candidates as holding positions closer to their own.

When asked directly to describe his politics, the governor is ambiguous, preferring broad terms such as "right of center" or "center-right."[48] He adds, "If someone says that I'm a moderate, that doesn't bother me. But I'm also a commonsense conservative." He's aware that those on the far right see him as a "squishy RINO," and those on the left think he's a "right-wing nut." But those voters are of little consequence to the governor: "If people on both extremes think you aren't one of them, then they are both right."[49] Years of being a Republican in a state defined by Democratic dominance didn't push Hogan to become a hardline ideologue. It convinced him that what people don't like are extremism and a one-party monopoly.

Geoffrey Kabaservice, the author of *Rule and Ruin* (2013), the definitive book on Republican moderates, contends that Hogan seems to hold "an ancestral view of what it means to be a Republican, rooted largely in the conservative but pragmatic positions of politicians like his father and Ronald Reagan." Kabaservice considers Hogan a Republican whose loyalties lie with an older version of the party that now has been almost entirely displaced by Trump and his brand of populism. For Hogan, Reagan's famous quote about why he switched parties might now be applied in reverse: "I didn't leave the Republican Party, the party left me."[50] To that point, perceptions of Hogan's politics are also likely a function of where he fits into the broader, polarized political environment during his first term. Analysis of the General Social Survey by *FiveThirtyEight* finds that Democrats have drifted leftward on many of their policy positions, whereas Republicans are more uniformly conservative.[51]

Policy-based or symbolic notions of ideological moderation aside, Hogan also leans into the public image that he's moderate in temperament, frequently chastising those on the right and left for inflammatory, divisive rhetoric and calling for other elected leaders to "turn down the temperature." The governor doesn't always live up to his standard—for example, early in his tenure, he described teachers union officials as "union thugs" and likened lawmakers in Annapolis to students on "spring break."[52] He also derided a 2017 measure that would have prohibited counties from being paid by the federal government to house immigration detainees as "sanctuary state legislation," calling it "absurd" before vetoing it.[53] Critics also contend that the governor is far from a beacon of moderation or civility, charging that he employs racist "dog whistle" rhetoric toward Baltimore City and its leadership.

Hogan is also a notoriously tough boss with a dominant personality, whom several staffers describe as demanding and hard-charging. He has little patience for those who can't meet his standards and even less for those who try to blame circumstance for their mistakes, and he does not attempt to hide his displeasure toward both offenses. He does listen to advisers, particularly those in his close-knit inner circle, but can be strident and stubborn in preference for his instincts. The modus operandi for Hogan staffers is to be prepared, succinct, and singularly focused on delivering for their boss and his agenda.

Staffers also note one of Hogan's governing superpowers that helps explain his effective public positioning as a moderate: an innate ability to immediately discern not just what average voters think but what issues they care about the most. A good sense of public preferences is an ability born out of necessity, given Maryland's heavily Democratic electorate, and undoubtedly bolstered by his vociferous consumption of scientific polling. He wants to be popular, is image-conscious, and loves to cite when the public is on his side of an issue. Hogan pays close attention to how he's perceived in the media and remembers those who have publicly criticized him. He's a prodigious consumer of opinion pieces and commentary—and not just about him. He pays attention to how other politicians communicate and are publicly discussed in the media.

As an important side note, particularly in the era of #MeToo and powerful male politicians being held accountable for sexist and abusive behavior, there is no evidence of a toxic "boys club" culture surrounding the Hogan administration or his campaign. From the beginning, the governor has promoted women to positions of power, as cabinet secretaries and in key staff positions.[54] There is a sense among female staffers that the governor values equal opportunity and accountability across gender lines.

In an August 22, 2017, column for the *New York Times*, David Brooks attempted to define what moderates believe in an era of Trump and hyperpolarization. "Moderation is not an ideology," he wrote. "It's a way of coping with the complexity of the world." He noted that moderates, unlike their rigid counterparts on the left and right, see the truth as plural, politics as syncretistic, and partisanship as necessary but blinding. Hogan fits within this definition of moderation. His governing style suggests a rejection of rigid purity for a malleable set of priorities grounded in traditional conservatism but constrained by the politically possible with a penchant for popular policy issues. And his broader governing philosophy, the larger view related to the role of government in the affairs of its citizens, is simple: "We need elected officials who will do their best to solve problems. . . . [M]y general philosophy is that we shouldn't be overtaxing people, that small businesses are the engine, where jobs come from . . . and that we should be focused on economic issues, be unabashedly pro-business, put more people to work."

Whether all this makes him a moderate or a conservative who strategically moderates is up for debate and heavily dependent on who you ask and to whom Hogan is compared. The journalist Ezra Klein once noted that "moderate is simultaneously one of the most powerful and least meaningful descriptions in politics."[55] And as it applies to Hogan, it seems Klein is right.

5

Go Ahead, Call Him a Socialist

"Well, boss, new game plan," longtime political consigliere Don Mohler remembers saying to Baltimore County Executive Kevin Kamenetz as election results rolled in on Tuesday, November 4, 2014.[1]

Larry Hogan's upset victory created a vacuum for leading Democratic contenders in 2018, and Kamenetz and others immediately changed course to fill it.

In their second and final terms, county executives—such as Kamenetz and Prince George's County Executive Rushern L. Baker III—were obvious choices. Others, such as Tom Perez, the U.S. Labor Secretary during the Obama administration, would weigh a run but ultimately decline the chance.

The field began to take shape after the 2017 General Assembly session in Annapolis. First to announce was Alec Ross, a technology policy expert who worked for Secretary of State Hillary Clinton. He was soon followed by Baker and Kamenetz, then by Ben Jealous, former leader of the National Association for the Advancement of Colored People (NAACP); Richard Madaleno, a state senator from the Washington, DC, suburbs; Jim Shea, former chairman of a prominent law firm; and Krish Vignarajah, a former policy director for First Lady Michelle Obama.

The large field fell into two camps: candidates who had worked in or around Maryland politics (Baker, Kamenetz, Madaleno, and Shea) and those who worked in national politics and lived in Maryland (Jealous, Ross, and Vignarajah).

As elected county executives, Baker and Kamenetz had similar levels of experience and strong geographic voter bases. Baker represented a vote-rich Democratic stronghold, while Kamenetz led politically diverse Baltimore County, considered a bellwether in state elections.

Madaleno was a wonky, outspoken lawmaker from Montgomery County. As vice chair of the Senate Budget and Taxation Committee, he regularly delivered unvarnished assessments of Hogan while displaying a deep understanding of the budgetary impacts of the progressive policies he championed.

Shea, a pragmatic lawyer, sought the moderate lane. He had never held public office but had deep connections in the state's power corridors, including among high-dollar donors.

Ross and Vignarajah represented the hopes of the Obama era. Both were smart, young Gen Xers with serious résumés from the highest levels of national politics. Yet they weren't as well known as Jealous, named "Marylander of the Year" by the *Baltimore Sun* in 2013 for his work advocating for marriage equality as president of the NAACP. This move was significant at the time, as Black Americans had been slower than their white counterparts to rally behind same-sex marriage rights.[2]

Jealous emerged early as a hard-line progressive. He helped launch the progressive group Our Revolution and served as a campaign surrogate for Bernie Sanders in the 2016 presidential campaign. That meant he also had a record of biting commentary on Hillary Clinton, who had bested Sanders in the 2016 Maryland primary by thirty points and was endorsed by most elected Democratic officials in the state. While Jealous lacked ties with Democrats in Maryland, he could capture the attention of voters who believed the party needed to learn from past errors and embrace progressive policies.

Fatal Distraction

As Hogan worked to solidify his image as a pragmatic, bipartisan moderate, his potential Democratic challengers traversed the state for a year, attempting to break from the pack.

But there was little daylight among them on many policy issues. Each supported increased funding for public education, reforming the criminal justice system, a more inclusive economy, and stronger environmental regulations. An ultimately defining exception was Jealous's plan for a state-level Medicare-for-all program. Jealous also supported free in-state tuition for Maryland's public colleges and universities.

But most Marylanders were ignoring the slog of town halls, debates, and public forums. Internal Kamenetz polling showed that voters weren't interested in the nuances of state policy. They wanted to know what the candidates could do about the maniac tweeting from the Oval Office, or they were too consumed by the next Trump-driven news cycle to think about the governor's race at all.

The same Trump effect that worked to bolster Hogan's image as a "different kind of Republican" became a fatal distraction to the Democratic candidates.

While they still discussed policy and made arguments about why they were the best suited to lead the state, Democratic candidates during much of the campaign focused on resisting Trump policies that they could do little more than talk about. Moreover, the Democrats in the Maryland General Assembly and Attorney-General Brian Frosh were already doing the substantive work of resistance—and voters were satisfied with how Hogan was handing Trump.

Public polls conducted from September 2017 to April 2018 told the same story: Baker, Jealous, and Kamenetz led, but none earned more than 20 percent. Nearly half of all Democratic primary voters were undecided. The fact that most voters were unable to say whether they had a favorable or unfavorable opinion of the candidates suggested few voters were paying attention.

The sleepy race dramatically changed in the early morning of May 10, 2018. Kamenetz, sixty years old and in outwardly good physical health, suffered a cardiac arrest and died on the way to the hospital. He left behind a wife and two teenage sons.

The sudden development ended the candidacy of a business-friendly leader who, many thought, had a chance to break out and match up well against Hogan in a general election. An aggressive fundraiser, Kamenetz had a massive television ad buy ready to run in the Baltimore and Washington, DC, markets during the final month of the spring primary campaign.

The *Washington Post* and *Baltimore Sun* conducted their final polls in late May and early June. The *Post* had Jealous with a slight advantage over Baker, the Prince George's County executive. The *Sun* had the candidates tied. Both found that about 40 percent of voters were still undecided.

The polls illuminated a bigger problem: not only did Hogan boast a double-digit advantage against every Democratic candidate, nearly a quarter of Democratic primary voters planned to vote for the Republican governor in the fall.

Keith Haller, a Democratic pollster with a long history in Maryland politics, told the *Washington Post*, "There's no question that the smart, large money appears to be staying out of the Democratic race for governor, largely because Hogan appears invulnerable and without a clear front-runner on the Democratic side."[3]

Then, in the final month before the primary, Baker's campaign sputtered, and Jealous pulled away.

Maryland's teachers' union and the Service Employees International Union, who endorsed Jealous, activated their ground games. National figures such as Ben Cohen, the liberal cofounder of Ben & Jerry's Ice Cream; the actor Lamman Rucker, who starred in several Tyler Perry movies; and the comedian Dave Chappelle appeared at campaign events. Outside groups and wealthy out-of-state liberals raised more than $1 million for get-out-the-vote efforts, mailers, and television ads. Jealous was telling voters on the stump that if they wanted to send a clear message to Donald Trump, they should send a civil rights leader to be their next governor.

Democrats who started to pay attention were growing excited by Jealous's clear progressive vision. Undecided voters broke hard his way.

Jealous earned 40 percent of the vote in the primary election, besting Baker by ten points overall. He dominated in the Baltimore region and earned a larger-than-expected margin in the DC suburbs.

In his victory speech, Jealous placed his win in a national context, telling supporters that the movement he was building would "make sure that everyone moves forward, no matter what happens in Donald Trump's Washington."[4]

The victory garnered headlines in the *New York Times*, the *Wall Street Journal*, and *NBC News*, bolstering a conversation about the rise of progressives during a time of Trump.

Writing for the *Atlantic*, Adam Serwer concluded that the Democratic Party might not have to choose between a populist economic agenda and one focused on civil rights and social justice. "Jealous's victory, along with others on Tuesday," Serwer wrote, "suggests that, in liberal strongholds at least, Democratic voters are comfortable pursuing both at once."[5]

That same day, Hogan received 100 percent of the vote in the Republican primary. Hogan didn't draw even a nominal primary challenger, despite grumbling from the most ardent Trump supporters. This was not wholly unexpected given his status as an incumbent, but it also reflected Hogan's effective navigation of the Trump effect on Maryland politics, not just in the eyes of Democrats, but also for Republicans. The governor's approval rating among those in his party held steady in the mid- to upper eighties, consistently higher than the marks earned by the president.

Trump never weighed in on the Maryland race. It was unclear exactly why. The president was often quick to lash out in response to even the most minor slights or perceived disloyalties, and Hogan was more outspoken against Trump than most elected Republicans. But the governor was, as evidenced in previous chapters, judicious with his critiques, especially early on. His criticism of Trump was never prolonged and rarely made a splash on cable news. Hogan never tagged @realDonaldTrump and referenced "Trump" directly only twice on Twitter between the president's inauguration and the midterm election.

A bigger concern for Hogan's advisers, particularly after the filing deadline for a primary opponent passed, was that Trump would offer words of support rather than condemnation. But as the campaign wore on, they grew confident in their ability to weather a presidential tweet storm of any variety.

A very different picture unfolded elsewhere across the country in 2018, where nearly every primary candidate Trump endorsed won and many incumbents chose to step aside rather than face a Trump-endorsed candidate. An analysis by *FiveThirtyEight* found that the GOP had the highest number of "pure" congressional retirements—those ending political careers and not seeking higher office—since 2008.[6]

The biggest names among those retiring were Senators Jeff Flake of Arizona and Bob Corker of Tennessee and House Speaker Paul Ryan of Wisconsin. All had clashed with Trump to some extent and, as a result, saw their power within the party wane.[7] For example, Flake's criticisms of Trump resulted in cratering poll numbers among Arizona Republicans and a primary challenge from the Make America Great Again (MAGA) firebrand Kelli Ward. The conservative senator served as a cautionary tale for Republicans. At the same time, Hogan was demonstrating the possibility that any Trump effect could be managed.

A Progressive Challenger

Hogan and his team remained tight-lipped during the primary, but many in his campaign were pleased that the Democratic nominee was Jealous. A key to Hogan's 2014 victory was appealing to the pocketbooks of voters clustered around the political center—and the Democratic nominee would allow the governor to continue those appeals. "If you like Martin O'Malley, you're gonna love this guy," Hogan told reporters the morning after the primary. "He's talking about tens of billions of dollars in tax increases that will cost us hundreds of thousands of jobs and devastate the great economy that we've made so much progress on."[8]

Jealous, too, was talking to journalists—but on the national platform of MSNBC. And he immediately made a misstep. Placing Jealous's win in a broader context, hosts Ali Velshi and Stephanie Ruhle asked the new nominee whether an emerging leftward Democratic swing would hinder the party in general elections. Jealous contended that his campaign was based on "people issues" rather than progressive issues, but Velshi and Ruhle were unsatisfied. They pressed him to answer directly.

A frustrated Jealous responded that Republicans could "call me the same things they called Obama, the same things they called Bernie, go ahead, *call me a socialist,* but it doesn't change the fact that I'm a venture capitalist."[9]

Doug Mayer, who was now Hogan's deputy campaign manager, was watching the interview and could hardly believe his luck. The candidate was repeating a core attack line against him. The Republican Governors Association (RGA) would later take Jealous up on the offer to call him a socialist—and now they could do it in his own words.

But first the RGA launched an ad depicting Jealous as a reckless "big spender." Perhaps ironically, Jealous was too broke after the primary to respond in kind.

Making matters worse for Jealous, the Democratic Governors Association and the progressive groups who helped secure his primary victory were focusing resources elsewhere. Stacey Abrams and Andrew Gillum—who, like Jealous, were Black, progressive, and endorsed by Our Revolution—won their primary contests for the open-seat races in Georgia and Florida, respectively. Early polling showed tight races in these states, while Maryland polls showed Jealous with a double-digit disadvantage. And the state of the race didn't improve by fall.

There were other problems unique to Jealous. He had won the primary, in part, by running against the Democratic establishment, and state party leaders felt no urgency to lend support to their nominee. On its end, the Jealous campaign did little in the way of meaningful outreach to many down-ballot Democrats. Some Democrats—notably, State Comptroller Peter Franchot and Montgomery County Executive Ike Leggett—publicly declined to endorse him (though Leggett would, months later). Others kept their distance or offered halfhearted offers of support.

Another ad from the RGA hit this point on what became a defining day on the campaign trail.[10] The Hogan campaign had worked to highlight its support from Democrats, part of a "permission to vote" strategy aimed at wooing groups not inclined to vote for Republican candidates. Hogan was particularly invested in this part of the campaign and was adamant that his team find Democrats of any profile willing to give their support publicly. The list was long in names but short in clout—most were older and out of office. But they secured a ringer in a crucial jurisdiction: Jim Brochin, a four-term state senator from Baltimore County who had just lost a primary for county executive by seventeen votes.

Brochin's endorsement announcement was scheduled for 10:30 A.M. on August 8 in front of the Baltimore County Courthouse in Towson and was expected to drive the day's headlines. It would reinforce the thirty-second RGA spot, which asked, "Why do so many fellow Democrats refuse to endorse Ben Jealous?" and answered, "Because Jealous is too extreme for Maryland," before cutting to a heavily edited MSNBC clip of Jealous saying, "Go ahead, call me a socialist." But because the Courthouse was a public venue, the Hogan campaign needed a permit, and word of the event leaked.

The Jealous campaign sent a barrage of emails, texts, and phone calls to organize their own endorsement event an hour earlier, featuring U.S. Representative John Sarbanes and a variety of state and local officials. The back-to-back morning events were a big draw for media. Jealous's team had set up its candidate to dominate the news cycle. But with one sentence the candidate turned opportunity into ashes.

After Jealous spoke, Erin Cox, a reporter for the *Washington Post*, asked him to respond to allegations from the Hogan campaign and RGA that he was a "far-left socialist." Jealous, with a laugh, responded by likening Hogan's messaging to name-calling reminiscent of what the Tea Party tried to do to Barack Obama and what Barry Goldwater did to Martin Luther King Jr. He ended by noting he was a venture capitalist.

Cox followed up: "Not to put too fine a point on it, but do you identify with the term 'socialist'?"

His answer: "Are you fucking kidding me?" Jealous smiled and asked Cox, with a brief chuckle, "Is that a fine enough point?"

But the profanity created unease and immediate recognition that Jealous had just undercut an otherwise successful press conference. It was written all over the faces of the elected officials standing behind their nominee. Reporters asked a few more questions, and the event soon ended.

While Cox didn't think Jealous was cursing at her and tweeted that she wasn't offended by the language, the f-bomb led media coverage of the day.

And the moment spread on Twitter to the national media. Fox News ran with the headline "Dem Candidate Ben Jealous Snaps at Reporter for Socialism Question: 'You F—ing Kidding Me?'" *USA Today* went with "'You F—ing Kidding Me': Maryland Governor Candidate Upset with Being Asked if He's a Socialist."[11] A spokesman from the RGA labeled Jealous "unhinged."

Hogan's team relished the opportunity to take the high ground and subtly compare Jealous to Trump. Mayer told reporters, "We need more people in public office who understand that words and tone matter, not fewer—we already have plenty who don't in Washington, DC."[12]

A few hours later, Jealous clarified his position on Twitter: "Let me answer @ErinatThePost's question once and for all. I'm a venture capitalist, not a socialist. I have never referred to myself as a socialist, nor would I govern as one."

But the damage was done, and the incident had staying power. The Hogan campaign found it popping up in focus groups and open-ended responses in internal polls well into the fall. The liberal-leaning outlet *Slate* had a different take on the day's events and noted that "the whole mess obscures the far more interesting part of this, which is that Jealous, a chief surrogate for Bernie Sanders two years ago, is so adamantly rejecting the socialist label."[13]

To that point, the socialist label, while championed by some on the political left, was problematic for large swaths of American voters. A Hill/HarrisX American Barometer poll conducted in July 2018 found that three-quarters of voters would not vote for a socialist for elected office. This number included 64 percent of Democrats, 63 percent of eighteen- to thirty-four-year-olds, and 72 percent of Black Americans—all groups Jealous hoped would help secure his victory.

In an August YouGov poll, 31 percent of voters weren't sure whether they held a favorable or unfavorable opinion on socialism, while 26 percent and 42 percent held favorable and unfavorable opinions, respectively.[14] Yet a Gallup poll found that 57 percent of Democrats and Democratic-leaning independents had a positive view of socialism.

A source of frustration among the progressive left is that socialism as a label is viewed as a net negative, yet the core philosophy of democratic socialism and related government programs—Social Security and Medicare, for example—are quite popular. The general notion that government should do more to solve problems and help people also enjoyed majority support both nationally and in Maryland; only a third of Maryland voters said that "the government is doing too many things better left to businesses and individuals," according to an April 2018 poll by Goucher College.[15] The Jealous campaign, constantly forced on defense by Hogan's team, could never turn these general attitudes into support for his platform.

Hard-Nosed Politics

The RGA and the Hogan campaign continued to hammer Jealous over the summer and into the fall. The governor likes to come across as the affable guy willing to work across party lines, but he's naturally pugnacious and assembled a team willing to throw sharp elbows on his behalf. They are adept at playing hard-nosed politics and came prepared to battle any issue.

A core group of high-level advisers met at least six days a week at 7:30 A.M. At these meetings, often held at Hogan's campaign headquarters in an Annapolis business park, Jim Barnett, the campaign manager, along with other key members of the team, reviewed long-term strategies and plans for the day. They would approve a daily email dubbed the "Sloofman Files" after their rapid response staffer, Scott Sloofman. This email was akin to an informal press release, highlighting the message for the day and media hits, with a positive spin from the campaign trail. It went out to reporters and other interested parties and reinforced the appearance of a campaign in forward motion. The research team painstakingly crafted a series of one-pagers on every potential policy or attack line that could be quickly converted into emails, social media posts, and talking points. They contested every shot the Jealous team took.

A core operating philosophy of the Hogan campaign was to work the media every day. This belief stemmed from the commonly held view among Republican operatives that reporters were predisposed to favor the Democratic perspective. A meticulous examination of media coverage was already a standard procedure for Hogan. Using a Public Information Act request early in Hogan's first term, an Associated Press story by Brian Witte detailed the governor's emailed complaints to his communications staff about press coverage and editorials he didn't like, even complaining that the aide who compiled press hits missed "a bunch of hogan christie stories and tv clips."[16]

Luke Broadwater, a *New York Times* reporter who was then covering the Maryland State House and 2018 campaign for the *Baltimore Sun*, remembers that Hogan's communications teams, always aggressive, were in hyperdrive during the campaign. "They would call reporters and read the number of sentences—even words—in a story that they perceived to be anti-Hogan versus pro-Hogan or neutral and demand there be equal number," says Broadwater. They pushed back on framing or analysis they disliked. And that behavior, Broadwater contends, came directly from the governor.[17]

Navigating a Blue Wave

Jealous was also working the media. Despite lackluster poll numbers, the Democratic campaign was pushing a narrative that a robust field operation would ultimately secure victory by turning out new voters and those who had stayed home in 2014. The campaign admitted it was down but contended it would win in the homestretch, as Hogan had four years earlier.

Focusing on bringing new voters into the electorate versus winning over a broad coalition of existing voters was a core difference between the Jealous and Hogan strategies. Jealous was an organizer at heart. His campaign believed that a progressive message combined with the building Blue Wave nationwide would bring the revolution sparked by Bernie Sanders in 2016 to Maryland. "If two million turn out, someone needs to get 1 million votes to win," said Travis Tazelaar, Jealous's campaign manager, at a meeting in Annapolis with reporters. "No Republican has ever come close."[18] This number was true. Hogan won with 884,400 votes in 2014. The only statewide candidate to break the million-vote barrier was O'Malley in 2010.

The seasoned Democratic pollster Fred Yang also weighed in at the meeting, showing reporters an internal campaign poll that had Hogan up by nine points, with 11 percent undecided in mid-July. Yang argued that the race would tighten when voters learned the platforms of the two candidates and that the most effective attack against Hogan would be that he "fails to stand up to Donald Trump and the

Republican Party." Voters who sat out 2014, Yang said, were more likely to vote for Jealous.

As expected, Hogan's campaign was dismissive of this assessment, telling reporters, "If the best-case scenario Ben Jealous can paint in his home-cooked poll is that he is losing by nine points in a state where Democrats outnumber Republicans by two to one, then he should be cursing his campaign strategists, not reporters."[19]

Democrats and the Jealous campaign were stuck. The governor had found a way to steer around the Trumpian land mines, yet a single misstep could quickly undermine his years of progress with Democrats and liberal-leaning independent voters. On this point, the Jealous and Hogan campaigns agreed: Trump presented the best opportunity to take Hogan down, but the focus on the president also detracted from the significant policy-centered differences between Jealous and Hogan.

The same polls that had Hogan leading the race also indicated he was out of step with some core policy preferences of Maryland voters. For example, large majorities of voters supported increasing the minimum wage to $15 per hour and legalizing recreational cannabis. Hogan directly opposed increasing the minimum wage and was noncommittal on recreational cannabis, although he supported bills expanding the medical marijuana industry. Voters, particularly Democrats, also expressed support for Medicare for all and Jealous's plan to offer free tuition at Maryland's state colleges and universities. Hogan opposed the broader policy of free tuition, although he did sign a bill to provide a no-cost community college education to low- and middle-income state residents. And while voters approved of the governor's handling of the economy, taxes, and transportation, they were divided on his handling of public education—an issue that consistently ranked as very important among Democratic voters and one that Hogan had lost support on over the year leading up to the campaign.[20]

Hogan was still a Republican in a state where Democrats vastly outnumber Republicans in what was shaping up to be a Democratic wave election year. Nothing could change that.

The Path to Victory

To win statewide in a high-turnout year, Hogan's campaign staff estimated that he needed to earn 25–30 percent of the Democratic vote.[21]

They cringed when Trump began tweeting about the "red wave" in early August and continued, without evidence, until Election Day. The president's boasts that Republican turnout would deliver GOP victories across the country were not something Hogan wanted Democratic voters to consider. Democratic voters entering polling places on Election Day with resistance on their minds could very easily cast a straight ticket for Democrats as a message of opposition to the president and his agenda. Indeed, voter hostility toward the opposing party can be a more significant motivator for political participation than positive feelings for one's own political party (Iyengar and Krupenkin 2018).

The path to victory in Maryland runs through a handful of the most populous counties and Baltimore City, where registered Democrats outnumber Republicans collectively by a margin of seven to one. Put another way, 56 percent of the state's nearly four million voters lived in Montgomery, Prince George's, and Baltimore counties and Baltimore City—all places where Democrats are organized and dominate every level of elected office.

Table 5.1 includes the voter registration numbers as of October 20, 2018. Counties with fewer than 100,000 registered voters are grouped by region. At first blush, those figures are evidence of why Jealous thought turning out new voters and engaging Democrats who sat out in 2014 could secure his victory.

Earlier in the year, Jealous even told voters in the Baltimore County suburb of Catonsville, "We're not going to win by tacking toward the middle. Hogan has already staked out that zone. We're going to run by tacking toward the people of the state."[22]

There were two problems with this strategy.

First, preelection polling indicated that a plurality of Maryland registered voters, including Democrats, identify themselves as moderates. Ceding the ideological middle to Hogan, especially when he was likely to win among the remaining conservative Democrats, only made it easier for the governor to get to the 25–30 percent of Democratic votes he needed to win.

And second, Jealous's perceived unwillingness to moderate or compromise on his politics was a mismatch with voter preferences, even though they found cohesion with him on some policy issues. About 80 percent of Democratic voters said that they preferred po-

TABLE 5.1. PARTY REGISTRATION IN MARYLAND BY COUNTY AND REGION (OCTOBER 2018)

	D (N)	D (%)	R (N)	R (%)	I (N)	I (%)	Other (N)	Total (N)	Total (%)
Maryland	2,173,884	55	1,008,369	26	708,012	18	63,762	3,954,027	100
Montgomery	390,400	60	112,995	17	142,173	22	9,847	655,415	17
Prince George's	456,702	79	40,500	7	68,270	12	14,051	579,523	15
Baltimore	310,019	56	142,739	26	91,948	17	9,231	553,937	14
Baltimore City	305,704	79	30,873	8	47,859	12	4,507	388,943	10
Anne Arundel	162,683	42	134,806	35	83,248	22	5,137	385,874	10
Howard	108,243	50	55,158	26	47,883	22	3,588	214,872	5
Harford	64,545	36	77,772	43	35,004	19	2,888	180,209	5
Frederick	64,669	37	67,012	39	39,092	23	2,134	172,907	4
Carroll	32,198	27	62,908	52	23,816	20	1,994	120,916	3
Charles	67,938	61	24,871	22	18,141	16	1,184	112,134	3
Eastern Shore	111,631	38	125,179	42	54,283	18	4,541	295,634	7
Western Maryland	49,813	32	76,688	49	28,699	18	2,560	157,760	4
Southern Maryland	49,339	36	56,868	42	27,596	20	2,100	135,903	3

Source: Maryland State Board of Elections
Notes: Eastern Shore includes Cecil, Wicomico, Worcester, Queen Anne's, Talbot, Dorchester, Caroline, Somerset, and Kent counties; western Maryland includes Washington, Garrett, and Allegany counties; southern Maryland includes Saint Mary's and Calvert counties. D = Democrat; R = Republican; I = Independent.

litical leaders who "compromise in order to get things done," compared with those who "stick to their beliefs even if less gets done," in an April 2018 Goucher College poll. They also viewed Hogan and the Democratic leadership as equally responsible when there was a lack of cooperation in state government.

The relentless campaign ads from the RGA defined Jealous as an ideologue. Hogan's campaign messaging reinforced his image as a moderate Republican who compromised with Democrats. And these frames worked in part because Jealous was steadfast in his positions and made little attempt to appeal to voters outside of his perceived base.

A Key Endorsement,
Minus the Enthusiasm

It was August, and Jealous still didn't have the money to run television ads. But progressive groups, unions, and lawmakers who strongly supported Jealous were pressuring elected Democrats to endorse their candidate. After all, Democratic voters had picked him, and by a comfortable margin.

Nearly two full months after Jealous won the primary, he secured several endorsements, including one from the powerful Senate President Mike Miller, who knew better than anyone what it takes to preserve allies and win elections in Maryland.

The *Washington Post* headline was bad: "Democratic Leaders Endorse Jealous, but Miller Is Less than Enthusiastic." The accompanying photograph of a frowning Miller during the event was worse. In his brief remarks, Miller mentioned the nominee just once and focused primarily on a new plan to improve public education in the state.

There was a backstory to Miller's mood.

Progressives in Maryland had grown tired of Miller's brand of centrist leadership and viewed him as a policy roadblock. They launched an effort in April 2018 to oust him in his primary, dubbing it "Take a Hike Mike" and declaring that "Miller time is over." Miller easily prevailed, but three of his closest legislative allies were defeated by more progressive candidates.[23]

The governor's popularity with moderate and conservative Democrats—the same ones Jealous wasn't particularly interested in reaching—now posed a threat to the veto-proof majority Miller had presided over for nearly three decades. If Republicans could capitalize on Hogan's strengths and pick up five seats in the forty-seven-member Senate, they could stop the at-will overrides that Miller could command

So a "Drive for Five" was underway, focusing on seats held by Democrats in districts that Hogan had carried in 2014. And three of those six seats were now open because of retirements.

The Maryland Republican Party, due to the Hogan's success, raised more money to spend on legislative races than in previous years. Hogan endorsed and campaigned for each Republican challenger save for one—a candidate who had made incendiary comments about Muslims and was an enthusiastic supporter of Trump. But he was far more focused on his race than on the legislative contests.

Democrats running in those competitive Senate districts wanted nothing to do with the Jealous campaign, sometimes actively rebuffing him. Jealous didn't have access to their political networks for canvassing or get-out-the-vote activities. One piece of direct mail funded by the Maryland Democratic Senate Caucus Committee, a political slate controlled by Miller, illustrated the disconnect between Jealous and the priorities of other elected Democrats. It featured a picture of Hogan alongside Baltimore County Senator Kathy Klausmeier, one of the Republicans' top targets, with the message, "Different political parties, same goal. Kathy Klausmeier is working with Governor Hogan for a better Baltimore County."[24]

Similar dynamics were at play in races for county executive in Baltimore, Howard, and Anne Arundel counties.

Baltimore County was the must-win for Hogan, and another place where Jealous's brand of progressivism was failing against the perception of Hogan as a bipartisan problem solver.

Like Jealous, John "Johnny O" Olszewski Jr. ran as the progressive in his primary race. The former state delegate from working-class Dundalk embraced free prekindergarten and community college, raising the minimum wage, and paid family leave. The difference was that Olszewski was well connected and liked in state Democratic politics and had a reputation as a pragmatist.

An early September internal poll from the Olszewski campaign illustrated why he kept his campaign untethered from the top of the ticket: only a third of likely voters in Baltimore County held a favorable view of Jealous, the same as for Trump. On the flip side, 77 percent of likely voters in Baltimore County held a favorable view of Hogan, and 64 percent planned to cast their ballots for him in November. Most voters indicated they wanted the next Baltimore County executive to work "across the party aisle" and "with the governor" to get things done.

When asked about supporting Jealous, Olszewski's response was a flat, "I'm a Democrat who supports Democrats."[25]

Minding the Gap

Hogan's approval rating suggested that he was sailing toward a second term, but a closer examination of the horse-race polling highlighted a weakness. A jarring gap between how voters viewed Hogan and their support for his reelection persisted throughout the campaign. The number of voters who said, "I like him, he's done a good job, but I'm not voting for him," was a significant concern for the campaign and led it to believe some of Hogan's support was soft.

Table 5.2 shows the gap between Hogan's approval rating and likely votes for him from the earliest horse-race polling against Jealous, conducted before he won the Democratic primary, to the final public poll against Jealous in early October 2018. Hogan's approval rating averaged a stunning eighteen points higher than his vote share throughout the campaign. Perhaps most interesting about the approval-reelection gap were the demographics and attitudes of the almost 20 percent of voters who fell into it at any given point.

A closer examination of polls conducted by Goucher College—one from February and one at the height of the general election campaign in mid-September—told the same story. Democrats, women, and those who said that Trump would have "some" or "a lot" of influence on their general election vote were the most likely to approve of the job Hogan was doing and plan to vote against him in November. Voters who thought Jealous was the better candidate on education and health care were also more likely to simultaneously approve of the job Hogan was doing and indicate they would vote for the Democratic nominee. There was little difference across racial lines: near-equal percentages among Black and white voters fell into the gap—though, to be sure, white voters were also far more likely than Black voters to approve of Hogan and support his reelection.

Hogan recalls his pollster telling the campaign, "We've never seen anything like this. Your job approval rating is in the seventies, your favorability is in the seventies, and you still could lose."[26]

There was good reason for Hogan to fear that Democrats would ultimately turn their backs on him at the ballot box. Voters are now more likely to hold strongly negative views of the opposing party than at any point in modern electoral history (Abramowitz and Webster

Poll Sponsor	Poll Field Dates	Total in Sample (n)	Hogan Approval Rating (RV, %)	Vote for Hogan (%)	Hogan Approval Vote	Vote for Jealous (%)	Hogan vs. Jealous
Mason-Dixon	September 27–30, 2017	625 (RV)	61	49	–12	33	Hogan +16
Gonzales Research	December 27, 2017– January 5, 2018	823 (LV)	71	49	–22	36	Hogan +13
Mason-Dixon	February 20–24, 2018	625 (RV)	63	50	–13	33	Hogan +17
Goucher College	April 14–19, 2018	449 (LV)	70	44	–26	31	Hogan +13
Washington Post	May 29–June 3, 2018	968 (RV)	74	51	–23	39	Hogan +12
Gonzales Research	June 4–10, 2018	800 (LV)	75	52	–23	34	Hogan +18
Gonzales Research	August 1–8, 2018	831 (LV)	71	52	–19	36	Hogan +16
Goucher College	September 11–16, 2018	472 (LV)	67	54	–13	32	Hogan +22
Mason-Dixon	September 24–26, 2018	625 (LV)	68	52	–16	37	Hogan +15
Gonzales Research	October 1–6, 2018	806 (LV)	72	54	–18	36	Hogan +18
Washington Post	October 4–7, 2018	648 (LV)	72	58	–14	38	Hogan +20
Average			69	51	–18	35	Hogan +16

TABLE 5.2. HOGAN VOTE-APPROVAL GAP AND HORSE RACE AGAINST JEALOUS

Sources: Mason-Dixon; Gonzales Research; Goucher College; *Washington Post*

Note: RV = registered voters; LV = likely voters.

2016). As a result, high levels of party loyalty and low levels of split-ticket voting characterize U.S. elections. Most troubling for Hogan and the Republican dream of breaking the veto-proof Democratic majority in the State Senate is that "negative partisanship," voting based on hostility toward the opposing party and its leaders, extends beyond just federal races and can play a role in state-level contests.

6

The Anatomy of a Landslide

The first campaign finance reports of the 2018 general election dropped on August 30 and showed the governor with a commanding advantage. The Hogan campaign was sitting on more than $9 million in available cash, compared with less than $400,000 for Ben Jealous, the Democratic nominee. Hogan's campaign manager, Jim Barnett, called the report "just the latest indignity to face the Jealous campaign."[1]

Sophia Silbergeld, a Democratic fundraiser, estimates that "transactional donors," the people who have specific interests in who wins and their relationship with the winner, make up about three-quarters of state donors.[2] Those donors had little interest in Jealous, a challenger who had never held office in Maryland and was trailing in the polls. Thus, Hogan's fundraising advantage was built in part by the political virtue of incumbency. And as a result, nearly all of Hogan's donations were from Maryland in the August report, compared with just 17 percent for Jealous.[3] Hogan's donors were also giving far more.

Jealous's campaign manager, Travis Tazelaar, tried to spin the disclosure, arguing that Hogan's money was no match for Democratic organization and enthusiasm. "All indicators point to the Blue

Wave coming to Maryland and being large enough that not even the millions of dollars in negative advertising from Larry Hogan will be enough to stave off a Ben Jealous victory," Tazelaar said, noting that the state Democratic Party had already doubled the number of field organizers from four years earlier.[4]

Hogan had more than enough money to invest in a sophisticated campaign structure that included staff, research, and advertising. His campaign invested heavily in data analytics—combining voter files with commercial databases and other sources—to create a broad universe of likely Hogan voters who could be targeted online and with traditional mailers.

But for most voters, the campaign's most visible feature was television advertisements—and Hogan's cash advantage meant there were far more of them for the Republican incumbent than his challenger.

After the Republican Governors Association (RGA) did the dirty work earlier in the summer, flooding airwaves with attacks on Jealous, the Hogan campaign chose to run only positive television advertisements. Without attack ads from the Hogan campaign, Jealous wouldn't get free media and an opportunity to define himself when reporters asked him to respond, a tactic that Hogan had used against Anthony Brown's negative ads four years earlier.

Hogan's first ad, "Maryland Strong," ran throughout the campaign and encapsulated Hogan's pitch to the public: he was a fiscally responsible governor who worked with Democrats to fund public schools, protect the environment, and fix infrastructure; he was decisive in the face of unrest in Baltimore; and he was grateful for a public who rallied around him when he had cancer.

A second statewide ad called "Affordability" was released in August and included messages on taxes and the reductions of tolls and fees—familiar themes from the 2014 campaign.[5] In a nod to the campaign's goals of reaching voters outside of the typical GOP base, it featured the voices of a Black female business owner and a white single mother. It reinforced the argument the RGA had spent $2.2 million making that summer: Jealous was reckless, whereas Hogan was fiscally responsible.

As public school students returned to classes, the next ads focused on education, including one that asked voters to support the "Hogan lockbox," a ballot initiative that would ensure that casino revenues went to public school funding. As noted in Chapter 4, while Hogan supported the lockbox as a policy, the actual ballot initiative was the work of Democratic lawmakers. A *Baltimore Sun* editorial chastised the ad as having "a comic disregard for the truth."[6] Undeterred, Hogan's campaign noted that the governor had signed a bill that put the lockbox amendment on the ballot and continued to run it.

Hogan's money afforded the campaign weeks of solo air time. Jealous would not release his first ad until mid-September, nearly three months after his primary victory.[7]

The sixty-second spot, called "Ready to Lead," laid out the challenger's progressive platform and highlighted his experience as a venture capitalist and time as chief executive of the national NAACP—a solid introduction but decidedly late for a largely unknown political entity.

Hogan's advertising advantage was getting results.

An early October survey by the *Washington Post* found that 60 percent of voters said they had seen a Hogan ad over the past few months, with almost half saying the ad had a positive message; 44 percent had seen an ad about Jealous, but fewer than a quarter described the ad as positive.[8]

Jealous tried to turn Hogan's massive cash advantage against him in mid-October by offering an ethics plan, criticizing how the governor handled his real estate development business while in office and accusing him of "cozying up" to a pair of high-power State House lobbyists—Bruce Bereano and Gerard Evans. Bereano and Evans have been convicted of fraud about two decades earlier.[9]

Unbeknownst to Jealous, Evans had casually ribbed some of Hogan's associates about the numerous phone calls he'd received from Jealous, claiming that maybe he'd cut a check to the Democrat. When Mayer caught word of the Jealous campaign's intentions to hit Hogan on his relationship with the lobbyists, he asked whether Evans had saved any of the voicemails. Evans provided the voicemails to the Hogan campaign and media outlets. He told reporters he was "amazed" and "dumbfounded" that Jealous would ask for a donation one day only to rebuke him publicly the next.[10] One voicemail was publicly played for Jealous by the *Daily Record* reporter Bryan Sears at a press gaggle near the Clarence M. Mitchell Jr. Courthouse in Baltimore City: *Gerry, hey, it's Ben Jealous calling. . . . Could really use your support.*[11] Jealous's campaign noted that the call was in error and that he would immediately have returned any check from Evans.

Hogan flooded the Baltimore airwaves with a powerful closing advertisement featuring Arthur "Squeaky" Kirk, a community activist Hogan met in West Baltimore while campaigning in 2014. The long-shot Republican candidate promised Kirk that he would help secure resources for a community center. Kirk assumed it was an empty campaign pledge. He didn't bother to save Hogan's cell phone number and answered a curt "Larry who?" when the governor-elect called.[12]

Hogan helped secure enough private donations to get the center off the ground, and Kirk repaid the favor by cutting a spot that included a line that spoke to Hogan's ability to connect with voters outside of his base: "You know, a white Republican governor. Hey, he acts like a regular human being to me." The ad worked because Kirk, an exceedingly generous and no-nonsense man, and Hogan have an authentic friendship.

In early October, the *Washington Post* conducted the last public poll on the race. Hogan was up by twenty points. Only a handful of voters remained undecided.

But the poll included another important number: 57 percent of voters wanted the state legislature to remain in Democratic control as a check on Hogan.

The campaign finance reports covering the period between August 22 and October 21 showed that Hogan had spent $6,384,584 on media, compared with $1,023,667 by Jealous.[13] With just over two weeks of the campaign left, Jealous had less than $300,000 to spend.

Still, Jealous and his campaign maintained that they didn't need massive fundraising or television advertising to win. "Our job in this race is to turn out Democrats and like-minded independents," Jealous told reporters in late October. "If you look at voting numbers, the big question is, 'How can we lose?'"[14] And at a rally on October 30 in Montgomery County that featured Senator Bernie Sanders, Jealous told the enthusiastic crowd, "I taught everyone in the primary one lesson: Polls don't vote."[15]

The Blue Wave Came but Didn't Swamp Hogan

Hogan's final internal poll, conducted on October 28–30, put Hogan at 51 percent and Jealous at 33 percent, with 16 percent undecided.

Like the *Washington Post* poll, the governor had a 70 percent approval rating and was viewed favorably by 63 percent of voters. Meanwhile, only 36 percent of voters held a favorable view of Jealous, while 31 percent held an unfavorable view and a third didn't know how to rate him.

The governor and his campaign team were optimistic. Hogan had invested millions to build a broad coalition of voters. He managed the Trump effect the best he could, and he ran a disciplined campaign.

But they worried that national Democratic momentum and voters who viewed the governor favorably but were nonetheless going with Jealous could still mean an upset loss for the incumbent. As Barnett sees it, "Waves break late and close to shore."[16]

Reports of massive turnout began to trickle in from the first day of Maryland's early voting period, which ran from October 25 to November 1. When polls closed on November 6, overall statewide turnout in Maryland had increased from 47.2 percent in 2014 to 59.1 percent, representing nearly a twelve-point overall bump. As happened elsewhere in the country, the Democratic Blue Wave had rolled into Maryland.

The Democratic candidate earned more than a million votes—1,002,639 to be exact—just shy of what former Governor Martin O'Malley had won in his reelection bid in 2010, making Jealous the third-largest vote getter in Maryland electoral history.

But it just wasn't enough.

Hogan won 1,275,644 total votes, the most of any statewide candidate in Maryland history, adding 391,244 more votes to his 2014 total.

Table 6.1 presents the statewide and Democratic turnout rates in 2014 and 2018 in order of the total votes cast in 2018. Counties with fewer than 100,000 registered voters are grouped by region. Democrats increased their turnout from 46.8 percent in 2014 to 61.5 percent in 2018—a 14.7 point jump—casting 1,337,541 of the total 2,335,128 votes; 57.3 percent of the state's votes were cast by Democrats, up from 54.5 percent in 2014.

TABLE 6.1. MARYLAND VOTER TURNOUT AND DEMOCRATIC VOTER TURNOUT (2014 AND 2018)

	All Voters				Democrats			
	Turnout, 2014 (%)	Total Votes, 2018	Turnout, 2018 (%)	Change, 2014–2018	Turnout, 2014 (%)	Total Votes, 2018	Turnout, 2018 (%)	Change, 2014–2018
Maryland	47.2	2,335,128	59.1	+11.8	46.8	1,337,541	61.5	+14.7
Montgomery	42.1	413,137	63.0	+20.9	45.4	267,302	68.5	+23.1
Baltimore (County)	51.1	328,973	59.4	+8.3	51.0	191,232	61.7	+10.6
Prince George's	40.6	323,352	55.8	+15.2	43.1	270,751	59.3	+16.2
Anne Arundel	52.0	231,897	60.1	+8.1	51.4	103,797	63.8	+12.4
Baltimore City	38.1	187,060	48.1	+9.9	40.4	154,659	50.6	+10.2
Eastern Shore	51.2	176,225	59.6	+8.4	48.2	66,430	59.5	+11.4
Howard	54.3	145,235	67.6	+13.3	55.8	77,596	71.7	+15.8
Harford	55.8	111,600	61.9	+6.1	52.3	40,453	62.7	+10.3
Frederick	53.6	108,782	62.9	+9.3	53.1	43,661	67.5	+14.4
Western Maryland	45.7	86,716	55.0	+9.2	42.5	27,824	55.9	+13.4
Southern Maryland	53.1	80,865	59.5	+6.4	52.4	30,338	61.5	+9.1
Carroll	57.4	75,733	62.6	+5.2	53.4	21,137	65.6	+12.2
Charles	47.6	65,553	58.5	+10.8	48.0	42,361	62.4	+14.3

Source: Maryland State Board of Elections
Notes: Eastern Shore includes Cecil, Wicomico, Worcester, Queen Anne's, Talbot, Dorchester, Caroline, Somerset, and Kent counties; western Maryland includes Washington, Garrett, and Allegany counties; southern Maryland includes Saint Mary's and Calvert counties.

The biggest increases in turnout from 2014 were in the heavily populated Democratic strongholds of Montgomery and Prince George's counties, where 68.5 percent and 59.3 percent of eligible Democrats cast their ballots, respectively.

More than 60 percent of the Democratic voters turned out in Baltimore and Anne Arundel counties, as did 71.7 percent in Howard County (the highest turnout in the state). This trio of battlegrounds was home to hotly contested county executive races and places where Hogan needed to put up big margins. Baltimore City's turnout rate was up from 2014, but at 50.6 percent Democratic turnout, it lagged behind the other large jurisdictions.

Consistent with the historical patterns of voting in midterm elections, statewide Republican turnout at 63.5 percent was even higher than that of Democrats but represented only a 4.7 point increase from 2014, reaching a total of 639,857 votes. This was not the "red wave" Trump had promised or evidence that Republican voters had sat out the election or disliked Hogan because of his lack of fealty to the president.

The state's independent voters cast 328,572 total votes with a 46.4 percent turnout rate, representing a 13.4 point increase in turnout from 2014. Voters representing other parties cast 29,158 total votes.

The results amounted to a double-digit shellacking. Hogan won 55.4 percent of the total 2,304,512 votes cast in the governor's race to Jealous's 43.5 percent.

Despite the Blue Wave, Hogan had won in a landslide.

Anatomy of a Landslide

An analysis of election results shows that Hogan did better in every area of the state than he had four years earlier. In heavily Democratic areas, such as Montgomery and Prince George's counties and Baltimore City, as well as in Charles County—a fast-growing area south of the District of Columbia—Hogan cut into Jealous's margins.

Given the party registration and turnout numbers in those jurisdictions, the only way to make those gains were by winning votes from Democrats. Hogan averaged nearly a ten-point gain from his 2014 numbers in the thirteen State Senate districts where Democrats cast more than three-quarters of the total votes.[17] Hogan also won in battleground areas and dominated in counties outside of the state's population centers. Table 6.2 includes the electoral results by county/region, as well as Hogan's gains in vote share from 2014.

State Senator William C. Smith, a Democrat who represents a heavily Democratic Senate district in Montgomery County where Hogan won 27.4 percent of the vote, points to several factors, including the structural advantages of incumbency and Hogan's well-financed and skilled campaign. "Montgomery County is not as progressive as it might appear at first blush," he said. "There are pockets of Republicans and a lot of moderate Democratic voters, so top-line issues such as taxes and his support for the Purple Line, as well as Hogan's relationships with the business community, really mattered."[18]

Elected officials such as Delegate Anne Kaiser, a long-serving lawmaker from Montgomery County, and Jolene Ivey, a member of the Prince George's County Council, said they heard a steady drumbeat in conversations with voters of "I don't know a lot about Ben Jealous, but Larry Hogan is doing a good job and it appears that he's working with Democrats, and things are going well in the state."[19] Those attitudes were reflected in public polling, mirroring Hogan's messaging strategy and governing priorities.

According to AP VoteCast, a massive nationwide phone and web survey by the National Opinion Research Center at the University of Chicago, Hogan won a third of the Democratic vote and 35 percent of voters who cast a ballot for a Democratic candidate in congressional elections. He earned nearly unified support from his Republican base and 70 percent of the state's unaffiliated voters.

As preelection polling suggested, the perception that Hogan was a moderate was a key factor. Hogan won 63 percent of the vote from moderates, while Jealous won just over a third.

Liberals made up a slight plurality of the vote in the AP VoteCast data (a somewhat higher percentage than in most preelection polling) and largely stood behind Jealous, as conservatives did for Hogan. Still, Hogan managed to earn 28 percent of the vote from self-described liberals.

The results also suggest that Hogan and his team were right to be fearful that any drop in his overall popularity could carry significant consequences. As preelection polling indicated, about a quarter of voters who said they had a favorable opinion of Hogan cast their votes

TABLE 6.2. ELECTORAL RESULTS BY COUNTY AND REGION (2018)

	Hogan Vote Count	Hogan Vote Share (%)	Jealous Vote Count	Jealous Vote Share (%)	Total Votes	Vote Margin	Hogan Gain (2014–2018)
Maryland	1,275,644	55.4	1,002,639	43.5	2,304,512	Hogan +11.8	+4.3
Montgomery	180,018	44.1	224,029	54.9	408,428	Jealous +10.8	+7.3
Baltimore	198,122	61.1	122,773	37.9	324,276	Hogan +23.2	+2.1
Prince George's	89,925	28.2	225,889	70.8	318,985	Jealous +42.6	+13.3
Anne Arundel	157,202	68.6	69,399	30.3	229,206	Hogan +38.3	+2.5
Baltimore City	58,360	31.6	123,609	66.9	184,691	Jealous +35.3	+9.7
Eastern Shore	131,649	75.8	39,986	23.0	173,657	Hogan +52.8	+4.4
Howard	80,574	56.2	61,146	42.6	143,383	Hogan +13.5	+4.7
Harford	85,259	77.1	24,012	21.7	110,579	Hogan +55.4	+0.6
Frederick	72,560	67.7	33,355	31.1	107,219	Hogan +36.6	+4.3
Western Maryland	67,461	79.4	16,274	19.1	84,999	Hogan +60.2	+4.6
Southern Maryland	60,313	75.7	18,300	23.0	79,678	Hogan +52.7	+4.8
Carroll	62,445	83.2	11,767	15.7	75,051	Hogan +67.5	+1.0
Charles	31,756	49.3	32,100	49.9	64,360	Jealous +0.5	+2.4

Source: Maryland State Board of Elections

Notes: Eastern Shore includes Cecil, Wicomico, Worcester, Queen Anne's, Talbot, Dorchester, Caroline, Somerset, and Kent counties; western Maryland includes Washington, Garrett, and Allegany counties; southern Maryland includes Saint Mary's and Calvert counties.

for Jealous, as did nearly all voters who held an unfavorable view of the governor. In comparison, 81 percent of voters who held a favorable opinion of Jealous voted for him over the incumbent. There were just far fewer of them. Jealous's inability to increase his positive name recognition against the pummeling of the RGA and mistakes on the campaign trail undoubtedly hurt him.

As expected, Trump was a factor in how Maryland voters cast their ballots. A majority of Maryland voters (53 percent) said that they voted to express opposition to the president. Hogan won about a third of these voters, a testament to the efforts his team made to mitigate the damage of a potential Trump drag. Hogan won nearly all the votes of those who were casting a ballot to support Trump, and he took home 70 percent of the votes of those who didn't consider Trump as part of their voting calculus.

Smith and other Democratic lawmakers noted that some voters could identify specific examples of how Hogan had pushed back on Trump and were largely satisfied with how the governor was handling the president. Table 6.3 shows the results of the AP VoteCast data by political factors.

Hogan also made inroads with voters who are becoming increasingly elusive to GOP candidates: young voters, college-educated voters, women, and people of color. Though Jealous won the under-forty vote, Hogan earned 39 percent of voters age eighteen to twenty-nine and 46 percent of those age thirty to thirty-nine.

College-educated voters, who broke hard against the GOP nationally that cycle, supported Hogan, but to a somewhat lesser extent than those without college degrees.[20]

Jealous fared better than Hogan in urban communities, households making less than $25,000 a year, and those who viewed their financial status as "falling behind." Hogan won among rural and small-town voters and suburban voters, as well as among voters from households making $25,000 or more a year and those who viewed their financial status as "holding steady" or "getting ahead."

Table 6.4 includes the results of the AP VoteCast data by demographic characteristics. The governor won handily among white voters and edged Jealous out among the state's small population of Asian voters. Hogan's campaign offers some anecdotal evidence that the

TABLE 6.3. AP VOTECAST RESULTS BY POLITICAL FACTORS			
	Hogan (%)	Jealous (%)	Total (*n*)
All voters	55	44	4,476
Party identification			
Democrat (61%)	33	66	2,724
Republican (30%)	96	4	1,337
Independent (9%)	70	25	415
Ideology			
Liberal (39%)	28	71	1,761
Moderate (36%)	63	36	1,622
Conservative (24%)	89	10	1,081
Opinion toward Hogan			
Favorable (70%)	74	26	3,147
Unfavorable (23%)	10	89	1,015
Don't know (7%)	19	74	314
Opinion toward Jealous			
Favorable (45%)	18	81	2,002
Unfavorable (38%)	93	6	1,693
Don't know (18%)	68	28	782
Trump factor in vote			
Voted to express support for Trump (17%)	94	5	725
Voted to express opposition to Trump (53%)	34	65	2,248
Trump was not a factor (30%)	70	28	1,268
Generic House ballot			
Democratic candidate (66%)	35	64	2,926
Republican candidate (30%)	97	2	1,333

Source: AP VoteCast data (2018) weighted to reflect final election results
Notes: Results rounded to nearest whole number. Table includes but does not present votes for "other" candidates or "don't know" responses, unless indicated.

presence of Yumi Hogan, the governor's Korean-born wife, and their three daughters on the campaign trail were vital to securing votes among some in the Asian community.[21] Jealous won among Black voters, Latinos, and other nonwhite voters, but at slimmer-than-expected margins.

The AP VoteCast data show that, nationwide, GOP gubernatorial and U.S. senatorial candidates during that cycle won just 12 percent and 7 percent of Black voters, respectively, whereas Hogan earned 28 percent. Hogan also earned more support from Latinos, Asians, and

TABLE 6.4. AP VOTECAST RESULTS BY DEMOGRAPHIC FACTORS

	Hogan (%)	Jealous (%)	Total (*n*)
All voters	55	44	4,476
Sex			
Men (40%)	60	39	1,786
Women (60%)	52	46	2,687
Race			
White (67%)	65	34	3,015
Black (19%)	28	70	865
Latino or Hispanic (4%)	44	54	190
Asian (4%)	52	48	155
Other (5%)	42	55	235
Age			
18–29 (14%)	39	59	628
30–39 (17%)	46	53	748
40–49 (15%)	54	45	663
50–64 (30%)	62	37	1,353
65 or older (24%)	65	35	1,066
Education			
Less than four-year degree (40%)	59	40	1,793
Four-year college degree or more (60%)	53	46	2,681
Community type			
Urban (16%)	37	61	705
Suburban (61%)	55	44	2,735
Small town (11%)	63	35	495
Rural (12%)	72	27	534
Income			
Under $25,000 (10%)	47	51	426
$25,000–$49,999 (15%)	52	46	662
$50,000–$74,999 (18%)	54	45	798
$75,000–$99,999 (16%)	58	41	728
$100,000 or more (40%)	58	42	1,812
View of financial situation			
Getting ahead (19%)	63	36	835
Holding steady (65%)	56	43	2,899
Falling behind (16%)	45	54	729

Source: AP VoteCast data (2018) weighted to reflect final election results

Notes: Results rounded to nearest whole number. Table includes but does not present votes for "other" candidates nor "don't know" responses, unless indicated.

other racial minorities than GOP gubernatorial and senatorial candidates did overall, though these groups make up a smaller part of the Maryland electorate.

Hogan bested Jealous among the state's female voters by a margin of 52 percent to 46 percent. This was primarily driven by the support of white women, independent women, and Republican women. A third of female Democrats voted for Hogan, as did about a quarter of Black women. By comparison, across all governor's races from the 2018 cycle, 53 percent of women voted for the Democratic nominee and 40 percent voted for Republicans (including just 11 percent of Black women).

Hogan's margins among women and Black voters made his victory in Maryland nationally significant and helped explain the difference between a narrow victory and his double-digit landslide. Chapter 7 provides a closer examination of how Hogan reached them.

Hogan's popularity and strengths were amplified by problems in the Jealous campaign.

Democratic lawmakers from different jurisdictions noted that their electoral slates funded campaign literature featuring Jealous and received little coordination from the Jealous campaign. Typically, walk pieces and mailers are funded and door knocking plans are organized by the top of the ticket.

Rush Baker IV, a member of the Prince George's County Democratic Central Committee and the son of Prince George's County Executive Rushern Baker, remembers that after his father endorsed Jealous immediately after the primary, no additional asks came in from the campaign. "I think [Jealous] thought the politicians were going to come to him," the younger Baker argued. "But he didn't have anything to offer them. He didn't have the campaign infrastructure or any money to spread around. So you're asking them to do all the work. And you haven't called them. And they don't know you."[22]

Some, such as State Senator Jill Carter, a Baltimore City Democrat who vocally supported Jealous, placed the blame on establishment Democratic figures who, they say, turned their backs on their nominee.[23] Other progressives echoed this critique. "We're absolutely frustrated with the political establishment in Maryland and how they've behaved," said Larry Stafford, executive director of Progressive Maryland, a statewide advocacy organization, in an interview with

Buzzfeed News. "They're legit just propping up a Republican governor in a state that we know we can win."[24]

None of the Democratic nominees for county executive in Baltimore County, Anne Arundel County, or Howard County actively campaigned for Jealous. Each of the Democratic nominees won, but Hogan also carried each county by a larger margin.

Cut-off Coattails

Hogan had built a personal brand and a diverse voter coalition that was strong enough to protect him against the antipathy toward Trump that fueled a huge increase in Democratic turnout. But the goodwill did not extend down-ballot, even for Republicans cut from similar cloth.

Perhaps no one felt this more acutely than Howard County Executive Allan Kittleman, a Republican incumbent. Like Hogan, Kittleman had publicly refused to endorse or vote for Trump. But unlike Hogan, he didn't have an RGA equivalent pounding his opponent for months or the protection of millions of dollars in sleek ads and a sophisticated data-driven campaign.

Kittleman's internal polling indicated he had consistently solid job approval ratings and was leading the race against his Democratic challenger, Calvin Ball. Kittleman also out-raised his challenger and had more cash on hand going into the election's final weeks.[25]

The incumbent knew his polls didn't accurately capture the massive increase in Democratic voters when the early voting numbers showed him down by more than six thousand votes. "A lot of new Democratic voters came out in that election, and they just didn't know me," he says. This was a strange place for a politician who had served in the Maryland State Senate for a decade and, before that, on the Howard County Council. As a final gesture that perhaps best exemplifies how fundamentally different Kittleman was from Trump, the defeated incumbent came to Ball's election night celebration to concede in person and offer his congratulations. "There's no doubt that Trump cut off Hogan's coattails," Kittleman says.[26]

Another Republican incumbent, Anne Arundel County Executive Steve Schuh, suffered the same fate as Kittleman, as did Al Redmer, the Republican nominee for the open-seat race for Baltimore County executive. Redmer was a serious candidate with deep county ties. He had saved the Hogan campaign from a headache by handily defeating a primary opponent the *Baltimore Sun* once dubbed "the Trump of Baltimore County."[27] He ultimately lost to Democrat John "Johnny O" Olszewski Jr. by a margin of 57.8 percent to 42 percent.

Hannah Marr, an alumnus of Hogan's first campaign who served as the communications director for Redmer, notes, "Throughout the campaign, we were getting a positive reception from community groups and on the ground. Voters agreed with us on many of the issues and liked Redmer's connection with Hogan." But on Election Day, Marr witnessed a telling interaction between Redmer and a female voter. "Are you a Republican?" the voter asked the candidate. When he said yes, she responded, "I'm not going for any Republican because of Trump" and promptly walked away.[28]

Schuh's loss to his Democratic challenger, the political newcomer Steuart Pittman, was perhaps the biggest upset of the night. Anne Arundel has a larger proportion of Republican voters than Howard and Baltimore counties and a strong and organized local Republican Party apparatus. Schuh won his seat in 2014 with 61.1 percent of the vote and lost with 47.6 percent of the vote in 2018—a precipitous drop.

Patrick O'Keefe, then serving as the executive director of the Maryland Republican Party, readily admits that the Trump-driven Democratic turnout was a problem for many Republicans in the state but offers a nuanced view of Hogan's coattails.[29] He believes that the election of Trump forced Hogan to choose between investing his significant resources in branding the Maryland Republican Party as the party of Hogan or rebranding himself as something different from the Republican Party. O'Keefe doesn't blame the governor for choosing the latter and recognizes the former as a riskier strategy, maybe even an impossible lift, albeit possibly better for down-ballot Republicans. "It's hard for Republican candidates to ride the coattails of a governor who is actively distancing himself from the party," O'Keefe says.

State Senator Justin Ready, a conservative Republican who represents Carroll County, doesn't think it was possible for Hogan—or any governor—to change how Republicans were viewed in their state, given Trump's position as the de facto head of the party.[30]

The lack of coattails meant that the state GOP's effort to eliminate the Democrats' veto-proof majority in the State Senate—the "Drive for Five"—would come up short. Republicans netted only one Senate seat, while Democrats in the House of Delegates widened their majority by picking up eight additional seats.[31] Miller and Busch would once again preside over veto-proof majorities in their respective legislative chambers, the check on Hogan that preelection polling suggested voters wanted.

"We would have been far worse off had Hogan been unpopular, but Hogan's popularity alone wasn't enough to protect or bolster down-ballot Republicans against the national headwinds," Ready says. "Our candidates needed to cultivate their own personal brand outside of the larger political environment."[32]

"People came out and expressed their frustration against just about all Republicans in our state with the exception of us," Hogan told reporters at a news conference the day after the election. "Last race, we had the biggest coattails of any Republican ever. This time we had a pretty big drag."[33]

7

Women and Black Voters
for Hogan

T he governor's phone started ringing as soon as the 2018 election
results were announced. Mixed with congratulations from supporters and calls from local reporters came a flood of requests
from national journalists suddenly interested in the two-term governor
of Maryland. They wanted to know how he had bested the Blue Wave
and what he thought about the current state of the Republican Party.

To be sure, Hogan was not the only Republican winner that election cycle. Ron DeSantis of Florida and Brian Kemp of Georgia both
beat progressive challengers by doubling down on appeals to the base.
The GOP also gained seats by flipping a trio of Senate seats in Florida,
Missouri, and North Dakota; each of those Republican victors had
been endorsed by Donald Trump. Charlie Baker and Phil Scott, Hogan's fellow blue-state Republican governors, also won their electoral
matchups by comfortable margins.

But the larger picture pointed to GOP electoral weaknesses outside of Republican-leaning jurisdictions. Democrats won a majority
in the House of Representatives and new control over seven governorships and six state legislatures. They broke the Republican supermajority in Pennsylvania and brought their Democratic trifectas in state
governments from eight to thirteen.

Exit polls, electoral returns, and campaign analyses all indicated that anti-Trump backlash drove suburban and college-educated voters, particularly women, to the Democratic Party. Some analysts suggested that Never Trump and Trump-skeptical Republican voters, though small in number, were part of the suburbanite exodus to Democrats.[1] And turnout was unusually high among voting blocs that lean Democratic: Black voters and other racial minorities, and young people.[2] It wasn't just a backlash to Trump. Polling indicated that health care was the biggest issue for voters, and Republican efforts to repeal the Affordable Care Act—efforts that Hogan opposed—were not popular.[3]

Hogan shared his ideas about what Republicans were doing wrong in an interview later that summer with KK Ottesen, writing for the *Washington Post Magazine*:

> I'm concerned—that the Republican Party is shrinking its appeal and its base down to a smaller and smaller group of only, you know, white males in a certain demographic. They're not trying to be the bigger tent that I would like to see. And they're getting away from traditional Republican values. I won in a landslide in a very blue state in a very blue year, with a huge blue wave. We won the suburban women vote overwhelmingly, where most in my party did not. We got nearly a third of the African American vote, when my party usually does not.[4]

So how was Hogan different from other Republicans when it came to winning women and making inroads with Black voters?

Narrowing the Gender Gap

As noted in Chapter 6, Hogan bested Ben Jealous among women in Maryland by an estimated margin of 52 percent to 46 percent.

The gender gap is one of the most studied and persistent features of contemporary American voting behavior and poses a significant electoral problem for Republicans.[5] Female voters supported Democratic presidential candidates by double digits in the 2012 and 2016 presidential contests and in the 2010 and 2014 midterms. Studies indicate that a race gap drives the gender gap: majorities of white women have voted for the Republican candidate since the 2000 presidential election, but much larger majorities of Black, Latina, and Asian women have supported the Democratic candidate (Junn and Masuoka 2020).[6]

Taken together, the large percentage of Democrats and the racial diversity of Maryland suggested that Hogan's electoral success was heavily reliant on earning the votes of women and his margins among women of color.

The Hogan campaign paid close attention to polling leading up to the 2018 midterms, which suggested that disdain for Trump would drive the gender gap to historic levels. The team was also painfully aware of the 2017 gubernatorial race in neighboring Virginia, where exit polling showed that Democrat Ralph Northam, in his 53.9 percent to 45 percent victory over Republican Ed Gillespie, won female voters by twenty-two points, even larger than Hillary Clinton's seventeen-point advantage in 2016.[7]

Hogan's team of strategic advisers included an expert on winning female voters: Ashley O'Connor.[8] Along with Christine Matthews and Katie Packer Gage, O'Connor had once headed up Burning Glass Consulting, a firm devoted to helping Republican candidates win female voters.[9] O'Connor reached out to Matthews, now the head of Bellwether Research and Consulting, to see whether she could assist in the Hogan campaign's efforts to reach female voters. Matthews had developed the Woman Advantage Panel, an online platform that captured the deliberative decision-making process of women.[10] It was what the campaign needed to track the attitudes of female voters and adjust its messaging accordingly during a campaign waged in the shadow of Trump.

Matthews recruited a diverse panel of approximately 110 Democratic and independent women who liked Hogan, hated Trump, and were undecided about the election for the Hogan campaign. The panel didn't include Republican women, as they already ranked among Hogan's most ardent supporters, and research suggested that they were unlikely to break GOP ranks, even in a Trump-fueled environment, to cast their ballots for Jealous over Hogan (Cassese and Barnes 2019; Ondercin and Lizotte 2021). It also didn't include Democratic and independent female voters who disapproved of Hogan's job as governor. Internal research suggested that those women were going to vote for Jealous regardless. The panelists answered a series of tracking questions and gave feedback on ads and messaging, helping the Hogan campaign fine-tune its strategy.

What the Panel Said

The first panel discussion gave a baseline for what the women thought of the candidates at the beginning of the campaign. Words in italics represent direct quotes. From the start, several women noted that, although they were Democrats, they liked that Hogan was a *moderate* and governed in *a bipartisan way*. A middle-aged panelist from Baltimore County wondered whether Jealous was *too similar to Bernie Sanders, a far-left politician.* One college-educated white woman from Montgomery County asked, *Is there a Democratic challenger who can do a better job than Hogan? Ben Jealous was chosen last week, and I don't know a lot about the man.*

Most panelists still weren't paying much attention to the race when they convened for a second time in mid-July. However, most had seen the "Big Spender" ad, released by the Republican Governors Association (RGA), prompting them to wonder whether Jealous could pay for his proposals. The ad *sums up my biggest concerns about Jealous,* one liberal woman said. *He has the huge ideas and no plan on enacting them. Sounds too similar to our current Orange-in-Chief. If Jealous wants to mount an actual campaign, he's going to need to create an actual plan.* And a Black woman from Howard County said, *I would sell my home and move out of the state before I would pay drastically higher taxes on every little thing that would likely not be used for the programs I am interested in.*

The third check-in came at the end of August, as many were preparing to send their kids back to school. Education was a top issue for the panelists, and many expressed skepticism about Hogan's commitment to public schools. A white, middle-aged Democrat from Anne Arundel said, *I want to know what Larry Hogan is doing to improve the education system. When you look at the best schools in Maryland, they are located in affluent areas. What is he going to do for the less affluent areas where other high schools are located?*

Concern over the inequality of public schools was frequently expressed, even by those who had positive things to say about their own schools. Some mentioned images that had made national news in January, of Baltimore City public school students freezing in winter jackets.[11] Others noted that some schools would be sweltering throughout September because they lacked air-conditioning.

I'm in Howard County, said a Black, college-educated Democrat. *We have the best school system in Howard County. Our children are doing amazing in the school system, and I, too, am a product of the school system. So for me—I would like to see stronger school systems in other counties within the state. I'd like all the counties to be top counties.*

The Hogan campaign had initially wavered on using the "Lockbox" ad, which promised to protect school funding, but the positive response from the panel pushed it into heavy rotation. Panelists' feedback also helped Hogan refine his message about education. Instead of simply noting that "every child in Maryland deserves access to a world-class education, regardless of what neighborhood they happen to grow up in," language often used by proponents of school choice, the campaign began to include the phrase "educational inequality" in ads and in Hogan's talking points.

The fourth session, in mid-September, focused heavily on Hogan's handling of Trump, who was growing more active on the campaign trail. Not surprisingly, the panelists' hatred for Trump was red-hot and unwavering, and they all liked when Hogan pushed back against the president. They also understood that it was necessary for Hogan to keep a working relationship with the federal government and appreciated that Hogan focused on Maryland instead of getting caught up in divisive national politics. A middle-aged woman noted, *I don't think [Hogan] supports Trump, but at the same time he is professional in his responses, as it will affect the state he is governing. I don't think he is running scared like other Republicans when it comes to Trump at all.*

In other words, while Democratic elected officials consistently accused Hogan of lacking forcefulness in his pushback, the female panelists (who, again, were all Democrats and independents) were largely satisfied with how the governor was handing Trump.

The panel also illuminated the growing view that Jealous was *in over his head* and *lacked the experience to be governor*, suggesting that the challenger's September television ad drop was doing little to combat the RGA's negative ads. The women also hadn't forgotten about

Jealous's f-bomb moment from the summer. A Black panelist from Howard County called it *not a good look*, adding, *Ben Jealous does not seem to be as polished as Governor Larry Hogan*. The best news for Hogan's team was that a majority of the panelists now believed that the governor was the better candidate on education, suggesting that his targeted ads and messaging could be working.

The group convened for a fifth time in late September, after the lone gubernatorial debate and the televised testimony of Supreme Court nominee Brett Kavanaugh and psychology professor Christine Blasey Ford. Blasey Ford convincingly and credibly accused Kavanaugh of sexual assault, and Kavanaugh had delivered a defiant denial. Republicans were pushing forward with his confirmation. A Montgomery County woman said she *cried in her car* after the hearings, which hit *especially close to home* because Kavanaugh had grown up there.

The women were uninterested in talking about the debate between Hogan and Jealous; more than half didn't watch or read news coverage of it. They did, however, know that Hogan had called for a full investigation of Kavanaugh prior to the confirmation process and that he supported an independent investigation of the allegations made by Blasey Ford.[12] They were angry at other Republicans for refusing to withdraw support for Kavanaugh but were largely satisfied with Hogan's response, viewing it as another example of Hogan *standing up for what's right*.

The Maryland Democratic Party put out two statements after the testimony of Blasey Ford and Kavanaugh. One asked whether Hogan believed Blasey Ford, and the second contended that the governor could either stand with Blasey Ford or with Trump. The Jealous campaign and other elected Democrats echoed these messages.

Hogan's internal polling, conducted in the aftermath of the testimonies, showed a small but troubling dip in support. Concerned that disdain over how Republicans and Trump had handled the confirmation process could drive Democratic voters to Jealous, the campaign asked Matthews to hold an additional emergency session with the panel that focused entirely on Kavanaugh.

Their fears were largely eased by what they heard. The women expressed similar attitudes regarding Hogan's response to Kavanaugh—

he had since declined to say whether he would confirm Kavanaugh if he were a member of the U.S. Senate—as they had in the previous panel meeting, and a majority indicated that it wasn't going to change their vote.[13] The next internal poll, taken a week later, showed Hogan's numbers had rebounded.

It remained tremendously important for the panelists that Hogan live up to his image as a Republican who was different from Trump. In the days before the penultimate panel in mid-October, the Hogan campaign released a web-only ad that mocked Jealous for making a series of verbal slip-ups, including one in which he said he was running for governor of Virginia. Barely any of the panelists had seen it. But when they were shown the ad their reactions were overwhelmingly negative. Earlier in the fall, Jealous had discussed his lifelong struggle with stuttering in a *Washington Post* interview and, in reaction to seeing the ad, told reporters that "while I can take it, it encourages the bullying of young people, and it's not okay. It is a new low in Maryland politics."[14]

Hogan's campaign insisted that it wasn't ridiculing Jealous for stuttering, just pointing out the candidate's mistakes. The panelists, however, thought that the ad was *bullying, something Trump would do,* and *so not who Hogan is.* The campaign kept the ad on its YouTube channel, not wanting to admit that it was a mistake, but pulled it from digital advertising rotations.

The last meeting of the panel asked the women how they planned to cast their ballots. About fifty of the women were solidly behind Hogan, and fewer than twenty were undecided. The rest planned to vote for Jealous. A Black Jealous voter from Prince George's County with a postgraduate degree noted that *Hogan did some good things* but thought *our country needs to rally against Trump in every way possible.*

But a Black voter from Baltimore City who had decided to vote for Hogan responded that he had *been good for Maryland,* conceding that might be due partly to the Democratic-led legislature providing a check. She noted that Hogan *was not a Trump Republican* and that *Jealous ran a poor campaign.* Another Hogan voter from Anne Arundel County, said she *found [Jealous] to be largely unprepared,* and *it's a shame that people still don't know who he is or what his position is.*

The Women's Vote

AP VoteCast data indicate that the campaign's careful attention to winning women paid off. A third of female Democrats cast their ballots for Hogan, as did 65 percent of female independents. As expected, Hogan captured nearly unified support (96 percent) from Republican women. Female conservatives and moderates, who made up 57 percent of all female voters, supported Hogan with 86 percent and 61 percent of their votes, respectively. Nearly 30 percent of liberal women voted for Hogan.

Hogan's team was largely successful in translating favorable opinions toward the governor into votes: 73 percent of women who held a favorable opinion of Hogan ultimately cast a ballot for him. More than half of female voters either couldn't rate Jealous or held an unfavorable opinion of him, and most of those voters picked Hogan.

Overall, Democratic and Republican women voted for Hogan at the same rates as their male counterparts. The biggest gender differences in Hogan support were among independents: nearly three-quarters of male independent voters supported Hogan, compared with 65 percent of female independent voters. Conservative men were slightly more supportive of Hogan than conservative women (93 percent compared with 86 percent), but there were no real differences between genders among moderates and liberals. Attitudes toward Jealous and Hogan had a similar effect on vote choice between men and women, although men held less favorable views toward Jealous and more favorable views toward Hogan than women overall. Table 7.1 includes the AP VoteCast data on the vote choice of female voters by political factors.

The results also show that Hogan split the votes with Jealous among female voters with a college degree and those from suburban areas. National-level data suggest that these voters were more motivated by health care and education than by immigration. But the chief reason these women left the GOP was that Trump was an "uncommonly divisive president" who created a "visceral repulsion" among many of these voters.[15] Hogan's personal style appealed to female voters, especially in comparison with Trump. Hogan was disciplined instead of erratic, self-deprecating instead of hubristic, every-

TABLE 7.1. AP VOTECAST RESULTS BY POLITICAL FACTORS AMONG FEMALE VOTERS

	Hogan (%)	Jealous (%)	Total (*n*)
All female voters	52	46	2,687
Party identification			
Democrat (66%)	33	66	1,770
Republican (26%)	96	3	699
Independent (8%)	65	27	219
Ideology			
Liberal (43%)	29	70	1,151
Moderate (36%)	61	37	970
Conservative (21%)	86	14	557
Opinion toward Hogan			
Favorable (67%)	73	27	1,807
Unfavorable (26%)	9	90	661
Don't know (8%)	17	76	217
Opinion toward Jealous			
Favorable (47%)	17	82	1,265
Unfavorable (33%)	92	7	883
Don't know (20%)	52	46	539

Source: AP VoteCast data (2018) weighted to reflect final election results
Note: Results are rounded to the nearest whole number. The table includes but does not present votes for "other" candidates or "don't know" responses, unless indicated.

man instead of reality TV star, agreeable instead of thin-skinned, and careful instead of brash.

Like other Republicans, Hogan earned the strongest support from white women: 64 percent of white women, compared with 27 percent of Black women, voted for Hogan, a thirty-seven-point difference. Still, that was considerably better than other Republicans' support. Nationwide, 8 percent of Black women cast a ballot for GOP candidates in 2018 and just 6 percent of Black women cast a ballot for Trump in 2020.

Hogan lost to Jealous among Maryland's relatively small populations of Hispanic women/Latinas (38 percent), Asian women (48 percent), and other women of color (30 percent) but again fared significantly better among these voters than Republicans did nationwide.

TABLE 7.2. AP VOTECAST RESULTS BY DEMOGRAPHIC FACTORS AMONG FEMALE VOTERS

	Hogan (%)	Jealous (%)	Total (n)
All female voters	52%	46%	2,687
Race			
White (65%)	64%	35%	1,758
Black (23%)	27%	71%	606
Latina or Hispanic (4%)	38%	60%	99
Asian (3%)	48%	51%	77
Other (5%)	30%	65%	138
Age			
18–29 (15%)	37%	61%	408
30–39 (19%)	45%	53%	500
40–49 (16%)	53%	46%	426
50–64 (30%)	59%	40%	815
65 and older (20%)	61%	38%	526
Education			
Less than four-year college (44%)	56%	42%	1,176
Four-year college degree (56%)	49%	50%	1,509
Community type			
Urban (16%)	38%	60%	427
Suburban (61%)	51%	48%	1,632
Small town (11%)	60%	38%	293
Rural (12%)	71%	28%	327
Income			
Under $25,000 (12%)	46%	51%	313
$25,000-$49,999 (17%)	51%	47%	455
$50,000-$74,999 (19%)	52%	47%	518
$75,000-$99,999 (17%)	53%	46%	444
$100,000 or more (35%)	55%	45%	925
View of financial situation			
Getting ahead (15%)	58%	41%	406
Holding steady (65%)	53%	46%	1,742
Falling behind (20%)	46%	53%	529

Source: AP VoteCast data (2018) weighted to reflect final election results
Note: Results rounded to nearest whole number. Table includes but does not present votes for "other" candidates nor "don't know" responses, unless indicated.

White and Black women both supported Hogan to a similar degree as their male counterparts (only a four-point difference, on average), but Hispanic men/Latinos, Asian men, and men of color were all more supportive of Hogan than their female counterparts (a sixteen-point difference, on average). The lack of robust data on racial groups outside of Black and white voters limits the ability to draw any broad conclusions as to why these differences exist.

Jealous bested Hogan among female voters making less than $25,000 a year and among those who said they were "falling behind" economically but lost among all other income categories and those who viewed their economic situation as "holding steady" or "getting better." Hogan's strongest support among women came from those age forty or older. Hogan earned somewhat higher margins among female voters under forty than other Republican candidates that cycle. Table 7.2 on the previous page includes the AP VoteCast data on the vote choice of female voters by demographic characteristics.

Inroads with Black Voters

A majority of Black voters consistently approved of the job Hogan was doing throughout his first term in office. Hogan's internal polling and public preelection polls indicated that about a third of Black voters intended to vote for him. But the campaign always assumed that support would waver when faced with the choice between a white Republican and a Black Democrat at the ballot box. The Hogan campaign was surprised and elated when it saw the exit polling. Moreover, electoral returns from the 2018 election indicated that Hogan had increased his vote share from 2014 in each majority-Black county and State Senate district. Table 7.3 includes those results.

Winning almost 30 percent of Black voters is highly unusual for a Republican. Since 1968, no Republican presidential candidate had received more than 13 percent of the Black vote, a trend that is generally reflected in down-ballot races, and surveys regularly show that upward of 80 percent of Black voters self-identify as Democrats.[16]

Numerous scholars of race in American politics have illuminated the reasons why Black voters are the most consistent voting bloc for Democrats. Seminal work by Michael C. Dawson (1995) posits that Black Americans prioritize the well-being of the group over their in-

TABLE 7.3. HOGAN VOTE SHARE AND GAIN IN MAJORITY-BLACK COUNTIES AND STATE SENATE DISTRICTS				
	Black Residents (%)	Hogan Vote Share, 2014 (%)	Hogan Vote Share, 2018 (%)	Hogan Gain, 2014–2018
Prince George's	64.4	14.9	28.2	+13.3
Baltimore City	62.4	21.9	31.6	+9.7
Charles	50.1	46.9	49.3	+2.4
Average	59.0	27.9	36.4	+8.5
25 Prince George's	86.0	6.8	21.3	+14.5
24 Prince George's	85.4	7.6	21.0	+13.4
26 Prince George's	76.7	11.2	24.6	+13.4
23 Prince George's	60.7	26.2	37.1	+10.8
41 Baltimore City	66.8	23.3	33.3	+10.0
22 Prince George's	52.5	17.3	26.6	+9.3
40 Baltimore City	67.8	17.6	26.4	+8.8
44 Baltimore City & County	66.3	27.3	35.9	+8.6
45 Baltimore City	73.8	20.6	28.8	+8.1
43 Baltimore City	64.8	19.1	26.1	+7.0
10 Baltimore County	57.3	35.3	41.0	+5.6
Average	68.9	19.3	29.3	+10.0
Source: American Community Survey, 2019 estimates; Maryland State Board of Elections				

dividual interests, considering what's best for all Black people because race is the predominant factor defining their collective American experience. Recent research has since built on Dawson's work—notably, Ismail K. White and Chryl N. Laird's book *Steadfast Democrats* (2020), which provides strong empirical evidence that decades of identification with the Democratic Party has created a norm within the Black community, entwining Black identity and partisanship: Black voters vote for Democrats as a show of solidarity, creating a social expectation even among those who have rational or policy reasons to choose Republicans. This helps explain why, as also explored in Tasha Philpot's *Conservative but Not Republican* (2017), an increasingly economically heterogeneous Black population and ideological conservatism do not translate into identification with the Republican Party, as they do for whites. Both Philpot and White and Laird provide robust overviews of the body of research on Black political behavior, and Michael Fauntroy (2007) provides a history of the policy and political choices that have kept Republicans from winning Black voters.

So what factors might explain why nearly 30 percent of Black voters picked Hogan over the Democratic nominee?

Black Maryland lawmakers and leaders largely credit Hogan's support from Black voters to his personal attributes, campaign outreach, and ideological appeal. They also point to Hogan's distancing from and criticism of Trump: multiple national polls indicated that Trump was viewed as a racist or biased against Black people by large swaths of Black voters, which also helped the governor win support.[17]

Others noted that having a white Republican governor, particularly one who was both personally popular among Black voters and was checked by a Democratic majority that included many Black lawmakers, wasn't viewed as a threat to the well-being of Black people in the same way a white Republican might be viewed in a state where Black people aren't as well represented in the political power structure. To that point, when Hogan was running for reelection in 2018, 51 of 188 members (28 percent) of the Maryland General Assembly were members of the Legislative Black Caucus; Prince George's County and Baltimore City had Black-majority councils and, along with Montgomery County, had Black executives. Other jurisdictions in the state and Maryland's congressional delegation also had Black elected officials.

Some Black leaders also viewed representation and access to power through the lens of accountability. In an interview with the *Washington Post* on October 29, 2018, Reverend Doug Miles, the former pastor of Koinonia Baptist Church and a community activist with the Baltimoreans United in Leadership Development (BUILD) community organization, noted that "fortunes in Baltimore have gone down rather than up," noting, "What you're seeing is the result of ineffectiveness of the Democratic Party over the past 25 years to deliver in a meaningful way for African Americans in Baltimore and Maryland."[18]

Stephanie Smith, a Black attorney who in the 2018 cycle was running for her first term in the Maryland House of Delegates, reflected on that dynamic and noted, "While the 2018 election was a profoundly disappointing moment for our [Democratic] party, there were some important lessons. The political dynamics in 2018 that left some Black Democratic voters feeling overlooked has given way to a new world where a broader bench of stakeholders see a place to turn the corner. We now have House Speaker Adrienne Jones, the only Black female presiding officer in the country, who has ushered forth an impressive agenda for closing the wealth gap for Black Marylanders while leading the nation on police reform."[19]

More than perhaps anything, Hogan's campaign wooed Black voters in the same way as white voters: through their pocketbooks. Polling conducted by Goucher College in September 2018 found that 63 percent of Black Marylanders thought state taxes were too high, compared with 51 percent of white residents.[20] Black voters were also less likely than white voters to say that they trusted the government to spend their tax dollars wisely. Rushern L. Baker III, the Black former Prince George's County executive, notes an underlying pragmatism among Black voters: "When they hear 'free,' they want to know 'what's the catch.' Jealous was great at explaining the benefits of his policy proposals, but not how to implement or pay for them. Moreover, Black Prince George's County homeowners are perpetually worried about their property taxes. They never want them raised. . . . They always think you're going to raise them."[21]

Then-Delegate Cory McCray was part of a trio of challengers who defeated candidates supported by powerful leaders to win a Democratic State Senate nomination in 2018. McCray has many concerns about Hogan's leadership but understands why some Black voters in his district were drawn to economy-focused messaging. When it comes to taxes in working-class jurisdictions, McCray says, "When you ain't got it already, you don't want to pay more. And that fiscally focused attitude isn't unique to white people."[22]

McCray said Hogan's decision to cancel the Red Line light-rail project in Baltimore did not resonate with many Black voters in his district to the extent many progressives and transit activists anticipated. While some Black voters were angry at Hogan, others were indifferent or even believed the move was fiscally wise—a view not shared by McCray. "Many just did not recognize the long-term impact of investing in the Red Line," he said. "The project would have increased job opportunities as well as mobility."[23]

TABLE 7.4. AP VOTECAST RESULTS BY POLITICAL FACTORS
AMONG BLACK VOTERS

	Hogan (%)	Jealous (%)	Total (*n*)
All Black voters	28	70	865
Party identification			
Democrat (88%)	24	75	760
Republican (4%)	84	13	32
Independent (8%)	49	44	72
Ideology			
Liberal (40%)	23	76	346
Moderate (47%)	31	67	401
Conservative (13%)	36	62	111
Opinion toward Hogan			
Favorable (54%)	46	53	470
Unfavorable (30%)	7	92	259
Don't know (16%)	7	89	136
Opinion toward Jealous			
Favorable (65%)	13	87	559
Unfavorable (15%)	76	22	132
Don't know (20%)	43	53	173

Source: AP VoteCast data (2018) weighted to reflect final election results
Note: Results rounded to nearest whole number. Table includes but does not present votes for "other" candidates nor "don't know" responses, unless indicated.

Exit polling showed little difference in support for Hogan across levels of income or among urban, suburban, and rural Black voters. The differences among Black voters were widest across political factors.

Black lawmakers also noted that Black voters are not as progressive as their white Democratic counterparts, a view supported by political science research and public opinion polls, suggesting an underlying ideological mismatch with Jealous.[24] A plurality of Black voters (47 percent) identified themselves as moderates; 40 percent, as liberals; and 13 percent, as conservatives.[25] About a third of both moderate and conservative Black voters supported Hogan's reelection effort, whereas fewer than one-quarter of liberal Black voters supported him. Table 7.4 above shows those results.

Reflecting national trends, 88 percent of Black voters in Maryland identified with the Democratic Party in the AP VoteCast data. Hogan won about a quarter of their votes. The small number of Black Republicans in Maryland largely supported Hogan, and the governor edged out Jealous among the 8 percent of Black voters who identified as independent. Research by Joshua Farrington (2016), Corey Fields (2016), and Leah Wright Rigueur (2015) offers a deep analysis of the motivation and politics of Black Republican voters.

The AP VoteCast data put Hogan's favorability rating at 54 percent among Black voters, mirroring what he had earned in preelection polling, but fewer than half who viewed Hogan favorably ultimately supported his reelection. However, most Black voters (87 percent) who held a favorable view of Jealous cast their ballots for him, as did those who held an unfavorable view of Hogan. Many Black voters held a positive opinion of Hogan and thought he was different from other Republicans—especially Trump, who consistently earned a single-digit approval rating among Black voters.

State Senator Jill Carter, a Black progressive from a storied family of civil rights leaders, was critical of Hogan's record on criminal justice, particularly his support for mandatory minimum sentencing and overall record regarding Baltimore City. She notes, however, that the view from some of her community members was that Hogan "came off like some regular guy who made $50,000 a year before he was governor. And even more than that, he wasn't uncomfortable around Black people—which is something, frankly, not a lot of white politicians do."[26] She also argued that television and print media in the state went easy on the governor, a criticism echoed by other Democrats.

Hogan attended community events in Prince George's County, frequently met with Black community and faith leaders, and opened a campaign office on North Avenue in Baltimore City. There he replaced the overhead billboard—where a local activist had spray-painted the poignant words "Whoever Died from a Rough Ride? The Whole Damn System" as a tribute to Freddie Gray—with a photo of Hogan and Lieutenant-Governor Boyd Rutherford and their wives. For some, the billboard represented Hogan's campaign presence in the city. Still, to others it was symbolic of a governor who didn't understand or care about the systemic problems facing Black Baltimoreans.[27]

To that point, Hogan was not free from criticism regarding race. In August, Larry Gibson, a professor at the University of Maryland Francis King Carey School of Law and longtime Democratic activist, condemned RGA ads that depicted Jealous as reckless, arguing that they pushed a racist "angry Black man" trope.[28] And in early October, the Hogan campaign was criticized for a mailer that used a black-and-white picture of Jealous with a claim that the Democratic candidate would "release thousands of violent and dangerous criminals into our neighborhoods." The Hogan campaign argued it was an accurate reflection of Jealous's stated positions on criminal justice; others saw shades of Willie Horton.[29] It's unclear how widely held this criticism of Hogan was among Black voters. As previously noted, a majority of Black voters consistently approved of the job Hogan was doing throughout his first term in office and viewed him favorably on Election Day. At the same time, while Hogan made inroads, far more Black voters cast ballots for Jealous.

The Quiet Power of Boyd

With few formal duties, the office of lieutenant-governor in Maryland is only as powerful as the governor wants it to be. In Rutherford, Hogan found a partner in governance and a balance in personality. The contrast between the men is clear in their different approaches to the local parades, a central feature of Maryland political life. The extroverted Hogan revels in these opportunities, darting from person to person, backslapping and posing for selfies. Rutherford, introverted by nature, looks for "a smiling older lady or a guy with a military hat on" and enjoys the one-on-one conversations a more leisurely pace allows.[30]

Preferring to discuss the nuances of procurement reform to seeking media attention, Rutherford spent considerable time speaking to community groups, visiting high schools, and meeting with faith leaders in predominantly Black parts of the state, out of the view of reporters. This presence led some Black leaders to conclude they had support from the Hogan administration even if it wasn't from the governor directly. "I went to a lot of church services in Baltimore," Rutherford remembers. He also points to an interesting nuance between the state's two largest majority-Black jurisdictions: "A small community association in Baltimore City has no problem asking me to come speak to an audience of 15 people—which I often did—but I didn't get those same requests from Prince George's County."[31] Jolene Ivey, a Prince George's County Council member who likes and respects Rutherford (though, she stresses, she does not share his politics), notes that, in her experience, "Boyd was someone you had a direct line to and was responsive to your requests."[32]

Sean Yoes, the Baltimore editor of *The Afro* during the 2018 election, also notes that "Boyd was present in the community, and he is respected among the Black business class."[33] The support from Black business owners was highlighted in an October ad featuring Kimberly Ellis, the owner of Breaking Bread Restaurant in Baltimore City. "Even though I'm registered as a Democrat, I really like what Hogan and Rutherford have been doing," Ellis said.

Rutherford is also a visible presence in governance. The lieutenant-governor frequently represented Hogan at meetings of the state Board of Public Works, which oversees all major spending; headed up the state's Heroin and Opioid Emergency Task Force; worked on the federal Opportunity Zones program; and stepped in to run the government while the governor was undergoing cancer treatments. In other words, a reason Hogan won Black voters was that he aligned himself with and empowered an effective and respected Black partner in governance.

Jealous's Parochial Problem

Finally, some Black leaders contend that Hogan's gains in the Black community reflected the failure of the Jealous campaign to adopt the parochial and retail-centered nature of a successful statewide campaign. Cory McCray notes that the Jealous campaign fell well short of what his voters expected from a candidate, particularly one who claimed Baltimore City roots. "Were you at that church?" he asked rhetorically. "Did you spend time in those neighborhoods, do you know where this street is, do you know this person on that block who is the unofficial 'mayor' of their respective neighborhood and did you kiss the ring?"[34] In his view, Jealous did not.

That sentiment was echoed by other prominent Black Democrats, including Rushern Baker. "It's not just about your platform. You have to be a constant presence at community events and people have to personally like you. And in the absence of community roots, you need validators to say 'I know this guy, he's one of us.'"[35] Although Hogan is obviously not a member of the Black community, he was born in Prince George's County, and as a successful developer, he had long-standing relationships with Black business leaders in the county and across the state.

Baker further contrasts Jealous's organization with his experience with Governor Martin O'Malley's campaign in his reelection bid against Robert Ehrlich in 2010: "I got a phone call the next day after the primary from the governor asking me to come to a rally. And when I got there, he gave me a schedule for the next couple months to turn out the vote." Baker remembers telling O'Malley, "You're going to win Prince George's County," and O'Malley countering, "We can't just win. We need to get the vote up. O'Malley made sure we—elected Democrats—were campaigning like everything was on the line."[36]

McCray ended his analysis with a warning for Democratic candidates regarding their most steadfast voting bloc so they don't cede Black voters to Republicans such as Hogan in the future: "Before you start chasing new voters, you need to understand that a sixty-something Black woman, who's lived in her neighborhood forever and is active in her church, really does not care about what mostly white progressive activists think she needs. She knows what she needs because she's lived it every day. The secret is to amplify her voice and take the time to learn her issues."[37]

Theodore Johnson, a senior fellow at the Brennan Center for Justice, perhaps best summed up the foundation of Hogan's appeal with Black voters: "To the extent that Republicans can deliver without being ridiculous on civil rights, they will have a receptive ear." He added, "It's really not that difficult. Black voters want what everyone else wants."[38]

Conclusion

The Future of the Hogan Coalition

To some attending Larry Hogan's second inauguration in January 2019, Jeb Bush seemed to be passing a baton from one un–Trump Republican to another. "Are we more humble? Or are we arrogant?" the former Florida governor and presidential candidate asked the crowd in Annapolis. "Do we strive to be transparent and truthful even when it is inconvenient? Or do we lie and deny facts?"[1] Hogan's remarks included more implicit criticism of Donald Trump, as he recalled that his father had put nation over party as the first Republican congressman to call for the impeachment of Richard M. Nixon.

It was a noticeable pivot for a governor who had spent the past year avoiding national politics, and like-minded thought leaders took notice. Bill Kristol, the founder of the conservative *Weekly Standard* and now editor-at-large of *The Bulwark*, told reporters that Hogan's speech was "more forward-leading than it had to be, [and] you couldn't help but see that he wanted to send a national message and maybe show some interest in the national stage."[2]

Hogan edged farther onto that stage a month later, at a conference at the Niskanen Center, a center-right think tank in Washington, DC, that had become the intellectual home of the Never Trump movement.³ His address on the virtues of civility, bipartisanship, and moderation sounded familiar to anyone following his reelection efforts. They were refreshing and welcome overtures to the group of politicos assembled at the event, which was named, "Starting Over: The Center-Right after Trump."

Speculation that Hogan was considering a presidential run, combined with widespread Republican losses in 2018 and the cloud of the ongoing investigation by Special Counsel Robert Mueller into Russian interference in the 2016 election, resulted in waves of national media coverage for Hogan in early 2019, including on the op-ed pages of the *New York Times* and the *Atlantic*. He visited Iowa, the first caucus state, for a meeting of the National Governors Association (NGA), and New Hampshire, where he spoke at "Politics & Eggs," the famed testing ground for presidential candidates at St. Anselm's College. Kristol and other Never Trumpers were lobbying Hogan to enter the 2020 primary contest.

But the pragmatic governor saw no realistic path forward against an incumbent president with unified institutional support. The results of the Mueller Report did not mortally wound Trump or lead to impeachment proceedings. (That would come later, twice.) And Republican voters were standing behind the president. While Hogan enjoyed the spotlight, he had no intention of sacrificing himself to the anti-Trump cause. On June 1, 2019, he told Robert Costa of the *Washington Post* that he was no longer considering a primary challenge. Instead, he planned to create a nationally focused advocacy organization called An America United. The following two years would give him ample opportunity to raise his national profile and position himself as a Republican alternative to Trumpism.

A Pandemic, a "Stolen" Election, and the Insurrection

Hogan became the chair of the NGA on July 26, 2019. He planned to use the platform to improve infrastructure and boost bipartisan cooperation. He struck a familiar tone in this first speech when he said, "To those who say that our political system, like our infrastructure, is too broken and can't be fixed, I would argue America's governors have already shown a better path forward."

Six months later, cases of a pneumonia-like disease detected in Wuhan, China, were first reported by the World Health Organization, and the world changed. Hogan and other governors found themselves on the political frontlines against the COVID-19 pandemic. As NGA chair, Hogan advocated on behalf of America's governors and the needs of states. Trump proved to be a difficult governing partner, often contradicting the advice of his own medical professionals and turning highly publicized novel coronavirus task force briefings into political theater. Unlike most Republicans who demurred and defended the president, Hogan publicly criticized Trump for sending mixed messages on COVID-19 response, downplaying the seriousness of the virus, and providing inadequate federal testing resources. During the height of the first wave of the coronavirus pandemic, Hogan became a fixture on national cable television news programs—and he's remained there since.

In March 2020, with the help of his Korean-born wife, Yumi, Hogan bypassed the federal government and secured a half-million coronavirus test kits from South Korean suppliers. The purchase was lauded by the national media and critiqued by Trump, who said Hogan didn't need to turn to South Korea but, instead, "needed to get a little knowledge."[4] Months later, a state audit examining the unusual procurement concluded that the South Korean test kits were flawed and were replaced at additional cost.[5] The state also faced problems handling the surge in unemployment claims. Many Marylanders reported difficulties using the state's website and delays in receiving their benefits.[6]

But despite broad criticisms from Democrats that he eased restrictions too quickly and from Republicans that he needlessly embraced mask mandates and other restrictions, Maryland residents consistently gave Hogan high marks for his handling of the pandemic. A poll by Goucher College taken in March 2022, a full two years after the first cases were detected in the state, found that 70 percent of residents approved of how Hogan managed the outbreak. Hogan was also a consistent, visible advocate for vaccines, and the state's vaccination rate is among the highest in the country.

The 2020 election contest further widened fissures between Hogan and Trump allies. Hogan supported mail-in balloting as Trump and other Republicans were undermining it. In June 2020, he ordered the Maryland State Board of Elections to send primary ballots to all state voters, and for the general election he ordered that all voters be sent a mail-in ballot application. The general election in Maryland, a mix of in-person and increased mail-in ballots, went off smoothly. Hogan didn't cast a ballot for Trump or Biden. He wrote in "Ronald Reagan," a decision that made national news but was panned by many political commentators.

After election night, while other Republicans hedged, humored, and even supported the defeated president's false claims of widespread voter fraud and a stolen election, Hogan was among the first elected Republicans to congratulate Joe Biden. "Everyone should want our president to succeed," he tweeted on November 7, "because we need our country to succeed."[7]

As Trump continued to refuse to acknowledge Biden's victory, Hogan told Trump via a tweet to "stop golfing and concede."

On January 6, 2021, as insurrectionists emboldened by the president stormed the U.S. Capitol, Hogan mobilized Maryland State Police and the National Guard. In a press conference, Hogan lambasted Trump, noting that he had received frantic calls from Democratic Majority Leader Steny Hoyer asking for help, but the authorization Hogan needed from the federal government to send National Guard troops was inexplicably delayed. "I think there's no question that America would be better off if the president would resign or be removed from office and if Mike Pence, the vice president of the United States, would conduct a peaceful transition of power over the next 13 days until President Biden is sworn in," Hogan said.[8]

Days later, amid the quickly convened impeachment trial of Trump on charges of "incitement of insurrection," Hogan told CNN's Jake Tapper that he would have voted to convict if he was a member of the U.S. Senate. Months later, Hogan warned Republicans not to "whitewash" the events of January 6, telling CBS News Chief Correspondent Major Garrett, "We need to get all the facts and find out exactly what happened. But there's no way to just overlook this and say it didn't happen. The nonsense about 'these were just peaceful tourists' is completely absurd."⁹ Hogan reiterated his position to a national audience on the one-year anniversary of the insurrection on *CBS Mornings*: "We can either embrace the truth of what happened with the election and on January 6 or we could be destroyed by lies."[10]

Hogan has remained popular since Trump departed the White House and as he approaches his last months as governor, but his second term has not been immune to controversy. For example, a lengthy investigation in *Washington Monthly* magazine concluded that the value of Hogan's private real estate holdings increased as he authorized state transportation money for road construction projects near land owned by his company.[11] No official inquiry has found him guilty of wrongdoing.

Hogan also made an uncharacteristic, high-level staffing mistake in late spring 2020. His new chief-of-staff, Roy McGrath, resigned after just eleven weeks, following media reports that he received a hefty severance package from his previous position at the Maryland Environmental Service, a quasi-public environmental projects agency. The investigations that followed led McGrath to be indicted on federal and state charges that he embezzled funds for personal purposes, illegally recorded phone calls with the governor and other Hogan staffers, and misled officials into paying him a six-figure severance. Hogan, who once called McGrath a "deeply valued member of our administration," denied previous knowledge of his alleged wrongdoing and said that he "actively assisted" in the criminal investigations.[12] As of this writing, the cases against McGrath are ongoing.

Hogan has remained one of Trump's and, more broadly, Trumpism's most prominent critics among elected Republicans. He frequently makes the rounds on evening cable television and appears on major news shows, such as *Good Morning America*, *CBS Mornings*, *Face the Nation*, *Fox News Sunday*, *Meet the Press*, and *State of the Union*. Further bolstering his bipartisan credentials, he now serves as national cochair of the No Labels Coalition, which promotes centrist political ideas. In September 2021, Alex Isenstadt, a reporter for *Politico*, outlined all the moves Hogan was making to build a national political apparatus capable of combating the forces of Trumpism in the GOP and launching a presidential bid in an article titled, "Larry Hogan's Audacious Bet: A Trump Critic Could Win the GOP's 2024

Nod."[13] But the path to the White House goes through a national Republican presidential primary, pitting Hogan's blue-state practicalities against an electorate that is hostile to them.

Hogan's Primary Problem

In a profile of Hogan published in the *Atlantic* in June 2020, McKay Coppins argued that Hogan is "catnip for a certain kind of centrist pundit who has long fantasized about the heroic moderate riding in on a white horse to deliver the GOP from barbarism."[14] But the "MAGAfication" of the party, Coppins concluded, is not easily undone. Polling in the aftermath of Trump's loss to Biden and the insurrection at the U.S. Capitol underscores this point. Among others, the Republican-leaning firm Echelon Insights has consistently found that Trump remains the front-runner among potential 2024 GOP candidates, and a sizable number of Republicans continue to identify themselves as "Trump first" rather than "Republican Party first" voters.[15] Other polls of GOP voters conducted throughout 2021 and early 2022 tell a similar story: Trump remains popular. Many Republicans want him to run for president again. A majority of Republicans believe Trump's loss resulted from illegal voting or election rigging, and many are motivated more by grievance and cultural issues than traditional conservative economic policies.

This political reality has led Republican operatives and conservative commentators to conclude that, while Hogan could hypothetically be a strong candidate in a national general election, he would face significant, perhaps insurmountable, challenges winning a GOP presidential primary. Political science research analyzing the 2016 Republican presidential primary and current attitudinal trends of GOP voters broadly supports their conclusions.

As John Sides, Michael Tesler, and Lynn Vavreck (2018) put it, "While Trump's nomination was hard to predict, it is not difficult to explain." Their research finds that Trump won the 2016 GOP presidential primary by activating long-standing and unacknowledged sentiments among Republican voters: hawkish views on immigration and relatively liberal views on economic policy. Other scholars find that authoritarian attitudes, racial animus, anti-immigration sentiment, xenophobia, nativism, and anti-Muslim prejudice are all at the root of Trump's primary victory in 2016 and his sustained appeal to Republican voters (Donovan 2019; Reny et al. 2019; Tucker et al. 2019). Trump's support among GOP primary voters also resulted from their underlying distrust in government (Dyck et al. 2018). None of this bodes particularly well for the un-Trump governor of Maryland.

Sarah Longwell, a Republican strategist who serves as the executive director of the Republican Accountability Project, wanted Hogan to challenge Trump in 2020 and considers herself a fan of the governor. Longwell has conducted thousands of hours of focus groups on Republican voters in the years since Trump took office. The results have convinced her that the path forward for a candidate such as Hogan has narrowed since 2020. She contends that "many white working-class voters are now culturally MAGA, and some of the college-educated, suburban white voters have switched to become Joe Biden Democrats." In her view, there is little room for Hogan to cobble together enough votes to win primary races. "The one scenario where Hogan could win is if he was the single candidate occupying the center-right lane against a field of Trump and Trump-like Republicans, and the approximately 30 percent of Republicans who want to move on from Trumpism got behind him." Plurality support, Longwell recalls, "was enough for Trump to break out in 2016."[16] Thinking about this scenario, Hogan represents a clean break from Trump, unlike some other rumored 2024 candidates who are now attempting to distance themselves from the former president.

Hogan's record on social issues may also present a challenge. He has avoided commenting on recent culture war issues such as critical race theory and transgender rights. He did take a pro-religious liberty stance in 2017 in response to a U.S. Fourth Circuit Court of Appeals ruling that the giant "Peace Cross," maintained with public money, "has the primary effect of endorsing religion and excessively entangles the government in religion."[17] Hogan called the decision, later overruled by the U.S. Supreme Court, "outrageous" and an "unacceptable overreach." He also sparred with County Executive Marc Elrich over the Democrat's ban of the controversial "thin blue line" flag from public space at police departments in Montgomery County.[18] The flag symbolizes support for the pro-police Blue Lives Matter movement, which some view as a racist response to the Black Lives Matter protests against police violence. Hogan posted a picture of himself in front of the thin blue line flag on Twitter with the message, "We are proud to hang these Thin Blue Line flags in Government House to honor our brave law enforcement officers."[19]

To that point, policing is one area where Hogan is more aligned with the average Republican. On several occasions, he has described efforts to defund the police as "dangerous, radical, far-left lunacy" and supports mandatory minimum sentencing for crimes committed with a gun. Most of his commentary regarding crime has focused on Baltimore, resulting in criticism from Democrats that he's villainizing the majority-Black city while ignoring rising crime rates elsewhere in the state. In 2021, he vetoed three bills from the General Assembly's police reform package. These bills included a repeal of the Law Enforcement Officers' Bill of Rights, required departments to provide body-worn cameras for on-duty officers, made certain officer misconduct records available for public inspection, and regulated the execution of search warrants. He signed other parts of the package that prohibited law enforcement agencies from procuring weaponized surplus military equipment and created a unit of the Attorney-General's Office to investigate fatal use-of-force incidents. During his last legislative session as governor, he pushed a "re-fund the police" plan to infuse millions of state dollars to support salary increases, bonuses, body cameras, and local and state police training. To be sure, while activist groups in the state have certainly advocated to "defund the police," policing in Maryland has not been defunded during Hogan's time in office. Maryland spends more on state and local police per capita than the national average.

The battle over abortion rights, poised to play a significant role in the 2024 cycle, could also hinder his primary chances. Hogan is a practicing Catholic and is personally opposed to abortion but has said it is not "a black or white issue."[20] Hogan's position is "acceptable" for the governor of a generally liberal state such as Maryland, says Tim Carney, a conservative *Washington Examiner* columnist and the author of *Alienated America: Why Some Places Thrive while Others Collapse* (2020). But "for pro-life voters to support him as president," Carney said, "he'd have to actually show that he's pro-life."[21] That would mean supporting a ban on federal funding for abortions and a commitment to nominating pro-life judges, positions that Hogan has not taken.

Hogan offered a glimpse into how he might position himself nationally on abortion during an appearance on *Meet the Press* on September 5, 2021, after the Supreme Court allowed a Texas law to take effect that effectively bans abortions after the sixth week of pregnancy and deputizes everyday citizens to sue anyone who "aids or abets" an unlawful abortion to collect at least $10,000 in bounty. He told the host, Chuck Todd, "I happen to be personally opposed to abortion, and I believe states do have rights to pass some reasonable restrictions. But certainly, in this case, this bill in Texas seems to be a little bit extreme with this problem of bounties for people that turn in somebody that drove someone to an abortion clinic."[22]

A Hogan primary candidacy would face a skeptical if not hostile conservative media environment. Jim Swift, a senior editor for *The Bulwark* and former Republican congressional staffer, believes that "at first, conservative outlets, especially the biggest player, Fox News, will suffocate his candidacy by refusing to give him coverage. But if he starts to make any discernible inroads with GOP voters, then they will get the knives out. Hogan is a threat to Trumpism, and for that, they'll shiv him."[23] Research on media consumption by the Pew Research Center shows wide partisan gaps in terms of trust in national mainstream media outlets and consumption patterns.[24] Simply put, Republicans are far more likely to get their news from Fox News and, increasingly, from One America News Network (OANN) and Newsmax and distrust mainstream media outlets. Americans, in general, are also increasingly more likely to get their news from social media, and there is evidence that online sources such as *The Federalist*, the *Daily Caller*, and *Daily Wire* enjoy wide readership among conservatives.[25]

Hogan would also face a structural disadvantage, notes Amanda Carpenter, a former communications director for Senator Ted Cruz and the author of *Gaslighting America: Why We Love It When Trump Lies to Us* (2018). "State party organizations control a lot of the events that give presidential hopefuls access to their voters," Carpenter says. Officials such as Kelli Ward, the chair of the Arizona Republican Party, "would probably tank a candidate like Hogan in any way they could. And the Republicans who put country over Trump have since left these organizations."[26]

Attacks on Hogan from primary rivals would come easily, notes Tim Miller, who cofounded America Rising, a Republican opposition research firm. If Miller, who has since become an outspoken critic of Trump and the current state of the Republican Party, were asked to build an opposition file against Hogan, he says that he "wouldn't even have to do real research. It would simply be that he's not a team player. Here's a clip [of] Hogan bashing Trump. Here's one where Hogan is sucking up to Democrats. Here's another of Hogan hanging out with his mainstream media friends. He's just not one of us or on our side. And that would be enough."[27]

Supporting Miller's point, levels of affective polarization—the tendency of Democrats and Republicans to dislike and distrust each other—is now an essential phenomenon in understanding voting behavior and current levels of polarization (Druckman and Levendusky 2019; Iyengar et al. 2019; Luttig 2017; West and Iyengar 2020). Earning the support of Democrats through explicitly adopting their policy positions and the lauding of cooperation helped Hogan popularly govern and win a second term. The same strengths in Maryland could quickly become his core weakness.

Matt Lewis, the conservative author of *Too Dumb to Fail: How the GOP Went from the Party of Reagan to the Party of Trump* (2016) and a columnist for the *Daily Beast*, is more bullish on Hogan. Trump wasn't ideologically conservative on most issues when he first entered the race, Lewis notes. But voters appreciated his perceived toughness. "Hogan—like Christie and even [Florida Governor Ron] DeSantis—presents a stylistically tough, everyman image that might resonate with the grassroots . . . if he's given a shot. He has no-bullshit authenticity," Lewis says. "That charisma and likeably that won over voters in Maryland could be contagious." If GOP voters grow to like Hogan personally, they might look past his moderate record or lack of purity on some issues, Lewis adds. "Would I buy low on a stock that puts Hogan as the dark horse in 2024?" he asks. "I think so."[28]

A Legacy in Formation

Larry Hogan's place in Maryland political history was solidified on November 6, 2018. He will always be just the second Republican ever to secure a second term as governor and is on course to leave office in January 2023 as one of the state's most popular leaders.

Despite his political success, some in Maryland continue to dismiss Hogan's acumen and discount his victories as having come against subpar opponents. But while both former Lieutenant-Governor Anthony Brown and former NAACP head Ben Jealous had shortcomings, they are both talented individuals. In the cycle after his loss to Hogan, Brown emerged from a crowded primary field to represent Maryland's 4th district in Congress. As a member of the Armed Services Committee, where he is now vice-chair, Brown is a consistent, visible advocate for service members and their families and was a leading voice against the Trump-era ban on transgender service in the military. Jealous has continued his civil rights work as president of People for the American Way, a national advocacy organization that fights for the voting rights of Black Americans, Latinos, and other minority communities. Their professional accomplishments aside, Brown, Jealous, and their respective campaigns undeniably made many, and ultimately fatal, mistakes during their races against Hogan. But continuing to view Hogan's victories only through the shortcomings of his opponents will ill prepare the next generation of Democratic hopefuls against the next Republican like him.

To that point, the focus of this book has been on how Hogan won in 2018 and what it might mean for Republicans. Considered another way, it could be a story about whether Jealous's loss was a lesson for Democrats. Maryland Democratic primary voters selected a candidate who offered a progressive vision that ultimately failed to gain widespread support. During a Trump-centered and highly polarized election cycle, nearly a third of Democrats chose a Republican over one of their own. Democrats nationwide chose a different path in 2020 and settled on a more moderate Joe Biden. Seth Masket's book *Learning from Loss: The Democrats, 2016–2020* (2020) provides a recent and comprehensive analysis of those dynamics within the Democratic Party.

Hogan bested a demographic disadvantage and considerable national headwinds through disciplined messaging, a pragmatic approach to governance, understanding voter preferences, and a strong personal brand. His ability to win the votes of conservative and moderate Democrats and like-minded independents while keeping Republicans unified offers the GOP a template for broadening their coalition. He also demonstrates that Republicans can earn back the support of suburban, college-educated voters who have fled the party during the time of Trump, win the women's vote, and make inroads with Black voters. At its best, the "Hogan Coalition" offers the GOP a pathway to a modern, more diverse version of Ronald Reagan's "big tent" and a chance at majoritarian rule in a diversifying America.

Falling short of a lofty national goal, Hogan demonstrates how Republicans can win state-level elections and popularly govern in blue states. It's still hard to execute in our current political environment, but the blueprint is simple: stick to pocketbook issues that make a tangible difference in people's lives and ignore the culture wars; be an independent voice willing to buck your party and embrace opportunities to work with the opposition; have core principles but be flexible on policy solutions; be guided by the signal of the average voter rather than the noise of the fringe; be willing to take your message to all voters and do the work to persuade them; and surround yourself with professionals who can execute on all of the above with skill and fierce loyalty.

A profile of Hogan by the conservative writer Jim Geraghty that ran in the *National Review* on March 29, 2018, noted that, while the governor hasn't been able to enact sweeping conservative reforms, he has "acted . . . like a goalie, deflecting bad ideas and keeping the opposition from scoring."[29] In other words, Hogan's budgetary powers combined with effective public communications provided a check on Democratic leadership that wouldn't have existed under a one-party monopoly. The governor points to reducing or eliminating tolls and fees charged by state agencies and a series of targeted tax breaks that would not have occurred under a Democratic governor. Other economic indicators, such as the state's gross domestic product, have improved since Hogan took office. Still, it's important to note that his time in office also coincides with the rebounding national economy since the Great Recession. Some evidence shows that the state's business climate has improved under Hogan—for example, Maryland jumped nineteen places, to twelfth in the nation, in CNBC's Top States for Business rankings in 2021. Lawrence Kurzius, the chief executive of McCormick, which makes Maryland's iconic Old Bay seasoning, once noted that "the difference in the attitude of state government towards business is night-and-day better in his administration than the previous one. . . . That's actually a bigger factor than you might think."[30] Many Democratic leaders view Hogan as a frustrating impediment to needed progressive change that could have helped marginalized groups, grown a more equitable economy, addressed the systemic causes of poverty and crime, and built a more robust public education system.

The governor gets a lot of fanfare for his enviable public approval rating, which thus far has averaged in the mid-sixties to low-seventies throughout his time in office. But public sentiment toward the state's overall direction is perhaps a more meaningful indicator. While most residents hold negative views toward the country's direction and national leadership during this divisive and polarized time in American history, Maryland residents continue to view their state as heading in the right direction. These attitudes are not singularly attributable to Hogan's leadership; they are also attributable to the governance of the Democratic-led General Assembly. The story of Hogan's time in office and reelection is also one of functional divided government defined more by incremental progress than partisan gridlock.

It is unclear whether Hogan's political ambitions and the reality of the national Republican Party will intersect. Hogan holds a unique position: he is one of the few elected Republicans free from any connection to Trump; vocal in his criticisms toward the former president and authoritarian and extremist elements in the party; and steadfast in his support of our democratic institutions. At the same time, unlike many anti-Trump Republicans, Hogan remains a staunch defender of the party and what he believes remain its guiding principles: fiscal discipline, low taxes and regulation, free-market capitalism, and self-determination. He hopes to refocus the party's efforts on winning the majority of voters through persuasion and broadening the base, perhaps even breathing new life into the goals of the long-dead GOP autopsy report. "There's going to be a fight for the soul of the Republican Party," Hogan told the *Washington Post*'s Robert McCartney just weeks after the January 6 insurrection. "There are an awful lot of people in one lane fighting to take on the mantle of Donald Trump. I would argue that I'm one of the leading voices on the other side to say that we've got to move in a completely different direction."[31]

Regardless of what the future holds, Hogan has a clear view of how he wants to be remembered in Maryland: "I want people to look back on my years as governor and say that I worked hard and tried to solve problems. And that I was a good governor. I'd be happy with that."[32]

Notes

Preface

1. William F. Zorzi, "Tawes: Crabs, Camaraderie, Campaigning. See, Some Things Never Change," *Maryland Matters*, January 12, 2019, https://www.mary landmatters.org/2018/07/19/tawes-crabs-camaraderie-campaigning-see-some -things-never-change.

2. Ovetta Wiggins and Teo Armus, "Two Gubernatorial Candidates. One Clambake. No Interaction," *Washington Post*, July 19, 2018, https://www.wash ingtonpost.com/local/md-politics/jealous-and-hogan-went-to-the-same-clam -bake-wednesday-but-still-didnt-speak/2018/07/18/0b5c3ce2-8a82-11e8-8aea 86e88ae760d8_story.html.

3. Larry Hogan, interview by the author, Annapolis, MD, June 3, 2021.

Introduction

1. Alana Wise, "Prince George's County Voters Faced Hours in Line Due to Ballot Shortage," WAMU.org, November 6, 2018, https://wamu.org/story/18/11/06/ voters-in-prince-georges-county-face-shortage-of-ballots-hours-in-line.

2. Doug Mayer, interview by the author, Annapolis, MD, April 27, 2020.

3. Luke Broadwater, "Maryland Gov. Larry Hogan Re-elected, Soundly Defeating Ben Jealous," *Baltimore Sun*, November 6, 2018, https://www.balti moresun.com/politics/bs-md-governor-20181105-story.html.

4. Marisa Fernandez, "America's Ideological Balance Continues to Lean Center-Right," Axios, January 9, 2020, https://www.axios.com/political-ideol ogy-2020-presidential-election-391db0b5-16ac-4aa0-8e48-f05cceb1c1e4.html.

5. For a full history of politics in Maryland, see Brugger 1996; Willis and Smith 2012.

6. The U.S. Census calculates its "diversity index" as the probability that two people chosen at random will be from a different race or ethnic group: see U.S. Census Bureau, *Racial and Ethnic Diversity in the United States: 2010 Census and 2020 Census*, Census.gov, August 12, 2021, https://www.census.gov/library/visualizations/interactive/racial-and-ethnic-diversity-in-the-united-states-2010-and-2020-census.html.

7. Ruth Igielnik and Abby Budiman, *The Changing Racial and Ethnic Composition of the U.S. Electorate*, Pew Research Center, Washington, DC, September 23, 2020, https://www.pewresearch.org/2020/09/23/the-changing-racial-and-ethnic-composition-of-the-u-s-electorate.

8. The composition of Maryland's electorate limits the ability to analyze other racial groups. For in-depth analysis of the contours of the Latino and Hispanic vote and its impact on American elections, as well as of the Republican Party more specifically, see, among others, Abrajano et al. 2008; Barreto and Segura 2014; Cadava 2020; Corral and Leal 2020; de la Garza and Cortina 2007; Francis-Fallon 2019; Galbraith and Callister 2020. For analysis of the political behavior of Asian American voters, see Masuoka, Han, Leung, and Zheng 2018; Masuoka, Ramanathan, and Junn 2019; Raychaudhuri 2020; Zheng 2019.

9. Erika Vallejo, "The 'Diploma Divide': Does It Exist for Racial and Ethnic Minorities?" *Michigan Policy Wonk* (blog), March 15, 2021, https://ippsr.msu.edu/public-policy/michigan-wonk-blog/diploma-divide-does-it-exist-racial-and-ethnic-minorities.

10. Jeffrey M. Jones, "Non-College Whites Had Affinity for GOP before Trump," Gallup News, April 12, 2019, https://news.gallup.com/poll/248525/non-college-whites-affinity-gop-trump.aspx.

11. "Maryland at a Glance: Workforce," *Maryland Manual On-line*, updated August 9, 2021, https://msa.maryland.gov/msa/mdmanual/01glance/economy/html/labor.html.

12. Henry Barbour, Sally Bradshaw, Ari Fleischer, Zori Fonalledas, and Glenn McCall, *Republican National Committee's Growth and Opportunity Project*, report, 2021, https://www.documentcloud.org/documents/624293-republican-national-committees-growth-and.html.

13. Beth Reinhard, "The GOP Establishment's Bid to Push Back the Tea Party Insurrection," *The Atlantic*, October 24, 2013, https://www.theatlantic.com/politics/archive/2013/10/gop-establishment-bid-to-push-back-the-tea-party-insurrection/309608.

14. Kyle Cheney, "Blame Game Follows Tea Party Defeats," *Politico*, August 8, 2014, https://www.politico.com/story/2014/08/2014-elections-republican-tea-party-109834.

15. Tim Miller, phone interview by the author, August 23, 2021.

16. "Live Election 2014: 'Republicans Had a Good Night,' Obama Says," *Los Angeles Times*, November 4, 2014, https://www.latimes.com/local/politics/elections/la-live-blog-election-day-2014-htmlstory.html.

17. Whit Ayres, phone interview by the author, February 3, 2021.

18. Jonathan Capehart, "What the 2016 Republicans Have in Common with the 1989 Democrats," *Washington Post*, March 31, 2015, https://www.washington post.com/blogs/post-partisan/wp/2015/03/31/what-the-2016-republicans-have -in-common-with-the-1989-democrats.

19. Kyle Cheney, "Trump Kills GOP Autopsy," *Politico*, March 4, 2016, https:// www.politico.com/story/2016/03/donald-trump-gop-party-reform-220222.

20. "Exit Polls," *CNN Politics*, https://www.cnn.com/election/2020/exit-polls /president/national-results/0.

21. Sean McElwee and Colin McAuliffe, "Progressives Control the Future," Data for Progress, June 14, 2020, https://www.dataforprogress.org/blog/6/14 /progressives-control-the-future.

22. Kevin Morris and Coryn Grange, *Large Racial Turnout Gap Persisted in 2020 Election*, Brennan Center for Justice, August 6, 2021, https://www.bren nancenter.org/our-work/analysis-opinion/large-racial-turnout-gap-persisted -2020-election.

23. Barbour et al., *Republican National Committee's Growth and Opportu- nity Project*, 6.

24. Larry Hogan, "A Conversation with Governor Larry Hogan," The Ron- ald Reagan Presidential Foundation and Institute, November 16, 2020, https:// www.reaganfoundation.org/reagan-institute/events/a-conversation-with-gov ernor-larry-hogan/.

Chapter 1

1. Larry Hogan, "Why Do Annapolis Leaders Do These Things? Because They Can," *Baltimore Sun*, April 17, 2012, https://www.baltimoresun.com/opin ion/op-ed/bs-ed-assembly-democrats-20120417-story.html.

2. Len Lazarick, "'Change Maryland' Looks for Middle Ground," Mary- landReporter.com, June 13, 2011, https://marylandreporter.com/2011/06/13 /change-maryland%E2%80%99-looks-for-middle-ground.

3. Larry Hogan, interview by author, Annapolis, MD, June 3, 2021.

4. Larry Hogan, "Maryland Redefines Definition of Rich," *Fox Busi- ness*, May 16, 2012, https://video.foxbusiness.com/v/1642529743001#sp=show -clips.

5. Annie Linskey, "End of an Era for Ehrlich, Maryland Republicans," *Bal- timore Sun*, November 3, 2010, https://www.baltimoresun.com/politics/bs-xpm -2010-11-03-bs-md-ehrlich-future-20101103-story.html.

6. "Shutdown Widened Republican-Tea Party Rift," Associated Press, Octo- ber 18, 2013, https://apnews.com/article/business-health-care-reform-house -elections-united-states-congress-united-states-government-fc05d2e34318428 e96d2737288357a36.

7. Brian Montopoli, "Tea Party Supporters: Who They Are and What They Believe," *CBS News*, December 14, 2012, https://www.cbsnews.com/news/tea -party-supporters-who-they-are-and-what-they-believe; "Section 6: Tea Party

and Views of Government Overreach," *Distrust, Discontent, Anger and Partisan Rancor*, Pew Research Center, Washington, DC, April 1, 2010, https://www.pewresearch.org/politics/2010/04/18/section-6-tea-party-and-views-of-government-overreach.

8. Jim Pettit, "Tax Data Maryland Needs—and Almost Lost," *Baltimore Sun*, December 19, 2012, https://www.baltimoresun.com/opinion/op-ed/bs-ed-taxpayer-migration-20121219-story.html.

9. "About Us," Hogan Companies website, http://hogancompanies.com/about_us.

10. Jacques Kelly, "Lawrence J. Hogan Sr., Former Congressman and Father of Governor, Dies," *Baltimore Sun*, April 20, 2017, https://www.baltimoresun.com/obituaries/bs-md-ob-lawrence-hogan-20170420-story.html.

11. Quoted in Lawrence O'Donnell, "The Honorable Republican in Nixon Impeachment Hearings," NBCNews.com, April 22, 2019, https://www.nbcnews.com/dateline/video/lawrence-s-last-word-the-honorable-republican-in-nixon-impeachment-hearings-1502753859993.

12. Matt Schudel, "Lawrence J. Hogan Sr., M[arylan]d Republican Who Called for Nixon's Impeachment, Dies at 88," *Washington Post*, April 22, 2017, https://www.washingtonpost.com/national/lawrence-j-hogan-sr-md-republican-who-called-for-nixons-impeachment-dies-at-88/2017/04/20/80fe7f5c-251e-11e7-a1b3-faff0034e2de_story.html.

13. Michael Dresser, "Hogan Charts a Pragmatic Republican Course," *Baltimore Sun*, June 9, 2014, https://www.baltimoresun.com/politics/bs-md-hogan-profile-20140609-story.html.

14. Arelis R. Hernández, "Ten Things to Know about TRIM," *Washington Post*, October 8, 2015, https://www.washingtonpost.com/news/local/wp/2015/04/08/ten-things-to-know-about-trim.

15. Eugene L. Meyer, "The Two Worlds of Larry Hogan," *Washington Post*, October 31, 1976, C1.

16. Timothy B. Wheeler, "Hogan Joining GOP Race for Governor," *Baltimore Sun*, January 20, 2014, https://www.baltimoresun.com/politics/bs-xpm-2014-01-20-bs-md-hogan-to-announce-20140117-story.html.

17. John Wagner, "Gansler Launches Campaign for M[arylan]d Governor, Pledging to Shake Up the Status Quo," *Washington Post*, September 24, 2013, https://www.washingtonpost.com/local/md-politics/gansler-set-to-officially-launch-campaign-for-maryland-governor-in-rockville/2013/09/24/1437889e-250b-11e3-b75d-5b7f66349852_story.html.

18. John Wagner, "Brown Gains Fundraising Edge over Gansler in Maryland's Campaign for Governor," *Washington Post*, January 15, 2014, https://www.washingtonpost.com/local/md-politics/brown-gains-the-fundraising-edge-over-gansler-in-marylands-campaign-for-governor/2014/01/15/e7ba5c6a-7e42-11e3-93c1-0e888170b723_story.html.

19. Wagner, "Gansler Launches Campaign for M[arylan]d Governor."

20. Erin Cox and Michael Dresser, "Gansler Says Breaking Up Teen Party Was Not His Job," *Baltimore Sun*, October 23, 2013, https://www.baltimoresun.com /politics/bs-md-gansler-party-20131023-story.html.

21. Lydia Saad, "Half in Illinois and Connecticut Want to Move Elsewhere," *Gallup News*, April 30, 2014, https://news.gallup.com/poll/168770/half-illinois -connecticut-move-elsewhere.aspx.

22. Michael Dresser, "Hogan Qualifies for Public Financing of Campaign," *Baltimore Sun*, May 21, 2014, https://www.baltimoresun.com/politics/bs-xpm -2014-05-21-bal-larry-hogan-qualifies-for-public-financing-story-story.html.

23. Erin Cox, Michael Dresser, and *Baltimore Sun*, "Brown, Hogan Win Primaries for Maryland Governor," *Baltimore Sun*, June 25, 2014, https://www .baltimoresun.com/politics/bs-md-governor-primary-20140624-story.html.

24. Robert McCartney, "Martin O'Malley Blames Anthony Brown's Campaign for M[arylan]d Democrats' Loss," *Washington Post*, January 10, 2015, https://www.washingtonpost.com/local/martin-omalley-blames-anthony -brown-not-his-own-record-for-md-democrats-loss/2015/01/10/f6f6e976-9874 -11e4-927a-4fa2638cd1b0_story.html.

25. Yvonne Wenger and Erin Cox, "Hogan Removes 'Zaching' Photo from Brown Attack Ad," *Baltimore Sun*, June 28, 2014, https://www.baltimoresun.com /politics/bal-hogan-removes-zaching-photo-from-brown-attack-ad-20140628 -story.html.

26. Michael Dresser, "Brown, D[emocratic] G[overnors] A[ssociation] Go Back Decades to Slam Hogan on Abortion," *Baltimore Sun*, September 27, 2014, https://www.baltimoresun.com/politics/bs-md-adwatch-brown-dga-abortion -20140925-story.html.

27. Jenna Johnson, "Larry Hogan's Daughter Says in New Ad That Her Dad Is Not 'Anti-Woman,'" *Washington Post*, September 26, 2014, https://www.washing tonpost.com/local/md-politics/larry-hogans-daughter-says-in-new-ad-that-her -dad-is-not-anti-woman/2014/09/26/998bab1a-458a-11e4-b437-1a7368204804 _story.html.

28. Gabriella Souza, "Inside Two Worlds: Yumi Hogan Brings an Artist's Eye to the Role of First Lady," *Baltimore Magazine*, June 2015, https://www.baltimore magazine.com/section/artsentertainment/yumi-hogan-brings-artists-eye-role -of-first-lady.

29. Darren Sands, "Chris Christie Is a 'Mercenary,'" *BuzzFeed News*, October 21, 2014, https://www.buzzfeednews.com/article/darrensands/chris-christie-is-a -mercenary.

30. Russ Schriefer, interview by the author, Annapolis, MD, June 8, 2021.

31. Phil Cox, phone interview by the author, January 14, 2020.

32. Andrew Metcalf, "Report: Christie Helps Raise $400,000 for Hogan in Bethesda," *Bethesda Magazine*, September 17, 2014, https://bethesdamaga zine.com/bethesda-beat/politics/report-christie-raises-400000-for-hogan-in -bethesda.

33. Wilson Perkins Allen Opinion Research, "State of the Maryland Gubernatorial Race," memorandum, October 29, 2014, https://www.realclearpolitics.com/docs/2014/WPA_MD_1014.pdf.

34. Erin Cox, "Cook Political Report Declares Governor's Race a 'Toss Up,'" *Baltimore Sun*, October 31, 2014, https://www.baltimoresun.com/politics/bal-cook-political-report-declares-governors-race-a-toss-up-20141031-story.html.

35. Schriefer interview.

36. John Wagner and Jenna Johnson, "Hogan Sworn In as Maryland's Governor," *Washington Post*, January 21, 2015, https://www.washingtonpost.com/local/md-politics/larry-hogan-to-become-next-md-governor/2015/01/20/37338c56-a112-11e4-b146-577832eafcb4_story.html.

37. "Larry Hogan's Inaugural Address Speech," *Baltimore Sun*, January 21, 2015, https://www.baltimoresun.com/politics/bs-md-hogan-inaugural-address-speech-20150121-story.html.

38. Maryland Department of Budget and Management, "Maryland Operating Budget Overview," n.d., https://dbm.maryland.gov/budget/pages/budget-process-overview.aspx.

39. Miller died on January 15, 2021. He was the nation's longest-serving president of a State Senate. Miller was a shrewd, pragmatic politician who was the cornerstone for much of the state's policy agenda for more than three decades. He remains an iconic figure in Maryland politics.

40. Busch died on April 7, 2019. He was the longest-serving State House speaker in Maryland's history. Along with a list of policy accomplishments, Busch is remembered for promoting women and Black lawmakers to key leadership posts. He was a rare politician who stood by principles and adapted with the changing times.

41. David Nitkin and Greg Garland, "Busch Rebuffs Latest Ehrlich Slots Proposal," *Baltimore Sun*, January 28, 2004, https://www.baltimoresun.com/politics/bal-md.slots28jan28001640-story.html.

42. Jennifer Skalka, "Hearings on State Firings Conclude," *Baltimore Sun*, May 23, 2006, https://www.baltimoresun.com/news/bs-xpm-2006-05-23-0605230125-story.html.

43. David Nitkin, "Steffen Defends Role in Targeting State Workers," *Baltimore Sun*, October 31, 2005, https://www.baltimoresun.com/maryland/bal-te.md.steffen31oct31-story.html.

44. Larry Hogan, interview by the author, Annapolis, MD, June 3, 2021.

45. Boyd Rutherford, interview by the author, Annapolis, MD, August 9, 2021.

46. Pamela Wood, "Maryland Gov. Hogan Says Governors Don't Usually Testify on Bills: Ex-Governors Say It Worked for Them," *Baltimore Sun*, March 10, 2020, https://www.baltimoresun.com/politics/bs-md-pol-ga-hogan-testify-20200310-cdmkdyx7pfat5oxb7hl6ohyrp4-story.html.

47. David Nitkin, phone interview by the author, May 7, 2020.

48. Josh Kurtz, phone interview by the author, June 4, 2020.

49. Dan Rodricks, "With New Governor, Maryland Gets New, Cheesy Greeting," *Baltimore Sun*, January 31, 2015, https://www.baltimoresun.com/opinion/bs-md-rodricks-0201-20150130-column.html.

50. Michael Dresser and Erin Cox, "Session Goes to Wire with Budget Issues, Hogan Agenda in Doubt," *Baltimore Sun*, April 11, 2015, https://www.baltimoresun.com/politics/bs-md-hogan-assembly-budget-dispute-2-20150411-story.html.

51. John Wagner and Scott Clement, "Poll: Marylanders Like Hogan, but Oppose Effort to Slow School Funding," *Washington Post*, February 10, 2015, https://www.washingtonpost.com/local/md-politics/poll-marylanders-like-hogan-but-oppose-effort-to-slow-school-funding/2015/02/10/d834928a-b099-11e4-827f-93f454140e2b_story.html?itid=lk_inline_manual_31.

52. Erin Cox, Michael Dresser, and Timothy Wheeler, "Assembly Session Ends in Acrimony over Budget," *Baltimore Sun*, April 14, 2015, https://www.baltimoresun.com/politics/bs-md-assembly-adjourns-20150413-story.html.

53. Matt Bush, "'Rain Tax' Bill Survives in Maryland, and Hogan Doesn't Care That It's Not His Own," WAMU, March 11, 2015, https://wamu.org/story/15/03/11/rain_tax_bill_survives_in_maryland_and_hogan_doesnt_care_that_its_not_his_own.

54. Office of Governor Larry Hogan, "Governor Larry Hogan Signs Rain Tax Repeal and Military Retiree Tax Relief Legislation," news release, May 12, 2015, https://governor.maryland.gov/2015/05/12/governor-larry-hogan-signs-rain-tax-repeal-and-military-retiree-tax-relief-legislation.

Chapter 2

1. German Lopez, "Camden Yards Briefly Closed Off as Freddie Gray Protests Intensify in Baltimore," Vox.com, April 25, 2015, https://www.vox.com/2015/4/25/8498435/freddie-gray-protests-riots.

2. Miguel Marquez and Steve Almasy, "Freddie Gray Death: Protesters Damage Cars; 12 Arrested," CNN.com, April 25, 2015, https://www.cnn.com/2015/04/25/us/baltimore-freddie-gray-protest/index.html.

3. "Baltimore Mayor: 'Gave Those Who Wished to Destroy Space to Do That,'" CBS Baltimore, April 25, 2015, https://baltimore.cbslocal.com/2015/04/25/baltimore-mayor-gave-those-who-wished-to-destroy-space-to-do-that.

4. Elizabeth Chuck, "Baltimore Mayor Stephanie Rawlings-Blake under Fire for 'Space' to Destroy Comment," *CBS News*, April 28, 2015, https://www.nbcnews.com/storyline/baltimore-unrest/mayor-stephanie-rawlings-blake-under-fire-giving-space-destroy-baltimore-n349656.

5. Justin Fenton and Erica L. Green, "Baltimore Rioting Kicked Off with Rumors of 'Purge,'" *Baltimore Sun*, April 27, 2015, https://www.baltimoresun.com/news/crime/bs-md-ci-freddie-gray-violence-chronology-20150427-story.html.

6. Tom Scocca, "'Those Kids Were Set Up,'" *Gawker*, April 28, 2015, https://www.gawker.com/those-kids-were-set-up-1700716306.

7. For a comparison and analysis of the 1968 riots and the 2015 Baltimore Uprising, see Crenson 2019.

8. Mistrust and conflicts with police are a persistent feature of life for many Black Baltimore City residents. For a thorough analysis of the systemic issues that led to what is now known as the Baltimore Uprising, see Brown 2021. For crucial insight into the larger community reaction, including the views of predominant city racial justice activists, see Moore and Green 2020. These sources provide a full account of the systemic causes and community response that are central to understanding the Baltimore Uprising.

9. Jessica Anderson, "Baltimore Riots Lead to 235 Arrests, 20 Injured Officers," *Baltimore Sun*, April 28, 2015, https://www.baltimoresun.com/news /crime/bs-md-ci-baltimore-riots-what-we-know-20150428-story.html.

10. Paul Schwartzman, Ovetta Wiggins, and Cheryl W. Thompson, "At a Key Point in the Baltimore Riots, the Governor Wanted to Talk to the Mayor; She Didn't Pick Up the Phone," *Washington Post*, May 10, 2015, https://www.washing tonpost.com/local/in-the-crucial-hours-before-guard-was-called-in-a-commu nication-breakdown/2015/05/10/a7d7d47e-f57e-11e4-bcc4-e8141e5eb0c9_story .html.

11. David Collins, "Gov. Larry Hogan Speaks on Freddie Gray's Death," WBALTV.com, April 22, 2015, https://www.wbaltv.com/article/gov-larry-hogan -speaks-on-freddie-gray-s-death/7093184.

12. "National and Local Reaction to Charges in Freddie Gray Case," *Baltimore Sun*, May 2, 2015, https://www.baltimoresun.com/maryland/baltimore -city/bs-md-ci-freddie-gray-reax-quotes-0502-20150501-story.html.

13. Alvin Hathaway, interview by the author, Baltimore, June 12, 2021.

14. Rebecca Klar, "Republican Governor Says Trump Sending Opposite Message of One That Should Come from White House," *The Hill*, May 31, 2020, https://thehill.com/homenews/state-watch/500331-republican-governor-says -trump-sending-opposite-message-of-one-that.

15. Pamela Wood, "In Upcoming Political Memoir, Maryland Gov. Hogan Calls 2015 Baltimore Unrest His 'Baptism of Fire,'" *Baltimore Sun*, July 14, 2020, https:// www.baltimoresun.com/politics/bs-pr-pol-hogan-book-20200714-yepqs2x5xfhdh kghn6zu4zfowa-story.html.

16. Justin Fenton, "Baltimore Officials Identify Possible Source of 'Purge' Flyer after Freddie Gray's Death, Dispute Hogan on Requests for More Police Help," *Baltimore Sun*, April 14, 2021, https://www.baltimoresun.com/news /crime/bs-pr-md-ci-cr-purge-flyer-riot-lawsuit-20210414-ydjalqwpsjf7zogerb prcvuofa-story.html.

17. Ovetta Wiggins and Jenna Johnson, "Maryland Gov. Larry Hogan Discloses That He Has 'Advanced' Cancer," *Washington Post*, June 22, 2015, https://www.washingtonpost.com/local/md-politics/maryland-gov-larry-hogan -announces-that-he-has-cancer/2015/06/22/6b00eae2-1917-11e5-ab92-c75ae 6ab94b5_story.html.

18. "Transcript: Governor Larry Hogan's Full Remarks on His Cancer," *Bal-*

timore Sun, June 22, 2015, https://www.baltimoresun.com/politics/bs-md-hogan -transcript-20150622-story.html.

19. Chase Cook, "Trump Discusses His Presidential Campaign at Linthicum GOP Dinner," *Capital Gazette*, June 23, 2015, https://www.capitalgazette.com /ph-ac-cn-trump-republican-dinner-0624-20150623-story.html.

20. Doug Mayer, interview by the author, Annapolis, MD, April 27, 2020.

21. "2016 Republican Presidential Nomination," RealClearPolitics, n.d., https://www.realclearpolitics.com/epolls/2016/president/us/2016_republican _presidential_nomination-3823.html.

22. Josh Hicks, "Gov. Hogan's Decisions Cause Rift with Baltimore Leaders," *Washington Post*, July 12, 2015, https://www.washingtonpost.com/local /md-politics/did-killing-baltimores-red-line-ruin-hogans-political-fortunes -in-the-city/2015/07/12/57e95fc8-2733-11e5-b72c-2b7d516e1e0e_story.html.

23. Michael Dresser and Luke Broadwater, "Hogan Says No to Red Line, Yes to Purple," *Baltimore Sun*, June 25, 2015, https://www.baltimoresun.com /politics/bs-md-hogan-transportation-20150624-story.html.

24. Colin Campbell, "Five Years Later, Many across Baltimore Bitterly Lament Gov. Hogan's Decision to Kill the Red Line Light Rail," *Washington Post*, September 12, 2020, https://www.washingtonpost.com/local/trafficand commuting/five-years-later-many-across-baltimore-bitterly-lament-gov-hogans -decision-to-kill-the-red-line-light-rail/2020/09/12/600f9b44-f529-11ea-bc45 -e5d48ab44b9f_story.html.

25. Ron Cassie, phone interview by the author, September 1, 2021.

26. Robert McCartney, "How Republican Gov. Larry Hogan Made His First Big Mass Transit Decision," *Washington Post*, June 27, 2015, https://www.wash ingtonpost.com/local/how-republican-gov-larry-hogan-made-his-first-big-mass -transit-decision/2015/06/27/13f48dbc-1ceb-11e5-93b7-5eddc056ad8a_story .html.

27. Campbell, "Five Years Later."

28. Sheryll Cashin, "How Larry Hogan Kept Blacks in Baltimore Segregated and Poor," *Politico*, July 18, 2020, https://www.politico.com/news /magazine/2020/07/18/how-larry-hogan-kept-black-baltimore-segregated-and -poor-367930.

29. Ron Cassie, phone interview by the author, September 1, 2021.

30. Michael Dresser, "NAACP, ACLU Challenge Hogan Administration over Scrapping Red Line," *Baltimore Sun*, December 21, 2015, https://www.baltimore sun.com/maryland/baltimore-city/bs-md-red-line-complaint-20151221-story .html.

31. John Fritze, "Feds Close Complaint into Canceled Baltimore Red Line," *Baltimore Sun*, July 14, 2017, https://www.baltimoresun.com/politics/bs-md-red -line-complaint-20170714-story.html.

32. Michael Dresser, "Two-Thirds in Poll Say Baltimore Is Not Maryland's Economic Engine," *Baltimore Sun*, February 21, 2018, https://www.baltimoresun .com/politics/bs-md-goucher-poll-baltimore-20180220-story.html.

33. Maryland Department of Commerce, "Maryland GDP by County, 2015–2018," n.d., https://commerce.maryland.gov/Documents/ResearchDocument/maryland-gdp-by-county-2020-03-05.pdf.

34. Lorraine Mirabella, "T. Rowe Price, Sinclair Broadcast, McCormick Make Fortune 500 List, the First Baltimore Firms since 2012," *Baltimore Sun*, June 2, 2021, https://www.baltimoresun.com/business/bs-bz-baltimore-com panies-for tune-500-20210602-wja3pxzixneffdfvpoe3ko4svi-story.html.

35. Goucher Poll, "Results on Politician Approval Ratings, Local Presidential Hopefuls, Transportation, Vaccines, and the Environment," news release, https://www.goucher.edu/hughes-center/documents/Goucher-Poll-Wednesday-Feb-25-Release-FINAL.pdf

36. Bryan Sears, phone interview by the author, July 7, 2020.

37. "Hogan Announces Toll Reductions in Maryland," NBC Washington, May 7, 2015, https://www.nbcwashington.com/news/local/toll-prices-will-drop-in-maryland-in-july/118653.

38. Justin Fenton and Luke Broadwater, "Gov. Hogan Announces 'Immediate' Closure of Baltimore Jail," *Baltimore Sun*, June 21, 2019, https://www.baltimore sun.com/maryland/baltimore-city/bs-md-hogan-city-jail-20150730-story.html.

39. Josh Hicks, "Poll: Hogan's School-Start Order Popular; M[arylan]d Residents Divided over Fracking," *Washington Post*, September 26, 2016, https://www.washingtonpost.com/local/md-politics/poll-hogans-school-start-order-popular-md-residents-divided-over-fracking/2016/09/26/cbe596cc-8401-11e6-92c2-14b64f3d453f_story.html.

40. Goucher Poll, "Marylanders Differ on Views Toward Policing, Hogan Popularity High," news release, October 5, 2015, https://www.goucher.edu/hughes-center/documents/Fall-2015-Goucher-Poll-Release-Monday-FINAL.pdf.

41. Josh Hicks, "Gov. Hogan's Cancer Is in Remission, 30 Days after He Completed Chemo," *Washington Post*, November 16, 2015, https://www.washingtonpost.com/local/md-politics/tests-show-gov-larry-hogan-is-now-cancer-free/2015/11/16/dec912f4-8c5f-11e5-ae1f-af46b7df8483_story.html.

Chapter 3

1. Philip Rucker, "Chris Christie Wears 'Hogan Strong' Bracelet for M[arylan]d Governor," *Washington Post*, July 2, 2015, https://www.washingtonpost.com/news/post-politics/wp/2015/07/02/chris-christie-wears-hogan-strong-bracelet-for-md-governor.

2. Chase Cook, "Hogan Endorses Chris Christie for President at Annapolis Event," *Capital Gazette*, July 15, 2015, https://www.capitalgazette.com/ph-ac-cn-christie-annapolis-announcement-0716-20150715-story.html.

3. Carla Astudillo, "See the Strange and Wild Journey of Christie's Approval Ratings," NJ.com, January 15, 2018, https://www.nj.com/data/2018/01/christie_approval_numbers_timeline.html.

4. Chris Christie, phone interview by the author, March 26, 2020.

5. Josh Hicks, "This M[arylan]d Congressman Really, Really Wants Gov. Hogan to Take a Stand on Trump," *Washington Post*, March 23, 2016, https://www.washingtonpost.com/local/md-politics/this-congressman-really-really-wants-larry-hogan-to-denounce-donald-trump/2016/03/23/62e68a70-f0f7-11e5-a61f-e9c95c06edca_story.html?tid=usw_passupdatepg.

6. Ovetta Wiggins, "M[arylan]d Gov. Hogan Says He Might Not Support Trump as Nominee," *Washington Post*, March 25, 2016, https://www.washingtonpost.com/news/post-politics/wp/2016/03/25/md-gov-hogan-says-he-might-not-support-trump-as-nominee.

7. Jonathan Martin, "Governor Larry Hogan of Maryland, a Republican, Says Donald Trump Shouldn't Be Nominee," *New York Times*, March 24, 2016, https://www.nytimes.com/politics/first-draft/2016/03/24/maryland-gov-larry-hogan-a-republican-says-donald-trump-shouldnt-be-nominee.

8. *Maryland's 2016 Criminal Justice Reform*, Pew Charitable Trusts, November 13, 2017, https://www.pewtrusts.org/en/research-and-analysis/issue-briefs/2017/11/marylands-2016-criminal-justice-reform.

9. Maryland Governor's Office of Crime Prevention, Youth, and Victim Services, "Governor Larry Hogan Signs Comprehensive Criminal Justice Reform into Law," news release, May 19, 2016, http://goccp.maryland.gov/governor-larry-hogan-signs-comprehensive-criminal-justice-reform-into-law.

10. Goucher Poll, untitled news release, February 27, 2017, https://www.goucher.edu/hughes-center/documents/Spring-2017-Goucher-Poll-Release-2.pdf.

11. Democratic Governors Association, "DGA Launches New Project to Track GOP Gov[ernor]s on Trump: 'The Silent 9,'" news release, May 4, 2016, https://democraticgovernors.org/news/dga-launches-new-project-to-track-gop-govs-on-trump-the-silent-9.

12. Josh Hicks and Ovetta Wiggins, "Hogan and His Deputy Not Backing Trump as Nominee," *Washington Post*, May 5, 2016, https://www.washingtonpost.com/local/md-politics/democrats-place-hogan-on-a-silent-9-trump-list/2016/05/04/8e5006ea-124f-11e6-81b4-581a5c4c42df_story.html.

13. Tessa Stuart, "27 Best Republican Excuses for Skipping Trump's RNC," *Rolling Stone*, July 18, 2016, https://www.rollingstone.com/politics/politics-news/27-best-republican-excuses-for-skipping-trumps-rnc-105251.

14. Michael Dresser, "Far from Republican Convention in Cleveland, Hogan Enjoys Good Will at Tawes Crab Feast," *Baltimore Sun*, July 20, 2016, https://www.baltimoresun.com/politics/bs-md-hogan-tawes-20160718-story.html.

15. Ovetta Wiggins, "Hogan Endorses Kathy Szeliga for U.S. Senate," *Washington Post*, July 19, 2016, https://www.washingtonpost.com/local/md-politics/hogan-endorses-kathy-szeliga-for-us-senate/2016/07/19/89e03b16-4d41-11e6-aa14-e0c1087f7583_story.html.

16. Josh Hicks, "New LGBT Protections to Take Effect without Gov. Hogan's Signature," *Washington Post*, May 24, 2015, https://www.washingtonpost.com

/local/md-politics/new-lgbt-protections-to-become-law-in-md-without-gov-ho gans-signature/2015/05/24/1c11e57a-018a-11e5-833c-a2de05b6b2a4_story.html.

17. "The Politics Hour: 2016 Maryland Senate Debate," *The Kojo Nnamdi Show,* October 7, 2016, accessed September 24, 2021, https://thekojonnamdishow .org/shows/2016-10-07/the-politics-hour-october-7-2016.

18. Sophia Silbergeld, interview by the author, Baltimore, May 3, 2020.

19. Larry Hogan, interview by the author, Annapolis, MD, June 3, 2021.

Chapter 4

1. The consent decree was eventually approved by U.S. District Judge James K. Bredar on April 6, 2017. He denied the Justice Department's request that he delay signing for thirty days to give Trump administration officials more time to evaluate the agreement.

2. Lauren Dezenski and Kevin Robillard, "Trump Makes Blue-State Republicans Squirm," *Politico,* February 1, 2017, https://www.politico.com/story/2017/02 /trump-hogan-baker-blue-states-234452.

3. Michael Dresser, "Hogan, despite Non-support in Election, Will Attend Trump Inauguration," *Baltimore Sun,* December 30, 2016, https://www.baltimore sun.com/politics/bal-hogan-despite-non-support-in-election-will-attend-trump -inauguration-20161230-story.html.

4. "Senator: Maryland Five-Year-Old among Those Detained at Dulles," CBS Baltimore, January 29, 2017, https://baltimore.cbslocal.com/2017/01/29 /senator-maryland-5-year-old-among-those-detained-at-dulles.

5. Ovetta Wiggins, "Maryland Plans to Join Lawsuit against Trump's Travel Ban," *Washington Post,* March 10, 2017, https://www.washingtonpost .com/local/md-politics/maryland-plans-to-join-lawsuit-against-trumps-travel -ban/2017/03/10/becb97a2-05d4-11e7-b1e9-a05d3c21f7cf_story.html.

6. Brandon Soderberg, "Thousands Flood B[altimore]/W[ashington] I[nternational Airport] to Rally against Trump's 'Muslim Ban,'" *Baltimore City Paper,* January 30, 2017, https://www.baltimoresun.com/citypaper/bcpnews-thou sands-flood-bwi-to-rally-against-trump-s-muslim-ban-20170130-story.html.

7. "What Maryland Elected Officials Are Saying on the Travel Ban," *Baltimore Sun,* January 30, 2017, https://www.baltimoresun.com/politics/bal-what -maryland-elected-officials-are-saying-on-the-travel-ban-20170130-story.html.

8. Aaron Blake, "Whip Count: Here's Where Republicans Stand on Trump's Controversial Travel Ban," *Washington Post,* January 31, 2017, https://www.wash ingtonpost.com/news/the-fix/wp/2017/01/29/heres-where-republicans-stand-on -president-trumps-controversial-travel-ban.

9. Eric Luedtke, "Hogan Must Stand Up to Trump," *Baltimore Sun,* January 31, 2017, https://www.baltimoresun.com/opinion/op-ed/bs-ed-hogan-travel-ban -20170131-story.html.

10. Maryland Democratic Party, "Shame: Larry Hogan Refuses to Condemn

Trump's Muslim Ban," news release, January 30, 2017, https://www.mddems.org/news-clips/shame-larry-hogan-refuses-condemn-trumps-muslim-ban.

11. Julian Sadur, "Hogan Says of Trump, 'I'm Not a Defender of the Administration,'" WMDT.com, February 14, 2017, https://www.wmdt.com/2017/02/hogan-says-of-trump-im-not-a-defender-of-the-administration.

12. Ovetta Wiggins, "New Video Is Latest Attempt by M[aryland]d Democrats to Tie Hogan to Trump," *Washington Post*, February 21, 2017, https://www.washingtonpost.com/local/md-politics/new-video-is-latest-attempt-by-md-democrats-to-tie-hogan-to-trump/2017/02/21/3363137e-f482-11e6-a9b0-ecee7ce475fc_story.html.

13. Institute on Taxation and Economic Policy, "30 Percent of Marylanders Would Pay More under GOP-Trump Tax Framework, but the State's Richest 1 Percent Would Pay Less," ITEP.org, October 4, 2017, https://itep.org/trumpgopplanmd.

14. Goucher Poll, untitled news release, February 27, 2017, https://www.goucher.edu/hughes-center/documents/Spring-2017-Goucher-Poll-Release-2.pdf.

15. "Washington Post News Poll," *Washington Post*, October 29, 2006, https://www.washingtonpost.com/wp-srv/politics/polls/postpoll_102906.htm.

16. Rachel M. Cohen, "Can a Blue Wave in a Blue State Make Ben Jealous Maryland's First African American Governor?" *American Prospect*, October 12, 2018, https://prospect.org/power/can-blue-wave-blue-state-make-ben-jealous-maryland-s-first-african-american-governor.

17. John Fritze, "Democratic Members of Congress Press Gov. Hogan on Health Care Bill," *Baltimore Sun*, March 20, 2017, https://www.baltimoresun.com/politics/bal-democratic-members-of-congress-press-hogan-on-health-care-bill-20170320-story.html.

18. Josh Hicks, "Hogan, McAuliffe Tell Congress to 'Immediately Reject' Obamacare Repeal Efforts," *Washington Post*, July 18, 2017, https://www.washingtonpost.com/local/md-politics/hogan-mcauliffe-tell-congress-to-immediately-reject-obamacare-repeal-efforts/2017/07/18/7757dd4a-6be1-11e7-96ab-5f38140b38cc_story.html.

19. Josh Hicks, "Hogan Adds Maryland to U.S. Climate Alliance—After Long Delay," *Washington Post*, January 10, 2018, https://www.washingtonpost.com/local/md-politics/hogan-adds-maryland-to-us-climate-alliance--after-long-delay/2018/01/10/31a2909c-f64c-11e7-b34a-b85626af34ef_story.html.

20. Editorial Board, "Did Hogan Really Spend a Record Amount on Education? Yes, but . . . ," *Baltimore Sun*, September 10, 2018, https://www.baltimoresun.com/opinion/editorial/bs-ed-0910-hogan-education-20180905-story.html.

21. Pamela Wood, "After Veto Override, Renewable Energy Sourcing Accelerates in Maryland," *Baltimore Sun*, February 2, 2017, https://www.baltimoresun.com/politics/bs-md-senate-renewable-veto-20170202-story.html.

22. Josh Hicks, "Maryland Lawmakers Give A[ttorney-]G[eneral] Blanket Authority to Sue Trump Administration," *Washington Post*, February 15, 2017,

https://www.washingtonpost.com/local/md-politics/maryland-lawmakers-give
-ag-blanket-authority-to-sue-trump-administration/2017/02/15/26d33dee-f303
-11e6-a9b0-ecee7ce475fc_story.html.

23. Ovetta Wiggins and Josh Hicks, "M[arylan]d Senate Backs Resolution Allowing Attorney General to Sue Federal Government," *Washington
Post*, February 11, 2017, https://www.washingtonpost.com/local/md-politics
/md-senate-backs-resolution-allowing-attorney-general-to-sue-federal-govern
ment/2017/02/11/c40e0b1c-efb5-11e6-b4ff-ac2cf509efe5_story.html.

24. Ovetta Wiggins and Josh Hicks, "Delay Denied, Maryland's GOP Senators Storm Out," *Washington Post*, February 9, 2017, https://www.washington
post.com/local/md-politics/marylands-gop-senators-storm-out-of-session
-over-resolution/2017/02/09/378d0954-eee3-11e6-b4ff-ac2cf509efe5_story
.html?utm_term=.bdc90c49e697&tid=a_inl_manual.

25. Associated Press, "Planned Parenthood Funding Guaranteed in Maryland if Feds Cut Support," *NBC News*, April 7, 2017, https://www.nbcnews.com
/news/us-news/planned-parenthood-funding-guaranteed-maryland-if-feds
-cut-support-n743891.

26. House Joint Resolution 9, "The Protection of the Federal Affordable Care
Act," Maryland House of Delegates, March 21, 2017, https://mgaleg.maryland
.gov/2017RS/bills/hj/hj0009T.pdf.

27. Chris Christie, phone interview by the author, March 26, 2020.

28. Erin Cox and Pamela Wood, "Hogan Promises 'I'm Not Going to Play the
Politics,'" *Baltimore Sun*, June 30, 2019, https://www.baltimoresun.com/politics
/bs-md-hogan-politics-20170111-story.html.

29. Erin Cox, "Hogan Proposes Expanded Job Tax Credit, State Writes Down
Revenue," *Baltimore Sun*, December 13, 2017, https://www.baltimoresun.com
/politics/bs-md-hogan-job-tax-credit-20171213-story.html.

30. Robert Zirkin, phone interview by the author, August 30, 2020.

31. Brian Witte, "Maryland Governor Signs Fracking Ban into Law," Associated Press, April 4, 2017, https://apnews.com/article/24eda3ec67404981bc56
2f9177c7871a.

32. Pamela Wood, "Maryland State House Trust Votes to Remove Taney
Statue," *Baltimore Sun*, August 16, 2017, https://www.baltimoresun.com/politics
/bs-md-taney-state-house-vote-20170816-story.html.

33. Larry Hogan, interview by the author, Annapolis, MD, June 3, 2021.

34. Larry Hogan (@GovLarryHogan), "The President's proposal to eliminate these pay raises is simply wrong. I urge Congress to take bipartisan action
to protect these hardworking employees & keep the promises made to them,"
Twitter, August 30, 2018, https://twitter.com/GovLarryHogan/status/10352815
08758695936?s=20.

35. Talia Richman, "Maryland Lawmakers, Mayor Pugh, Gov. Hogan Condemn Trump's Comments on Immigrants," *Baltimore Sun*, January 12, 2018,
https://www.baltimoresun.com/politics/bs-md-trump-immigrants-countries
-20180111-story.html.

36. Larry Hogan (@GovLarryHogan), "I remember when President Ronald Reagan called the Soviet Union the evil empire. Not much has changed. Putin is a thug & his actions against our democracy are despicable. On this I agree with our intelligence community. President Trump failed to stand up for our country yesterday," Twitter, July 17, 2018, https://twitter.com/GovLarryHogan/status/10 19215052870742016?s=20.

37. Andrea McDaniels, "Hogan Says Alabama GOP Candidate Moore Is 'Unfit for Office,' Criticizes His Defenders," *Capital Gazette*, November 11, 2017, https:// www.capitalgazette.com/politics/bs-md-hogan-moore-20171111-story.html.

38. Frank Bruni, "Is the Republican Party Donald Trump's—or Larry Hogan's?" *New York Times*, August 4, 2018, https://www.nytimes.com/2018/08/04/opinion /sunday/republicans-donald-trump-larry-hogan.html.

39. Robert McCartney, "Breakthrough in Maryland on Metro Funding, as Hogan and Legislature Come Together," *Washington Post*, March 2, 2018, https:// www.washingtonpost.com/local/trafficandcommuting/breakthrough-in-mary land-on-metro-funding-as-hogan-and-legislature-come-together/2018/03/02 /ef1c5e7a-1e36-11e8-ae5a-16e60e4605f3_story.html.

40. Erin Cox, "Hogan, Franchot See Their Bipartisan Friendship as a Model," *Baltimore Sun*, October 21, 2016, https://www.baltimoresun.com/politics/bs-md -hogan-franchot-relationship-20161021-story.html.

41. William F. Zorzi, "State House School Construction Fight Boils Over," *Maryland Matters*, March 30, 2018, https://www.marylandmatters.org/2018/03/30 /state-house-school-construction-fight-boils-over.

42. Morgan Gstalter, "GOP Governor: I Would Reject an NRA Endorsement," *The Hill*, July 20, 2018, https://thehill.com/homenews/state-watch/398133-gop -maryland-governor-i-would-reject-an-nra-endorsement.

43. Rachel Chason, "A Bisexual Maryland Lawmaker Says Her Dad—a State Senator—Suggested Conversion Therapy; Now, She's Speaking Out," *Baltimore Sun*, April 5, 2018, https://www.washingtonpost.com/local/md -politics/a-bisexual-maryland-lawmaker-says-her-dad--a-state-senator--suggest ed-conversion-therapy-now-shes-speaking-out/2018/04/05/ccc5e44e-3854-11e8 -9c0a-85d477d9a226_story.html.

44. John Riley, "Maryland Governor Signs Conversion Therapy Bill into Law," *MetroWeekly*, May 15, 2018, https://www.metroweekly.com/2018/05/maryland -governor-signs-conversion-therapy-bill-into-law.

45. Committee on Arrangements for the 2016 Republican National Convention, "Republican Platform 2016," 2016, https://prod-cdn-static.gop.com/media /documents/DRAFT_12_FINAL percent5b1 percent5d-ben_1468872234.pdf.

46. Will Drabold, "Here's What Mike Pence Said on LGBT Issues over the Years," *Time*, July 15, 2016, https://time.com/4406337/mike-pence-gay-rights-lgbt -religious-freedom.

47. Eric Cortellessa, "Opinion: Larry Hogan Is No Moderate," *Washington Post*, October 31, 2018, https://www.washingtonpost.com/blogs/all-opinions-are -local/wp/2018/10/31/larry-hogan-is-no-moderate.

48. Hogan interview.
49. Hogan interview.
50. Geoffrey Kabaservice, phone interview by the author, June 6, 2012.
51. Maddie Sach, "Why the Democrats Have Shifted Left over the Last 30 Years," *FiveThirtyEight*, December 16, 2019, https://fivethirtyeight.com/features /why-the-democrats-have-shifted-left-over-the-last-30-years; Perry Bacon, "The Republican Party Has Changed Dramatically since George H. W. Bush Ran It," *FiveThirtyEight*, December 1, 2018, https://fivethirtyeight.com/features/the-repub lican-party-has-changed-dramatically-since-george-h-w-bush-ran-it.
52. Luke Broadwater, "Maryland Democrats Deride Gov. Hogan's Pledge of Bipartisanship as He Withholds Money Intended for Baltimore," *Baltimore Sun*, July 7, 2019, https://www.baltimoresun.com/politics/bs-md-hogan-democrats -20190705-story.html.
53. Erin Cox and Pamela Wood, "Hogan: Limiting Cooperation with Immigration Enforcement Is 'Absurd,'" *Baltimore Sun*, March 22, 2017, https://www .baltimoresun.com/politics/bs-md-trust-act-hogan-senate-20170321-story.html.
54. Hogan promoted Amelia Chassé Alcivar, his former communications director, to chief of staff in October 2020. Chassé Alcivar is the first woman ever to serve as chief of staff to a Maryland governor.
55. Ezra Klein, "No One's Less Moderate than the Moderates," *Vox*, February 26, 2015, https://www.vox.com/2014/7/8/5878293/lets-stop-using-the-word -moderate.

Chapter 5

1. Don Mohler, interview by the author, Towson, MD, April 6, 2019.
2. "Changing Attitudes on Same-Sex Marriage," Religion and Public Life Project, Pew Research Center, December 31, 2019, https://www.pewforum.org /fact-sheet/changing-attitudes-on-gay-marriage.
3. Steve Thompson, "Jealous, Shea Raise More Cash than Other Democrats; Baker Lags Behind," *Washington Post*, May 23, 2018, https://www.washington post.com/local/md-politics/jealous-shea-raise-more-cash-than-other-democrats -baker-lags-behind/2018/05/22/738256bc-5ddc-11e8-b2b8-08a538d9dbd6_story .html.
4. Erin Cox and Luke Broadwater, "Ben Jealous Wins Maryland Democratic Primary Race for Governor," *Baltimore Sun*, June 26, 2018, https://www.balt imoresun.com/politics/bs-md-governor-primary-20180626-story.html.
5. Adam Serwer, "What Ben Jealous's Win Means for Democrats," *The Atlantic*, October 9, 2018, https://www.theatlantic.com/politics/archive/2018/06/ben -jealous-win/563870.
6. Nathaniel Rakich, "Here Are All the Republicans Retiring from Congress in 2018," *Fivethirtyeight*, July 26, 2018, https://fivethirtyeight.com/features/here -are-all-the-republicans-retiring-from-congress-in-2018.
7. "Why Senator Jeff Flake Says He Won't Run for Re-election to the Sen-

ate," AZcentral.com, October 24, 2017, https://www.azcentral.com/story/news/politics/arizona/2017/10/24/why-senator-jeff-flake-says-he-wont-run-drops-out-race-trump-gop-politics/795497001.

8. Ovetta Wiggins, Arelis R. Hernández, and Robert McCartney, "Ben Jealous Wins Maryland Primary, Vows to Topple Republican Gov. Larry Hogan," *Washington Post*, June 27, 2018, https://www.washingtonpost.com/local/md-politics/maryland-democrats-choose-between-insurgents-and-party-establishment-in-crowded-primary/2018/06/26/a3aabc9a-77a8-11e8-80be-6d32e182a3bc_story.html.

9. Stephanie Ruhle and Ali Velshi, "What the Stunning Primary Upsets Mean for Democrats," MSNBC, June 27, 2018, https://www.msnbc.com/velshi-ruhle/watch/what-the-stunning-primary-upsets-mean-for-democrats-1265323587880.

10. Republican Governors Association, "'RGA Releases New TV Ad in Maryland Governor's Race: 'Too Extreme,'" news release, August 8, 2018, https://www.rga.org/rga-releases-new-tv-ad-maryland-governors-race-extreme.

11. Christal Hayes, "'You F------ Kidding Me': Maryland Governor Candidate Upset with Being Asked If He's a Socialist," *USA Today*, August 8, 2018, https://www.usatoday.com/story/news/politics/onpolitics/2018/08/08/ben-jealous-maryland-candidate-curses-when-asked-if-hes-socialist/942308002.

12. Pamela Wood, "Asked Whether He's a Socialist, Ben Jealous Drops F-Bomb at Baltimore County News Conference," *Baltimore Sun*, August 8, 2018, https://www.baltimoresun.com/politics/bs-md-jealous-profanity-20180808-story.html.

13. Josh Voorhees, "An F-Bomb about the S-Word," *Slate*, August 9, 2018, https://slate.com/news-and-politics/2018/08/ben-jealous-drops-the-f-bomb-to-reject-the-socialism-label.html.

14. YouGov, "Daily Survey: Socialism," August 1–2, 2018, https://d25d2506s fb94s.cloudfront.net/cumulus_uploads/document/0ltegcolu7/tabs_YG_Social ism_20180801.pdf.

15. Goucher College Poll, April 14–19, 2018, https://www.goucher.edu/hughes-center/documents/APR18_TUESDAY_Release_FINAL_crosstabs.pdf.

16. Brian Witte, "Hogan Watches Media Closely, Doesn't Hold Back in Emails," *Baltimore Sun*, March 14, 2016, https://www.baltimoresun.com/politics/bal-hogan-watches-media-closely-doesnt-hold-back-in-emails-20160314-story.html.

17. Luke Broadwater, phone interview by the author, April 7, 2021.

18. Luke Broadwater, "Ben Jealous Lays Out His Path to Victory: He Plans to Get More than 1 Million Voters to the Polls," *Baltimore Sun*, August 8, 2018, https://www.baltimoresun.com/politics/bs-md-jealous-path-20180808-story.html.

19. Ibid.

20. Robert McCartney, Emily Guskin, and Rachel Chason, "Marylanders Are More Liberal than Gov. Hogan, but They Like Him Anyway," *Washington Post*, June 6, 2018, https://www.washingtonpost.com/local/md-politics/mary

landers-are-more-liberal-than-gov-hogan-but-they-like-him-anyway/2018/06
/06/5cfb06fa-68e5-11e8-bea7-c8eb28bc52b1_story.html.

21. Jim Barnett, phone interview by the author, June 4, 2021.

22. Adam Serwer, "Is Ben Jealous What Progressives Want?" *The Atlantic*, June 25, 2018, https://www.theatlantic.com/politics/archive/2018/06/ben-jealous -a-former-naacp-chief-tries-to-reclaim-populism/563597.

23. Ovetta Wiggins, "Progressive Group Launches 'Take a Hike Mike' Campaign against M[aryland]d Senate President," *Washington Post*, April 9, 2018, https://www.washingtonpost.com/local/md-politics/progressive-group-launch es-a-take-a-hike-mike-campaign-against-the-countrys-longest-serving-senate -president/2018/04/09/70ceaf52-3c02-11e8-974f-aacd97698cef_story.html.

24. John Rydell, "Balt[imore] County Senator Draws Criticism for Implying She Was Endorsed by Gov. Hogan," *Fox Baltimore*, September 13, 2018, https:// foxbaltimore.com/news/local/balt-county-senator-draws-criticism-for-implying -she-was-endorsed-by-gov-hogan.

25. Michael Dresser and Pamela Wood, "As Ben Jealous Runs to the Left, Some Democrats Keep Distance or Embrace Hogan," *Baltimore Sun*, September 23, 2018, https://www.baltimoresun.com/politics/bs-md-jealous-democrats -20180917-story.html.

26. Larry Hogan, interview by the author, Annapolis, MD, June 3, 2021.

Chapter 6

1. Josh Kurtz, "Lies, Damned Lies and (Gubernatorial Fundraising) Statistics," *Maryland Matters*, August 28, 2018, https://www.marylandmatters .org/2018/08/28/lies-damned-lies-and-gubernatorial-fundraising-statistics.

2. Sophia Silbergeld, phone interview by the author, Baltimore, July 12, 2021.

3. Editorial Board, "Alternative Fact of the Week: The 'Hogan Lockbox,'" *Baltimore Sun*, August 30, 2018, https://www.baltimoresun.com/opinion/editorial /bs-ed-0831-hogan-lockbox-20180828-story.html.

4. Luke Broadwater, "Democrat Ben Jealous Trails Gov. Larry Hogan by $9 Million in Cash in Maryland Governor's Race," *Baltimore Sun*, August 28, 2018, https://www.baltimoresun.com/politics/bs-md-jealous-fundraising-2018 0828-story.html.

5. Michael Dresser, "Gov. Larry Hogan Blankets Maryland with Positive TV Ads as Ben Jealous Watches," *Baltimore Sun*, August 27, 2018, https://www.balti moresun.com/politics/bs-md-hogan-ad-campaign-20180824-story.html.

6. Editorial Board, "Alternative Fact of the Week."

7. Ovetta Wiggins, "In M[aryland]d Governor's Race, Jealous Releases His First Ad since Primary," *Washington Post*, September 16, 2018, https://www.washing tonpost.com/local/md-politics/in-md-governors-race-jealous-releases-his-first -ad-since-primary/2018/09/16/8242d63e-b9ff-11e8-bdc0-90f81cc58c5d_story .html.

8. Erin Cox, Emily Guskin, and Ovetta Wiggins, "Gov. Larry Hogan Leads Democrat Ben Jealous by 20 Points, Post–U[niversity of] M[arylan]d Poll Finds," *Washington Post*, October 9, 2018, https://www.washingtonpost.com/local/md-politics/gov-larry-hogan-leads-democrat-ben-jealous-by-20-points-post-u-md-poll-finds/2018/10/09/c1d23f40-cb40-11e8-a360-85875bac0b1f_story.html.

9. Thomas Waldron and Greg Garland, "Top Lobbyist Convicted of Fraud," *Baltimore Sun*, July 15, 2000, https://www.baltimoresun.com/news/bs-xpm-2000-07-15-0007150207-story.html.

10. Bruce DePuyt, "Jealous Releases Ethics Plan but Lobbyist and GOP Hit Back Hard," *Maryland Matters*, October 18, 2018, https://www.marylandmatters.org/2018/10/18/jealous-releases-ethics-plan-but-lobbyist-and-gop-hit-back-hard.

11. Bryan Sears, "Jealous Asks Convicted Lobbyist for Help, Contradicting Ethics Reform Proposal," *Maryland Daily Record*, October 18, 2018, https://thedailyrecord.com/2018/10/17/jealous-asks-convicted-lobbyist-for-help-contradicting-ethics-reform-proposal.

12. Arthur Kirk, interview by the author, Baltimore, July 6, 2021.

13. Michael Dresser, "Maryland Governor's Race: Key Numbers from Hogan and Jealous' Campaign Finance Reports," *Baltimore Sun*, October 29, 2018, https://www.baltimoresun.com/politics/bs-md-campaign-finance-numbers-20181027-story.html.

14. Michael Dresser, "Ben Jealous: Democrat Has Ambitious Plans for Maryland as He Runs for Governor, but Some Fault Cost," *Baltimore Sun*, October 20, 2018, https://www.baltimoresun.com/politics/bs-md-jealous-profile-20181002-story.html.

15. Michael Dresser, "Sanders Rallies with Jealous as Maryland Gov. Hogan Seeks to Boost Redmer in Baltimore County," *Baltimore Sun*, October 30, 2018, https://www.baltimoresun.com/politics/bs-md-jealous-sanders-20181030-story.html.

16. Jim Barnett, phone interview by the author, June 4, 2021.

17. These districts include, in order of Hogan's gains from 2014 to 2018, MD-25 (Prince George's), +14.5; MD-24 (Prince George's County), +13.4; MD-26 (Prince George's County), +13.4; MD-23 (Prince George's County), +10.8; MD-47 (Prince George's County), +10.4; MD-41 (Baltimore City), +10.0; MD-22 (Prince George's County), +9.3; MD-20 (Montgomery County), +8.9; MD-40 (Baltimore City), +8.8; MD-44 (Baltimore City and County), +8.6; MD-45 (Baltimore City), +8.1; MD-43 (Baltimore City), +7.0; and MD-10 (Baltimore City), +5.6.

18. William C. Smith, phone interview by the author, July 13, 2021.

19. Anne Kaiser, phone interview by the author, July 19, 2021; Jolene Ivey, interview by the author, Landover Hills, MD, July 15, 2021.

20. Chuck Todd, Mark Murray, and Carrie Dann, "The 2018 Midterms Showed Us America's Great Education Realignment," *NBC News*, November 15, 2018, https://www.nbcnews.com/politics/first-read/full-display-midterms-america-s-great-education-realignment-n936556.

21. Rachel Chason, "Before Campaign Kickoff, Gov. Hogan Woos Asian American Supporters," *Washington Post*, June 3, 2018, https://www.washington post.com/local/md-politics/before-campaign-kickoff-gov-hogan-woos-asian -american-supporters/2018/06/03/eeca0772-678a-11e8-9e38-24e693b38637 _story.html.

22. Rush Baker VI, phone interview by the author, July 20, 2021.

23. Jill Carter, phone interview by the author, July 29, 2021.

24. Ryan Brooks, "Progressives Think the Democratic Establishment Has Abandoned Their Candidate in Maryland," *BuzzFeed News*, October 25, 2018, https://www.buzzfeednews.com/article/ryancbrooks/ben-jealous-maryland-gov ernor-progressives-democratic.

25. Danielle E. Gaines and Bruce DePuyt, "Fundraising Totals From Five Key Elections for County Executive," *Maryland Matters*, October 29, 2018, https:// www.marylandmatters.org/2018/10/29/fundraising-totals-from-five-key-elec tions-for-county-executive.

26. Allan Kittleman, phone interview by the author, July 13, 2021.

27. "The Trump of Baltimore County," *Baltimore Sun*, December 18, 2015, https://www.baltimoresun.com/opinion/bs-ed-mcdonough-20151218-story .html.

28. Hannah Marr, phone interview by the author, July 26, 2021.

29. Patrick O'Keefe, phone interview by the author, July 20, 2021.

30. Justin Ready, phone interview by the author, July 24, 2021.

31. Danielle E. Gaines, "With Absentee Ballots Counted, Democrats Run Up Their House Majority," *Maryland Matters*, November 18, 2018, https://www .marylandmatters.org/2018/11/18/with-absentee-ballots-counted-democrats -run-up-their-house-majority.

32. Ready interview.

33. Doug Donovan and Michael Dresser, "No Coattails: Maryland Voters Backed Republican Gov. Hogan, but Also Showed Their Disdain for Trump," *Baltimore Sun*, November 7, 2018, https://www.baltimoresun.com/politics/bs -md-hogan-coattails-20181107-story.html.

Chapter 7

1. Jane Coaston, "How Trump-Skeptical Republicans Swung the 2018 Mid-terms," *Vox*, November 15, 2018, https://www.vox.com/2018/11/15/18078974 /trump-gop-midterms-2018-arizona-texas-never-trump.

2. William H. Frey, "2018 Voter Turnout Rose Dramatically for Groups Favor-ing Democrats, Census Confirms," *Brookings*, May 2, 2019, https://www.brook ings.edu/research/2018-voter-turnout-rose-dramatically-for-groups-favoring -democrats-census-confirms.

3. Public Religion Research Institute, "Partisan Polarization Dominates Trump Era: Findings from the 2018 American Values Survey," PRRI.org, June

18, 2020, https://www.prri.org/research/partisan-polarization-dominates-trump-era-findings-from-the-2018-american-values-survey.

4. KK Ottesen, "Maryland Gov. Larry Hogan: 'At Some Point, There's No Longer Going to Be a Donald Trump Party,'" *Washington Post*, July 30, 2019, https://www.washingtonpost.com/lifestyle/magazine/maryland-gov-larry-hogan-at-some-point-theres-no-longer-going-to-be-a-donald-trump-party/2019/07/29/c8fa2684-9ce1-11e9-85d6-5211733f92c7_story.html.

5. For a comprehensive overview of the women's vote in American elections, see Wolbrecht and Corder 2020.

6. "Presidential Vote Choice," Center for American Women in Politics, Rutgers University, February 24, 2021, https://cawp.rutgers.edu/gender-gap-presvote.

7. "Exit Poll Results: How Different Groups of Virginians Voted," *Washington Post*, accessed October 11, 2021, https://www.washingtonpost.com/graphics/2017/local/virginia-politics/governor-exit-polls.

8. Ashley O'Connor, interview by the author, Annapolis, MD, July 16, 2021.

9. Jonathan Martin, "A New Firm Sets out to Secure Women's Votes for a Vulnerable GOP," *New York Times*, November 12, 2013, https://www.nytimes.com/2013/11/12/us/politics/a-new-firm-sets-out-to-secure-womens-votes-for-a-vulnerable-gop.html.

10. Christine Matthews, phone interview by the author, July 15, 2021.

11. Katie Reilly, "Baltimore Schools Closed after Students Sit in Cold Classes," *Time*, January 4, 2018, https://time.com/5088435/baltimore-schools-cold-winter-storm.

12. Jesus Rodriguez, "GOP Governors Call for Delaying Kavanaugh Vote," *Politico*, September 27, 2018, https://www.politico.com/story/2018/09/27/kavanaugh-governors-847804.

13. Ovetta Wiggins, "Hogan: 'I Don't Feel Educated Enough' to Make a Decision on Kavanaugh's Nomination," *Washington Post*, October 5, 2018, https://www.washingtonpost.com/local/md-politics/hogan-i-dont-feel-educated-enough-to-make-a-decision-on-kavanaughs-nomination/2018/10/05/8b21ca3e-c8d3-11e8-b1ed-1d2d65b86d0c_story.html.

14. Ovetta Wiggins, "Jealous Accuses Hogan of Bullying: 'A New Low in Maryland Politics,'" *Washington Post*, October 10, 2018, https://www.washingtonpost.com/local/md-politics/jealous-accuses-hogan-of-bullying-a-new-low-in-maryland-politics/2018/10/09/cc933f00-cbc3-11e8-920f-dd52e1ae4570_story.html.

15. Dylan Scott, "What Do the Suburbs Want?" *Vox*, December 19, 2018, https://www.vox.com/policy-and-politics/2018/12/19/18129448/suburbs-midterms-2018-democrats-republicans-congress.

16. "Democratic Edge in Party Identification Narrows Slightly," Pew Research Center, March 25, 2021, https://www.pewresearch.org/politics/2020/06/02/democratic-edge-in-party-identification-narrows-slightly.

17. Marwa Eltagouri, "Most Americans Think Trump Is Racist, According to a New Poll," *Washington Post*, March 29, 2019, https://www.washingtonpost

.com/news/politics/wp/2018/03/01/ap-norc-poll-most-americans-say-trump-is
-racist.

18. Paul Schwartzman and Ovetta Wiggins, "Once Wary, Black Voters Have Warmed Up to Republican Larry Hogan in Maryland," *Washington Post*, October 30, 2018, https://www.washingtonpost.com/local/md-politics /once-wary-black-voters-have-warmed-up-to-republican-larry-hogan-in -maryland/2018/10/29/a6e1ede2-d631-11e8-aeb7-ddcad4a0a54e_story.html.

19. Stephanie Smith, phone interview by the author, August 10, 2021.

20. "Marylanders Support a $15 Minimum Wage and Legalization of Recreational Marijuana, View State Taxes as Too High," Goucher College poll, accessed October 11, 2021, https://www.goucher.edu/hughes-center/documents /SEPT18_Goucher_Poll_Part_One.pdf.

21. Rushern L. Baker III, phone interview by the author, July 22, 2021.

22. Cory McCray, phone interview by the author, July 5, 2021.

23. Ibid.

24. Hannah Gilberstadt and Andrew Daniller, "Liberals Make Up the Largest Share of Democratic Voters, but Their Growth Has Slowed in Recent Years," Pew Research Center, August 28, 2020, https://www.pewresearch.org/fact-tank /2020/01/17/liberals-make-up-largest-share-of-democratic-voters.

25. Forthcoming research by Hakeem Jefferson challenges the use of traditional ideological scale in defining the politics of Black Americans. Using data from the American National Election Study, Jefferson finds that "the terms 'liberal' and 'conservative' are unfamiliar to many Black Americans, rendering the commonly used 7-point liberal-conservative measure of ideology invalid for this population": Hakeem Jefferson, "The Curious Case of Black Conservatives: Construct Validity and the 7-Point Liberal-Conservative Scale," *SSRN*, July 6, 2020, https://ssrn.com/abstract=3602209.

26. Jill Carter, phone interview by the author, July 29, 2021.

27. Ethan McLeod, "Hogan Campaign Office Opening in Old Bank Building in Station North," *Baltimore Fishbowl*, August 2, 2018, https://baltimorefishbowl .com/stories/hogan-campaign-office-opening-in-old-bank-building-in-station -north.

28. Larry S. Gibson, "RGA's Larry Hogan Ads Are 'Blatantly Racist,'" *Baltimore Sun*, June 2, 2019, https://www.baltimoresun.com/opinion/readers-respond /bs-ed-rr-0815-rga-racist-ads-20180814-story.html.

29. David Zurawik, "Hogan Attack on Jealous Extends into Fliers Arriving in Mailboxes This Week," *Baltimore Sun*, June 1, 2019, https://www.baltimore sun.com/opinion/columnists/zurawik/bs-fe-zontv-hogan-jealous-media-fliers -20181005-story.html.

30. Boyd Rutherford, interview by the author, Annapolis, MD, August 9, 2021.

31. Ibid.

32. Jolene Ivey, interview by the author, Landover Hills, MD, July 15, 2021.

33. Sean Yoes, phone interview by the author, July 7, 2021.

34. McCray interview.
35. Baker interview.
36. Ibid.
37. McCray interview.
38. Schwartzman and Wiggins, "Once Wary, Black Voters Have Warmed up to Republican Larry Hogan in Maryland."

Conclusion

1. David Collins, "Gov. Larry Hogan Sworn in for Historic Second Term," WBAL-TV, January 16, 2019, https://www.wbaltv.com/article/jeb-bush-to -introduce-gov-larry-hogan-at-inauguration/25894219.

2. Ovetta Wiggins and Arelis Hernandez, "At Inaugural, Hogan Calls for Government 'More Noble than the Politics of Today,'" *Washington Post*, January 17, 2019, https://www.washingtonpost.com/local/md-politics/maryland-gov -hogan-is-scheduled-to-be-sworn-in-on-wednesday-at-noon/2019/01/15/2cd c174c-191c-11e9-88fe-f9f77a3bcb6c_story.html.

3. For a full overview of the Never Trump movement and key players, see Saldin and Teles 2020.

4. William Cummings, "Republican Governor of Maryland Says He Has 'No Idea Why' Trump Blasted Him at Briefing," *USA Today*, April 23, 2020, https:// www.usatoday.com/story/news/politics/2020/04/21/larry-hogan-responds -trump-criticism/2997095001.

5. Steve Thompson, "Audit Criticizes Maryland's $9 Million Purchase from South Korean Company of Coronavirus Tests That Had to Be Replaced," *Washington Post*, April 2, 2021, https://www.washingtonpost.com/local/md -politics/korean-coronavirus-tests-audit/2021/04/02/9c456726-9342-11eb -9668-89be11273c09_story.html.

6. Phil Davis and Lorraine Mirabella, "Nearly One in Five Maryland Workers Have Filed for Unemployment as Gig Workers Join Flood of Claims," *Baltimore Sun*, May 7, 2020, https://www.baltimoresun.com/coronavirus/bs-md-unemploy ment-claims-april-25-20200507-c2p7w2mrbbcajj6gsnbply5iqy-story.html.

7. Kaelan Deese, "Hogan Congratulates Biden, Harris on Election Victory: 'Everyone Should Want Our President to Succeed,'" *The Hill*, November 7, 2020, https://thehill.com/homenews/state-watch/524978-hogan-congratulates-biden -harris-on-election-victory-everyone-should.

8. Brian Witte, "Hogan Describes Delayed Permission to Send National Guard," Associated Press, January 7, 2021, https://apnews.com/article/donald-trump -district-of-columbia-inaugurations-larry-hogan-electoral-college-1a2caceca 5b08a4e4360995183df4e6c.

9. Jacob Rosen, "Maryland Governor Larry Hogan Doesn't Want Any GOP 'Whitewashing' of January 6 Riots," *CBS News*, July 24, 2021, https://www .cbsnews.com/news/governor-larry-hogan-doesnt-want-gop-whitewashing-janu ary-6-riots-the-takeout-podcast.

10. "Maryland Governor Larry Hogan on Future of GOP One Year after January 6 Capitol Insurrection," *CBS News*, January 6, 2022, https://www.cbsnews.com/video/maryland-governor-larry-hogan-on-future-of-gop-one-year-after-january-6-capitol-insurrection/#x.

11. Alex Pareene, "The Most Popular Crook in America," *New Republic*, October 10, 2021, https://newrepublic.com/article/156183/popular-crook-america.

12. Hannah Gaskill, "Roy McGrath, Governor's Former Chief of Staff, Faces Federal, State Criminal Charges," *Maryland Matters*, October 6, 2021, https://www.marylandmatters.org/2021/10/05/roy-mcgrath-governors-former-chief-of-staff-indicted-for-federal-state-charges.

13. Alex Isenstadt, "Larry Hogan's Audacious Bet: A Trump Critic Could Win the GOP's 2024 Nod," *Politico*, September 28, 2021, https://www.politico.com/news/2021/09/28/hogan-anti-trump-2024-514453.

14. McKay Coppins, "Larry Hogan Isn't Coming to Save the Republican Party," *The Atlantic*, July 23, 2020, https://www.theatlantic.com/politics/archive/2020/07/larry-hogan-betting-his-future-post-trump-gop/614494.

15. Marc Caputo, "GOP 2024 Hopefuls Tread Carefully around Trump," *Politico*, September 14, 2021, https://www.politico.com/news/2021/09/13/gop-2024-hopefuls-511617.

16. Sarah Longwell, phone interview by the author, September 10, 2021.

17. Robert O'Brien, "Hogan Joins Culture War with Peace Cross Stance," *Baltimore Fishbowl*, October 23, 2017, https://baltimorefishbowl.com/stories/hogan-joins-culture-war-with-peace-cross-stance.

18. Dominique Bonessi, "Hogan, Elrich 'Blue Line' Flag Controversy Goes Much Deeper," National Public Radio, November 6, 2019, https://www.npr.org/local/305/2019/11/05/776581242/hogan-elrich-blue-line-flag-controversy-goes-much-deeper.

19. The full tweet reads, "We are proud to hang these Thin Blue Line flags in Government House to honor our brave law enforcement officers. A local elected official prohibiting police from displaying a flag given to them by a grateful child is disgraceful": Larry Hogan (@GovLarryHogan), Twitter post dated November 3, 2019, https://twitter.com/govlarryhogan/status/1191095631424753664?lang=en.

20. Robert Costa and Erin Cox, "'I Haven't Abandoned My Principles': Hogan, Pondering Challenge to Trump, Casts Himself as a Traditional Republican," *Washington Post*, March 18, 2019, https://www.washingtonpost.com/politics/i-havent-abandoned-my-principles-hogan-pondering-challenge-to-trump-casts-himself-as-a-traditional-republican/2019/03/17/3862b274-48d3-11e9-9663-00ac73f49662_story.html.

21. Tim Carney, phone interview by the author, August 9, 2021.

22. *Meet the Press*, NBCNews.com, September 5, 2021, https://www.nbcnews.com/meet-the-press/meet-press-september-5-2021-n1278543.

23. Jim Swift, phone interview by the author, May 19, 2021.

24. Jeffrey Gottfried and Jacob Liedke, "Partisan Divides in Media Trust Widen, Driven by a Decline among Republicans," Pew Research Center, August

30, 2021, https://www.pewresearch.org/fact-tank/2021/08/30/partisan-divides-in -media-trust-widen-driven-by-a-decline-among-republicans.

25. Amy Mitchell, Mark Jurkowitz, J. Baxter Oliphant, and Elisa Shearer, "Americans Who Mainly Get Their News on Social Media Are Less Engaged, Less Knowledgeable," Pew Research Center, August 27, 2020, https://www.pew research.org/journalism/2020/07/30/americans-who-mainly-get-their-news-on -social-media-are-less-engaged-less-knowledgeable; Rebecca Heilweil, "Right-Wing Media Thrives on Facebook; Whether It Rules Is More Complicated," *Vox*, September 9, 2020, https://www.vox.com/recode/21419328/facebook-conserva tive-bias-right-wing-crowdtangle-election.

26. Amanda Carpenter, phone interview by the author, August 10, 2021.

27. Tim Miller, phone interview by the author, August 23, 2021.

28. Matt Lewis, phone interview by the author, August 4, 2021.

29. Jim Geraghty, "Hogan's Heroics," *National Review*, March 29, 2018, https://www.nationalreview.com/magazine/2018/04/16/hogans-heroics.

30. Erin Cox, "Hogan Promised Fiscal Prudence and Economic Turn-around; Has He Delivered?" *Washington Post*, October 28, 2018, https://www .washingtonpost.com/local/md-politics/hogan-promised-fiscal-prudence-and -economic-turnaround-has-he-delivered/2018/10/27/4526bb32-d21c-11e8-b2d2 -f397227b43f0_story.html.

31. Robert McCartney, "Larry Hogan, the GOP's Anti-Trump, Hopes to Reverse the Party's Direction and 'Purge' Its Extremists," *Washington Post*, January 25, 2021, https://www.washingtonpost.com/local/md-politics/larry-hogan -the-gops-anti-trump-hopes-to-reverse-the-partys-direction-and-purge-its -extremists/2021/01/24/c9bb1b5a-5ccf-11eb-8bcf-3877871c819d_story.html.

32. Larry Hogan, interview by the author, Annapolis, MD, June 3, 2021.

References

Abrajano, Marisa A., R. Michael Alvarez, and Jonathan Nagler. "The Hispanic Vote in the 2004 Presidential Election: Insecurity and Moral Concerns." *Journal of Politics* 70, no. 2 (2008): 368–382.

Abramowitz, Alan, and Jennifer McCoy. "United States: Racial Resentment, Negative Partisanship, and Polarization in Trump's America." *Annals of the American Academy of Political and Social Science* 681, no. 1 (2019): 137–156.

Abramowitz, Alan I., and Steven Webster. "The Rise of Negative Partisanship and the Nationalization of U.S. Elections in the 21st Century." *Electoral Studies* 41 (2016): 12–22.

Ahler, Douglas J., and David E. Broockman. "The Delegate Paradox: Why Polarized Politicians Can Represent Citizens Best." *Journal of Politics* 80, no. 4 (2018): 1117–1133.

Amira, Karyn. "Do People Contrast and Assimilate Candidate Ideology? An Experimental Test of the Projection Hypothesis." *Journal of Experimental Political Science* 5, no. 3 (2018): 195–205.

Arceneaux, Kevin, and Stephen P. Nicholson. "Who Wants to Have a Tea Party? The Who, What, and Why of the Tea Party Movement." *PS: Political Science and Politics* 45, no. 4 (2012): 700–710.

Ayres, Whit. *2016 and Beyond: How Republicans Can Elect a President in the New America.* Alexandria, VA: Resurgent Republic, 2015.

Barreto, Matt, and Gary M. Segura. *Latino America: How America's Most Dynamic Population Is Poised to Transform the Politics of the Nation.* New York: PublicAffairs, 2014.

Beyle, Thad. "Governors." In *Politics in the American States*, 8th ed., edited by Virginia Gray and Russell Hanson, 194–232. Washington, DC: CQ Press, 2004.

Blum, Rachel M. *How the Tea Party Captured the GOP: Insurgent Factions in American Politics*. Chicago: University of Chicago Press, 2020.

Bordo, Susan. *The Destruction of Hillary Clinton*. Brooklyn, NY: Melville House, 2018.

Brown, Lawrence T. *The Black Butterfly: The Harmful Politics of Race and Space in America*. Baltimore: Johns Hopkins University Press, 2021.

Brugger, Robert J. *Maryland, a Middle Temperament: 1634–1980*. Baltimore: Johns Hopkins University Press, 1996.

Cadava, Geraldo. *The Hispanic Republican: The Shaping of an American Political Identity, from Nixon to Trump*. New York: HarperCollins, 2020.

Carney, Timothy P. *Alienated America: Why Some Places Thrive while Others Collapse*. New York: Harper, 2020.

Carpenter, Amanda. *Gaslighting America: Why We Love It When Trump Lies to Us*. New York: HarperCollins, 2018.

Cassese, Erin C., and Tiffany D. Barnes. "Reconciling Sexism and Women's Support for Republican Candidates: A Look at Gender, Class, and Whiteness in the 2012 and 2016 Presidential Races." *Political Behavior* 41, no. 3 (2019): 677–700.

Converse, Philip E. "The Nature of Belief Systems in Mass Publics." In *Ideology and Discontent*, edited by David Apter, 206–261. New York: Free Press, 1964.

Corral, Álvaro J., and David L. Leal. "Latinos por Trump? Latinos and the 2016 Presidential Election." *Social Science Quarterly* 101, no. 3 (2020): 1115–1131.

Crenson, Matthew A. *Baltimore: A Political History*. Baltimore: Johns Hopkins University Press, 2019.

Dawson, Michael C. *Behind the Mule: Race and Class in African-American Politics*. Princeton, NJ: Princeton University Press, 1994.

de la Garza, Rodolfo O., and Jeronimo Cortina. "Are Latinos Republicans but Just Don't Know It? The Latino Vote in the 2000 and 2004 Presidential Elections." *American Politics Research* 35, no. 2 (2007): 202–223.

Devine, Christopher J. "Ideological Social Identity: Psychological Attachment to Ideological In-groups as a Political Phenomenon and a Behavioral Influence." *Political Behavior* 37, no. 3 (2015): 509–535.

Donovan, Todd. "Authoritarian Attitudes and Support for Radical Right Populists." *Journal of Elections, Public Opinion and Parties* 29, no. 4 (2019): 448–464.

Druckman, James N., and Matthew S. Levendusky. "What Do We Measure When We Measure Affective Polarization?" *Public Opinion Quarterly* 83, no. 1 (2019): 114–122.

Dyck, Joshua J., Shanna Pearson-Merkowitz, and Michael Coates. "Primary Distrust: Political Distrust and Support for the Insurgent Candidacies of Donald Trump and Bernie Sanders in the 2016 Primary." *PS: Political Science and Politics* 51, no. 2 (2018): 351–357.

Ellis, Christopher, and James A. Stimson. *Ideology in America.* Cambridge: Cambridge University Press, 2012.

Farrington, Joshua D. *Black Republicans and the Transformation of the GOP.* Philadelphia: University of Pennsylvania Press, 2016.

Fauntroy, Michael K. *Republicans and the Black Vote.* Boulder, CO: Lynne Rienner, 2007.

Fields, Corey. *Black Elephants in the Room: The Unexpected Politics of African American Republicans.* Berkeley: University of California Press, 2016.

Francis-Fallon, Benjamin. *The Rise of the Latino Vote.* Cambridge, MA: Harvard University Press, 2019.

Free, Lloyd A., and Hadley Cantril. *The Political Beliefs of Americans: A Study of Public Opinion.* New Brunswick, NJ: Rutgers University Press, 1967.

Galbraith, Quinn, and Adam Callister. "Why Would Hispanics Vote for Trump? Explaining the Controversy of the 2016 Election." *Hispanic Journal of Behavioral Sciences* 42, no. 1 (2020): 77–94.

Green, Jon, and Sean McElwee. "The Differential Effects of Economic Conditions and Racial Attitudes in the Election of Donald Trump." *Perspectives on Politics* 17, no. 2 (2019): 358–379.

Halliez, Adrien A., and Judd R. Thornton. "Examining Trends in Ideological Identification: 1972–2016." *American Politics Research* 49, no. 3 (2021): 259–268.

Happer, Catherine, Andrew Hoskins, and William Merrin. *Trump's Media War.* Cham, Switzerland: Palgrave Macmillan, 2019.

Iyengar, Shanto, and Masha Krupenkin. "The Strengthening of Partisan Affect." *Political Psychology* 39 (2018): 201–218.

Iyengar, Shanto, Yphtach Lelkes, Matthew Levendusky, Neil Malhotra, and Sean J. Westwood. "The Origins and Consequences of Affective Polarization in the United States." *Annual Review of Political Science* 22 (2019): 129–146.

Junn, Jane, and Natalie Masuoka. "The Gender Gap Is a Race Gap: Women Voters in U.S. Presidential Elections." *Perspectives on Politics* 18, no. 4 (2020): 1135–1145.

Kabaservice, Geoffrey. *Rule and Ruin: The Downfall of Moderation and the Destruction of the Republican Party, from Eisenhower to the Tea Party.* New York: Oxford University Press, 2013.

Knuckey, Jonathan, and Komysha Hassan. "Authoritarianism and Support for Trump in the 2016 Presidential Election." *Social Science Journal* (2020): 1–14.

Lewis, Matt K. *Too Dumb to Fail: How the GOP Went from the Party of Reagan to the Party of Trump.* New York: Hachette, 2016.

Luttig, Matthew D. "Authoritarianism and Affective Polarization: A New View on the Origins of Partisan Extremism." *Public Opinion Quarterly* 81, no. 4 (2017): 866–895.

Malka, Ariel, and Yphtach Lelkes. "More than Ideology: Conservative-Liberal Identity and Receptivity to Political Cues." *Social Justice Research* 23, nos. 2–3 (2010): 156–188.

Masket, Seth. *Learning from Loss: The Democrats, 2016–2020.* Cambridge: Cambridge University Press, 2020.

Mason, Lilliana. "Ideologues without Issues: The Polarizing Consequences of Ideological Identities." *Public Opinion Quarterly* 82, no. S1 (2018): 866–887.

Masuoka, Natalie, Hahrie Han, Vivien Leung, and Bang Quan Zheng. "Understanding the Asian American Vote in the 2016 Election." *Journal of Race, Ethnicity, and Politics* 3, no. 1 (2018): 189–215.

Masuoka, Natalie, Kumar Ramanathan, and Jane Junn. "New Asian American Voters: Political Incorporation and Participation in 2016." *Political Research Quarterly* 72, no. 4 (2019): 991–1003.

Moore, Wes, and Erica L. Green. *Five Days: The Fiery Reckoning of an American City.* New York: One World, 2020.

Ondercin, Heather Louise, and Mary Kate Lizotte. "You've Lost That Loving Feeling: How Gender Shapes Affective Polarization." *American Politics Research* 49, no. 3 (2021): 282–292.

Parker, Christopher S., and Matt A. Barreto. *Change They Can't Believe In.* Princeton, NJ: Princeton University Press, 2014.

Philpot, Tasha S. *Conservative but Not Republican: The Paradox of Party Identification and Ideology among African Americans.* Cambridge: Cambridge University Press, 2017.

Raychaudhuri, Tanika. "Socializing Democrats: Examining Asian American Vote Choice with Evidence from a National Survey." *Electoral Studies* 63 (2020): 102114.

Reny, Tyler T., Loren Collingwood, and Ali A. Valenzuela. "Vote Switching in the 2016 Election: How Racial and Immigration Attitudes, Not Economics, Explain Shifts in White Voting," *Public Opinion Quarterly* 31, no. 1 (2019): 91–113.

Saldin, Robert P., and Steven M. Teles. *Never Trump: The Revolt of the Conservative Elites.* New York: Oxford University Press, 2020.

Sides, John, Michael Tesler, and Lynn Vavreck. "Hunting Where the Ducks Are: Activating Support for Donald Trump in the 2016 Republican Primary." *Journal of Elections, Public Opinion and Parties* 28, no. 2 (2018): 135–156.

Skocpol, Theda, and Vanessa Williamson. *The Tea Party and the Remaking of Republican Conservatism.* Oxford: Oxford University Press, 2016.

Tolbert, Caroline J., David P. Redlawsk, and Kellen J. Gracey. "Racial Attitudes and Emotional Responses to the 2016 Republican Candidates." *Journal of Elections, Public Opinion and Parties* 28, no. 2 (2018): 245–262.

Tope, Daniel, Justin T. Pickett, and Ted Chiricos. "Anti-minority Attitudes and Tea Party Movement Membership." *Social Science Research* 51 (2015): 322–337.

Tucker, Patrick D., Michelle Torres, Betsy Sinclair, and Steven S. Smith. "Pathways to Trump: Republican Voters in 2016." *Electoral Studies* 61 (2019): 102035.

West, Emily A., and Shanto Iyengar. "Partisanship as a Social Identity: Implications for Polarization." *Political Behavior* (2020): 1–32.

White, Ismail, and Chryl N. Laird. *Steadfast Democrats: How Social Forces Shape Black Political Behavior.* Princeton, NJ: Princeton University Press, 2020.

Williamson, Vanessa, Theda Skocpol, and John Coggin. "The Tea Party and the Remaking of Republican Conservatism." *Perspectives on Politics* 9, no. 1 (2011): 25–43.

Willis, John T., and Herbert C. Smith. *Maryland Politics and Government: Democratic Dominance.* Lincoln: University of Nebraska Press, 2012.

Wolbrecht, Christina, and J. Kevin Corder. *A Century of Votes for Women: American Elections since Suffrage.* Cambridge: Cambridge University Press, 2020.

Wright Rigueur, Leah. *The Loneliness of the Black Republican: Pragmatic Politics and the Pursuit of Power.* Princeton, NJ: Princeton University Press, 2015.

Zheng, Bang Quan. "The Patterns of Asian Americans' Partisan Choice: Policy Preferences and Racial Consciousness." *Social Science Quarterly* 100, no. 5 (2019): 1593–1608.

Index

MILEAH K. KROMER is Associate Professor of Political Science and Director of the Sarah T. Hughes Center for Politics at Goucher College. She is the founder of the Goucher College Poll, which measures the opinions of Maryland residents and voters on important policy, social, and economic issues.